Acclaim for
CHUCK KLOSTERMAN
and
FARGO ROCK CITY

"The best music book ever to cause me to spend not one red cent shopping for new CDs, an unusual bargain. But whether or not you take the bait and undertake a massive reconsideration of Ratt, Poison, Def Leppard and their ilk, you'll glimpse your lonely hearted and dreamy teenage self in Klosterman's confessions."
—Jonathan Lethem, *Crawdaddy*

"It's easily the most implausible (and the most comically agile) piece of wildcat criticism I've come across in years. . . . Klosterman's book is terrific for a lot of reasons—it's an act of cultural bravery, a convincing argument for why this cranked-up music was important to a generation of kids, and a delicious attack on the pretensions of baby-boomer rock critics, who hated this stuff. What makes *Fargo Rock City* sing, however, is Klosterman's good-natured enthusiasm. . . . Thanks to *Fargo Rock City* and another book, *Bebe Buell's Rebel Heart*, this has been the best year in recent memory for fresh and heartfelt American rock writing."
—Dwight Garner, *The New York Times Book Review*

"This is what Lester Bangs would have written had he been a farmboy raised on a diet of Skid Row and KISS. Unfailingly smart and demonically opinionated. . . . "
—*Kirkus Reviews*

"Klosterman starts up with a bang, shifts gears often, and rarely idles. [*Fargo Rock City*] will strike a power chord. . . . "
—*Publishers Weekly*

D0263318

"Klosterman's hilarious heavy metal odyssey will flick the Bic of every headbanger who's ever found salvation in a great Mötley Crüe riff. His sly, swaggering prose struts across the page like Axl Rose in his prime."

—Marc Weingarten, author of *Station to Station: The Secret History of Rock and Roll on Television*

"I spend about half my time thinking and writing about music and this is the best damn book I've read in several years. Nothing written about metal comes close. It deserves a place alongside Dave Marsh's *The Heart of Rock and Soul*, Greil Marcus' *Mystery Train*, Peter Guralnick's *Sweet Soul Music*, and Gary Giddins' *Visions of Jazz* at the very top of the list of the best books ever written about American music."

—Craig Werner, author of A *Change Is Gonna Come: Music, Race & the Soul of America*

"Though often analytical, *Fargo Rock City* is so much fun that it feels more like a tribute than an intellectual exercise. In reality, it's both . . . perhaps the best book written on the topic."

—*Billboard*

Fargo Rock City

A HEAVY METAL ODYSSEY
IN RURAL NÖRTH DAKÖTA

CHUCK KLOSTERMAN

Scribner

This paperback edition first published by Scribner, 2002
An imprint of Simon & Schuster UK Ltd
A Viacom Company

1 3 5 7 9 10 8 6 4 2

Simon & Schuster UK Ltd
Africa House
64–78 Kingsway
London WC2B 6AH

www.simonsays.co.uk

Simon & Schuster Australia
Sydney

A CIP record for this book is
available from the British Library

ISBN 0-7432-3157-0

Printed and bound in Great Britain
by Bath Press, Bath

Dedicated to my parents

(who I hope never actually read this book),

and in memory of Thad Holen

(who I wish could have had the chance).

Acknowledgments

When given the opportunity to make "acknowledgments" for the creation of a book, it's tempting to list every person you've ever met in your entire life. That was my original intention when I started writing this page, but I suppose that's kind of ridiculous and sort of risky, so I'm not even going to try. Instead, I'm only mentioning a select few.

The first person I need to thank is my agent, Todd Keithley, who believed in this project with the intensity of a wolverine on crack. I also must mention Matthew Kalash and his associate Sid Jenkins, who innocently introduced me to Todd and changed the course of my career. I'm just as thankful for the brilliant work of my editor at Scribner, Brant Rumble, who understood this book immediately and actually seemed to like it, even though it never mentions Liam Gallagher or Greg Maddux.

I would also like to thank the multitudes of people who read this manuscript at its various stages, particularly David Giffels and Michael Weinreb (who both provided the necessary competition) and Ross Raihala (who helped shape the way I think about popular music). I am forever indebted to Mark J. Price, who's got to be the only copy editor in the universe who knows AP style *and* the original lineup for Stryper. Bob Ethington provided some bonus editing down the stretch. And though I can't mention them all by name, I want to acknowledge my entire family, the UND Posse, my colleagues from the *Dakota Student* (especially my superfoxy lawyer, Amy Everhart), my past and current coworkers at *The Forum* newspaper and the *Akron Beacon Journal*, and everyone else who ever wasted time with me. If we've had more than two conversations, you're probably in this book. I would also like to apologize to any girl I've ever dated, partially for using you in this story but mostly for anything else I might have done along the way.

Finally, I would like to personally thank everyone who buys this book, and even those of you who just look at it in a bookstore and decide it isn't worth the money. As a writer, there is nothing more flattering than having someone invest their thoughts into something you wrote. And if you hate this book, feel free to call me at home. My phone number is (330) 867-1883. The only thing I ask is that you promise not to talk about heavy metal (except for maybe KISS).

Fargo Rock City

You know, I've never had long hair.

I don't think there has ever been a day when the back of my neck wasn't visible. In fact, I think I've had pretty much the same Richie Cunningham haircut for the past twenty-seven years (excluding a three-year stretch from 1985 to 1988, when I parted my hair down the middle and feathered it back). It seems like I spent half my life arguing with my parents over this issue, and it was a debate I obviously lost every single time. As a ninth-grader, I once became so enraged about the length of my hair that I actually spit on our kitchen floor. Remarkably, that clever gesture did not seem to influence my mother's aesthetics.

What my mom failed to understand was that I didn't even want long hair—I *needed* long hair. And my desire for protracted, flowing locks had virtually nothing to do with fashion, nor was it a form of protest against the constructions of mainstream society. My motivation was far more philosophical.

I wanted to rock.

To me, rocking was everything. As a skinny white kid on a family farm in North Dakota, it seemed to be the answer to all the problems I thought I had. I couldn't sing and I played no instruments, but I knew I had the potential to rock. All night long I slapped Mötley Crüe and Ratt cassettes into my boom box (which we called a "ghetto blaster," which I suppose would now be considered racist) and rocked out in my bedroom while I read *Hit Parader* and played one-on-none Nerf hoop basketball. Clearly, I was always ready to rock—*but I needed the hair*. I didn't care if it was blond and severe like Vince Neil's or black and explosive like Nikki Sixx's—I just needed *more* of it. It would have been my singular conduit to greatness, and it was the only part of my life that had a hope of mirroring the world of the

1

Crüe: They lived in L.A., they banged porn stars, they drank Jack Daniel's for breakfast, and they could spit on their kitchen floor with no repercussions whatsoever. They were like gods on Mount Olympus, and it's all because they understood the awe-inspiring majesty of rock. Compared to Nikki and Vince, Zeus was a total poseur.

Sadly, the Crüe proved to be ephemeral, coke-addled deities. Rock critics spent an entire decade waiting for heavy metal to crash like a lead zeppelin, and—seemingly seconds after Kurt Cobain wore a dress on MTV's *Headbanger's Ball*—they all got their shovels and began pouring dirt on the graves of Faster Pussycat, Winger, Tesla, Kix, and every other band that experimented with spandex, hairspray, and flash pots. Metal had always been a little stupid; now it wasn't even cool. This was the end. Yngwie Malmsteen, we hardly knew ye.

I became a cultural exile; I wandered the 1990s in search of pyrotechnic riffs and lukewarm Budweiser. It didn't matter how much I pretended to like Sub Pop or hip-hop—I was an indisputable fossil from a musical bronze age, and everybody knew it. My street cred was always in question. Like a mutant species of metal morlocks, my fellow headbangers and I went into hiding, praying that the cute alternachick who worked at the local coffeehouse would not suss out our love for Krokus.

But that era of darkness is going to end.

It is time for all of us to embrace our heavy metal past. It is time to admit that we used to rock like hurricanes. It is time to run for the hills and go round and round. It is time for us to *Shout at the Devil*. We've got the right to choose it, there ain't no way we'll lose it, and we're not gonna take it anymore.

Quite simply, that's why I wrote this book: to recognize that all that poofy, sexist, shallow glam rock *was* important (at least to the kids who loved it). I'm not necessarily claiming that the metal genre was intellectually underrated, but I feel compelled to insist it's been unjustifiably ignored.

In 1998, I was in a Borders bookstore, browsing through the music section. Chain bookstores always amaze me, because it

seems like someone has written a book about absolutely everything. I think that's why bookstores have become the hot place
for single adults to hook up—bookstores have a built-in pickup
line that always fits the situation. You simply walk up to any
desirable person in the place, look at whatever section they're in,
and you say (with a certain sense of endearing bewilderment),
"Isn't it insane how many books there are about _____?" Fill in
the blank with whatever subject at which the individual happens
to be looking, and you will always seem perceptive. *Of course*
there's going to be a ridiculous number of books on draft horses
(or David Berkowitz, or the pipe organ renaissance, or theories
about the mating habits of the Sasquatch, or whatever), and you
will both enjoy a chuckle over the concept of literary overkill.
The best part of this scheme is that it actually seems sponta-
neous. Bookstores have always been a great place for liars and
sexual predators.

ANYWAY, I was shocked to realize this phenomenon does not
apply to heavy metal. There are plenty of books about every
other pop subculture—grunge, disco, techno, rap, punk, alt
country—but virtually nothing about 1980s hard rock. All you find
are a few rock encyclopedias, a handful of "serious" metal exam-
inations, and maybe something by Chuck Eddy.

At first blush, that shouldn't seem altogether surprising. I
mean, nobody literate cares about metal, right? But then something else occurred to me: I like metal, and I'm at least semilit-
erate. In fact, a lot of the most intelligent people I knew at
college grew up on metal, just like me. And we were obviously not
alone.

Let's say you walked into the average American record store on
a typical summer day in 1987 (and for sake of argument, let's say
it was June 20). What was selling? Well, U2's *The Joshua Tree* was
No. 1 on the charts—but Whitesnake was No. 2. Mötley Crüe's
Girls Girls Girls was No. 3. Bon Jovi's commercial monster *Slippery When Wet* was still No. 4 (in fact, three Bon Jovi records
were in the Top 200). Poison was No. 5. Ozzy Osbourne's live
Tribute to Randy Rhoads was No. 6. Cinderella's *Night Songs* was

a year old, but it was hanging on at No. 27. Ace Frehley was showing his windshield-scarred face at No. 43. Tesla's *Mechanical Resonance* was outperforming R.E.M.'s *Dead Letter Office* by eleven spots (and—perhaps even more telling—*Dead Letter Office* featured a cover of Aerosmith's "Toys in the Attic"). Christ, even Stryper's *To Hell with the Devil* was at No. 74.

There were between twenty and twenty-five metals bands on the *Billboard* Top 200 album chart that week (depending on your definition of "heavy metal"), and—in reality—there almost certainly should have been more. Remember, this was before Soundscan, and metal acts were faced with the same problem that plagued rappers and country artists: They were often ignored by the record store owners who reported the sales, usually by pure estimation. This was clearly illustrated in the summer of 1991, when Soundscan was finally introduced and Skid Row's *Slave to the Grind* immediately debuted at No. 1. The Skid's eponymous first record sold three times as many units as its follow-up, but *Billboard* had never placed *Skid Row* higher than No. 7 and forced it to crawl up the chart, one position per week. It almost certainly flew off shelves far faster (and far more often).

In the 1980s, heavy metal *was* pop (and I say that to mean it was "*pop*ular"). Growing up, it was the soundtrack for my life, and for the life of pretty much everyone I cared about. We didn't necessarily dress in leather chaps and we didn't wear makeup to school, but this stuff touched our minds. Regardless of its artistic merit, Guns N' Roses' 1987 *Appetite for Destruction* affected the guys in my shop class the same way teens in 1967 were touched by Paul McCartney and John Lennon. Commercial success does not legitimize musical consequence, but it does legitimize cultural consequence. And this shit was everywhere.

I walked out of that Borders bookstore thinking that someone needed to write a book about the cultural impact of heavy metal from a *fan's* perspective (Deena Weinstein's *Heavy Metal: A Cultural Sociology* is arguably brilliant, but Deena never reminded me of anyone I ever hung out with). As I drove home, the classic rock station on my car radio played Thin Lizzy's "Cowboy Song."

I was struck by how much it reminded me of "Wanted Dead or Alive," the best Bon Jovi song there ever was. Obviously, my youth makes this process work in reverse; members of the generation that came before me were more likely reminded of Phil Lynott when they first heard Jon Bon Jovi talk about riding his steel horse. However, I don't think historical sequence matters when you're talking about being personally affected. I'd like to think my memories count for *something*.

You know, if someone wrote an essay insisting Thin Lizzy provided the backbone for his teen experience in the mid 1970s, every rock critic in America would nod their head in agreement. A serious discussion on the metaphorical significance of *Jailbreak* would be totally acceptable. I just happen to think the same dialogue can be had about *Slippery When Wet*.

Whenever social pundits try to explain why glam metal died, they usually insist that "It wasn't real" or that "It didn't say anything." Well, it was certainly real to me and all my friends. And more importantly, it *did* say something.

It said something about us.

October 26, 1983

The worldwide release of Mötley Crüe's
Shout at the Devil.

It's easy for me to recall the morning I was absorbed into the cult of heavy metal. As is so often the case with this sort of thing, it was all my brother's fault.

As a painfully typical fifth-grader living in the rural Midwest, my life was boring, just like it was supposed to be. I lived five miles south of a tiny town called Wyndmere, where I spent a lot of time drinking Pepsi in the basement and watching syndicated episodes of *Laverne & Shirley* and *Diff'rent Strokes*. I killed the rest of my free time listening to Y-94, the lone Top 40 radio station transmitted out of Fargo, sixty-five miles to the north (in the horizontal wasteland of North Dakota, radio waves travel forever). This was 1983, which—at least in Fargo—was the era of mainstream "new wave" pop (although it seems the phrase "new wave" was only used by people who never actually listened to that kind of music). The artists who appear exclusively on today's "Best of the '80s" compilations were the dominant attractions: Madness, Culture Club, Falco, the Stray Cats, German songstress Nena, and—of course—Duran Duran (the economic backbone of *Friday Night Videos*' cultural economy). The most popular song in my elementary school was Eddy Grant's "Electric Avenue," but that was destined to be replaced by Prince's "Let's Go Crazy" (which would subsequently be replaced by "Raspberry Beret").

Obviously, popular music was not in a state of revolution, or turbulence, or even contrived horror. The only exposure anyone in Wyndmere had to punk rock was an episode of *Quincy* that focused on the rising danger of slam dancing (later, we found out that Courtney Love had made a cameo appearance in that particular program, but that kind of trivia wouldn't be worth knowing until college). There were five hundred people in my hometown, and exactly zero of them knew about Motorhead, Judas Priest, or anything loud and British. Rock historians typically describe this as the period where hard rock moved "underground," and that's the perfect metaphor; the magma of heavy metal was thousands of miles below the snow-packed surface of Wyndmere, North Dakota.

Was this some kind of unadulterated tranquillity? Certainly not. As I look back, nothing seems retroactively utopian about Rick Springfield, even though others might try to tell you differently. Whenever people look back on their grammar school days, they inevitably insist that they remember feeling "safe" or "pure" or "hungry for discovery." Of course, the people who say those things are lying (or stupid, or both). It's revisionist history; it's someone trying to describe how it felt to be eleven by comparing it to how it feels to be thirty-one, and it has nothing to do with how things really were. When you actually *are* eleven, your life always feels exhaustively normal, because your definition of "normal" is whatever is going on at the moment. You view the entire concept of "life" as *your* life, because you have nothing else to measure it against. Unless your mom dies or you get your foot caught in the family lawn mower, every part of childhood happens exactly as it should. It's the only way things *can* happen.

That changed when my older brother returned from the army. He was on leave from Fort Benning in Georgia, and he had two cassettes in his duffel bag (both of which he would forget to take back with him when he returned to his base). The first, *Sports*, by Huey Lewis and the News, was already a known quantity ("I Want a New Drug" happened to be the song of the moment on

Y-94). However, the second cassette would redirect the path of my life: *Shout at the Devil* by Mötley Crüe.

As cliché as it now seems, I was wholly disturbed by the *Shout at the Devil* cover. I clearly remember thinking, Who the fuck *are* these guys? Who *the fuck* are these guys? And—more importantly—Are these guys even *guys*? The blond one looked like a chick, and one of the members was named "Nikki." Fortunately, my sister broached this issue seconds after seeing the album cover, and my brother (eleven years my senior) said, "No, they're all guys. They're really twisted, but it's pretty good music." When my brother was a senior in high school, he used to drive me to school; I remembered that he always listened to 8-tracks featuring Meat Loaf, Molly Hatchet, and what I later recognized to be old Van Halen. Using that memory as my reference point, I assumed I had a vague idea what Mötley Crüe might sound like.

Still, I didn't listen to it. I put Huey Lewis into my brother's trendy Walkman (another first) and fast-forwarded to all the songs I already knew. Meanwhile, I read the liner notes to *Shout at the Devil*. It was like stumbling across a copy of Anton LaVey's *Satanic Bible* (which—of course—was a book I had never heard of or could even imagine existing). The band insisted that "This album was recorded on Foster's Lager, Budweiser, Bombay Gin, lots of Jack Daniel's, Kahlua and Brandy, Quakers and Krell, and Wild Women!" And they even included an advisory: *Caution: This record may contain backwards messages.* What the hell did that mean? Why would anyone do that? I wondered if my brother (or anyone in the world, for that matter) had a tape player that played cassettes backward.

The day before I actually listened to the album, I told my friends about this awesome new band I had discovered. Eleven years later I would become a rock critic and do that sort of thing all the time, so maybe this was like vocational training. Everyone seemed mildly impressed that the Crüe had a song named "Bastard." "God Bless the Children of the Beast" also seemed promising.

Clearly, this was a cool band. Clearly, I was an idiot and so were all my friends. It's incredible to look back and realize how effectively the Mötley image machine operated. It didn't occur to anyone that we were going to listen to Mötley Crüe for the same reason we all watched *KISS Meets the Phantom of the Park* in 1978, when we were first-graders who liked Ace Frehley for the same reasons we liked Spider-Man.

Yet I would be lying if I said the only thing we dug about Mötley Crüe was their persona. Without a doubt, their image was the catalyst for the attraction—but that wasn't the entire equation. I say this because I also remember sitting on my bed on a Sunday afternoon and playing *Shout at the Devil* for the first time. This may make a sad statement about my generation (or perhaps just myself), but *Shout at the Devil* was my *Sgt. Pepper's*.

The LP opens with a spoken-word piece called "In the Beginning." The track doesn't make a whole lot of sense and would seem laughable on any record made after 1992, but I was predictably (and stereotypically) bewitched. The next three songs would forever define my image of what glam metal was supposed to sound like: "Shout at the Devil," "Looks That Kill," and the seminal "Bastard." Although the instrumental "God Bless the Children of the Beast" kind of wasted my precious time, the last song on side one was "Helter Skelter," which I immediately decided was the catchiest tune on the record (fortunately, I was still a decade away from understanding irony). I was possessed, just as Tipper Gore always feared; I had no choice but to listen to these songs again. And again. And again.

It was three months before I took the time to listen to side two.

It can safely be said that few rock historians consider *Shout at the Devil* a "concept album." In fact, few rock historians have ever considered *Shout at the Devil* in any way whatsoever (the only exception might be when J. D. Considine reviewed it for *Rolling Stone* and compared it to disco-era KISS). Bassist Nikki Sixx wrote virtually every song on *Shout*, and he probably didn't see it as a concept record either. But for someone (read: me) who had never really listened to albums before—I had only been exposed to singles on the radio—*Shout at the Devil* took on a conceptual quality that Yes would have castrated themselves to achieve. Like all great '80s music, it was inadvertently post-modern: The significance of *Shout at the Devil* had nothing to do with the concepts it introduced; its significance was the concept of what it literally *was*.

I realize this argument could be made by anyone when they discuss their first favorite album. My sister probably saw epic ideas in the Thompson Twins. That's the nature of an adolescent's relationship with rock 'n' roll. Sixx himself has described Aerosmith as "my Beatles." Using that logic, Mötley Crüe was "my Aerosmith," who (along these same lines) would still ultimately be "my Beatles."

Yet this personal relationship is only half the story, and not even the half that matters. There is another reason to look at the Crüe with slightly more seriousness (the operative word here being "slightly"). As we all know, '80s glam metal came from predictable sources: the aforementioned Aerosmith (seemingly every glam artist's favorite band), early and midperiod KISS (duh), Alice Cooper (but not so much musically), Slade (at least according to Quiet Riot), T. Rex (more than logic would dictate), Blue Cheer (supposedly), and—of course—Black Sabbath and Led Zeppelin (although those two bands had just as much effect on Pearl Jam, Soundgarden, and all the Sasquatch Rockers who would rise from the Pacific Northwest when metal started to flounder). In other words, this wasn't groundbreaking stuff, and no one is trying to argue otherwise. Sonically and visually, heavy metal was (and is) an unabashedly derivative art form.

But those sonic thefts are only half the equation, and maybe even less than that. We have to consider when this happened. The decade of the 1980s is constantly misrepresented by writers who obviously did not have the typical teen experience. If you believe unofficial Gen X spokesman Douglas Coupland (a title I realize he never asked for), every kid in the 1980s laid awake at night and worried about nuclear war. I don't recall the fear of nuclear apocalypse being an issue for me, for anyone I knew, or for any kid who wasn't trying to win an essay contest. The imprint Ronald Reagan placed on Children of the '80s had nothing to do with the escalation of the Cold War; it had more to do with the fact that he was the only president any of us could really remember (most of my information on Jimmy Carter had been learned through *Real People*, and—in retrospect—I suspect a bias in its news reporting).

In the attempt to paint the 1980s as some glossy, capitalistic wasteland, contemporary writers tend to ignore how unremarkable things actually were. John Hughes movies like *The Breakfast Club* and *Sixteen Candles* were perfect period pieces for their era—all his characters were obsessed with overwrought, self-centered personal problems, exactly like the rest of us. I suppose all the '80s films about the raging arms race are culturally relevant, much in the same way that Godzilla films are interesting reflections on the atomic age. But those films certainly weren't unsettling to anyone who didn't know better. *WarGames* and the TV movie *The Day After* were more plausible than something like *Planet of the Apes*, but—quite frankly—*every* new movie seemed a little more plausible than the stuff made before we were born. Anything could happen and probably would (sooner or later), but nothing would really change. Nobody seemed too shocked over the abundance of nuclear warheads the Soviets pointed at us; as far as I could tell, we were supposed to be on the brink of war 24/7. That was part of being an American. I remember when *Newsweek* ran a cover story introducing a new breed of adults called "Yuppies," a class of people who wore Nikes to the office and were money-hungry egomaniacs. No fifteen-year-old saw anything unusual about this. I mean, wouldn't that be normal behavior? The single biggest influence on our lives was the inescapable *sameness* of everything, which is probably true for most generations.

Jefferson Morley makes a brilliant point about inflation in his 1988 essay "Twentysomething": "For us, everything seemed normal. I remember wondering why people were surprised that prices were going up. I thought, That's what prices did." Consider that those sentiments come from a guy who was already in high school during Watergate—roughly the same year I was born. To be honest, I don't know if I've ever been legitimately *shocked* by anything, even as a third-grader in 1981. That was the year John Hinckley shot Ronald Reagan, and I wasn't surprised at all (in fact, it seemed to me that presidential assassinations didn't happen nearly as often as one would expect). From what I could tell, the world had always been a deeply underwhelming place; my generation inherited this paradigm, and it was perfectly fine with me (both then and now).

Mötley Crüe was made to live in this kind of world. *Shout at the Devil* injected itself into a social vortex of jaded pragmatism; subsequently, it was the best album my friends and I had ever heard. We never scoffed at the content as "contrived shock rock." By 1983, that idea was the norm. Elvis Costello has questioned whether or not '80s glam metal should even be considered rock 'n' roll, because he thinks it's a "facsimile" of what legitimate artists already did in the past. What he fails to realize is that no one born after 1970 can possibly appreciate any creative element in rock 'n' roll. By 1980, there was no creativity left. The freshest ideas in pop music's past twenty years have come out of rap, and that genre is totally based on recycled, bastardized riffs. Clever facsimiles are all we really expect.

The problem with the current generation of rock academics is that they remember when rock music seemed new. It's impossible for them to relate to those of us who have never known a world where rock 'n' roll wasn't *everywhere*, all the time. They remind me of my eleventh-grade history teacher—a guy who simply could not fathom why nobody in my class seemed impressed by the *Apollo* moon landing. As long as I can remember, all good rock bands told lies about themselves and dressed like freaks; that was part of what defined being a "rock star." Mötley Crüe was a little more overt about following this criteria, but that only made me like them *immediately*.

In fact, I loved Mötley Crüe with such reckless abandon that I didn't waste my time learning much about the band. I consistently mispronounced Sixx's name wrong (I usually called him

"Nikki Stixx"), and I got Tommy Lee and Mick Mars mixed up for almost a year.

Until 1992, I didn't even know that the cover art for the vinyl version of *Shout at the Devil* was a singular, bad-ass pentagram that was only visible when the album was held at a forty-five-degree angle. The reason this slipped under my radar was because *Shout at the Devil* was released in 1983, a period when the only people who were still buying vinyl were serious music fans. Obviously, serious music fans weren't buying Mötley Crüe. I've never even *seen* Mötley Crüe on vinyl; I used to buy most of my music at a Pamida in Wahpeton, ND—the only town within a half hour's drive that sold rock 'n' roll—and the last piece of vinyl I recall noticing in the racks was the soundtrack to *Grease*. The rest of us got *Shout at the Devil* on tape. The cassette's jacket featured the four band members in four different photographs, apparently taken on the set for the "Looks That Kill" video (which is probably the most ridiculous video ever made, unless you count videos made in Canada). By the look of the photographs, the band is supposed to be in either (a) hell, or (b) a realm that is remarkably similar to hell, only less expensive to decorate.

Like a conceptual album of the proper variety, *Shout at the Devil* opens with the aforementioned spoken-word piece "In the Beginning." It describes an evil force (the devil?) who devastated society, thereby forcing the "youth" to join forces and destroy it (apparently by shouting in its general direction). This intro leads directly into "Shout . . . shout . . . shout . . . shout . . . shout . . . shout . . . shout at the Devil," a textbook metal anthem if there ever was one.

Humorless Jesus freaks always accused Mötley Crüe of satanism, and mostly because of this record. But—if taken literally (a practice that only seems to happen to rock music when it shouldn't)—the lyrics actually suggest an anti-Satan sentiment, which means Mötley Crüe released the most popular Christian rock record of the 1980s. They're not shouting *with* the devil or *for* the devil: They're shouting *at* the devil. Exactly what they're shouting remains open to interpretation; a cynic might speculate

Tommy Lee was shouting, "In exchange for letting me sleep with some of the sexiest women in television history, I will act like a goddamn moron in every social situation for the rest of my life." However, I suspect Sixx had more high-minded ideas. In fact, as I reconsider the mood and message of these songs, I'm starting to think he really *did* intend this to be a concept album, and I'm merely the first person insane enough to notice.

There are two ways to look at the messages in *Shout at the Devil*. The first is to say "It's elementary antiauthority language, like every other rock record that was geared toward a teen audience. Don't ignore the obvious." But that kind of dismissive language suggests there's no reason to look for significance in *anything*. It's one thing to realize that something is goofy, but it's quite another to suggest that goofiness disqualifies its significance. If anything, it *expands* the significance, because the product becomes accessible to a wider audience (and to the kind of audience who would never look for symbolism on its own). I think it was Brian Eno who said, "Only a thousand people bought the first Velvet Underground album, but every one of them became a musician." Well, millions of people bought *Shout at the Devil*, and every single one of them remained a person (excluding the kids who moved on to Judas Priest and decided to shoot themselves in the face).

Fifteen years later, I am not embarrassed by my boyhood idolization of Mötley Crüe. The fact that I once put a Mötley Crüe bumper sticker on the headboard of my bed seems vaguely endearing. And if I hadn't been so obsessed with shouting at the devil, the cultural context of heavy metal might not seem as clear (or as real) as it does for me today.

Through the circumstances of my profession (and without really trying), I've ended up interviewing many of the poofy-haired metal stars I used to mimic against the reflection of my old bedroom windows. But in 1983, the idea of talking with Nikki Sixx or Vince Neil wasn't my dream or even my fantasy—it was something that never crossed my mind. Nikki and Vince did not seem like people you talked to. I was a myopic white kid who had never drank, never had sex, had never seen drugs, and had never even been in a fight. Judging from the content of *Shout at the Devil*, those were apparently the *only* things the guys in Mötley Crüe did. As far as I could deduce, getting wasted with strippers and beating up cops was their full-time job, so we really had nothing to talk about.

March 24, 1984

Van Halen's "Jump" holds off
"Karma Chameleon" and "99 Luftballoons"
for a fifth consecutive week to remain
America's No. 1 single.

Now, don't get me wrong—just because I lived in North Dakota doesn't mean I was some rube who had no idea that something called "heavy metal" existed. Quiet Riot's "Metal Health (Bang Your Head)" and Van Halen's "Jump" were hugely popular with my elementary school posse, and everyone knew those hooligans were widely considered to be heavy metal bands. However, they didn't seem particularly *heavy* (particularly for those of us who discovered VH via *1984*). "Panama" sounded different than most radio fare (sort of), and we could tell it improved when it was played at a higher volume, but it was essentially just a good party song (in as much as sixth-graders "party"). Girls generally liked it, and the video wasn't threatening at all (actually, it was kind of cute). At this point in their career, Van Halen didn't sound that far removed from pop life, and I was still too naive to realize rock 'n' roll is more about genres and categories than it is about how anything actually *sounds*. In short, I was too stupid to be affected by the greater stupidity of marketing.

Part of this confusion was probably due to my youthful unwillingness to accept that all of "heavy metal" could be classified under a singular umbrella. Van Halen, Judas Priest, and Slayer were all indisputably metal groups, but I really don't know if they had anything else in common. I can't think of any similarity between Warrant and Pantera, except that they used to appear in the same magazines. Since there was so much loud guitar rock in the 1980s, describing a band as *metal* was about as precise as describing a farm animal as a *mammal*. For attentive audiences, the more critical modifier was whatever word preceded "metal"—these included adjectives like *glam, speed,* and *death.* Those designations became even more important when the original precursor—the word "heavy"—became utterly useless by about 1987.

Taken out of context, "heavy metal" tells us very little. It's almost redundant; I suppose it indicates that Mötley Crüe doesn't have anything to do with aluminum. In other subcultures, "heavy" is a drug term constituting anything that requires a great deal of thought. My ex-girlfriend and I used to smoke pot every day we were together, and—at least for us—*heavy* could mean a lot of different things. Sometimes it referred to the relationship between God and science; sometimes it referred to who would put new batteries in the remote control; all too often, it referred to locating cereal. Regardless of the scenario, whenever we used the word "heavy," it had something to do with taking a hard look at a perplexing, previously ignored problem. Of course, the only time we ever described something as "heavy" was while we were stoned, which was pretty much all the time, which made for an abundance of perplexing problems (and if I recall correctly, we had a tendency to label every especially unsolvable problem as a "remarkable drag").

But what makes metal "heavy"? Good question. It becomes a particularly difficult issue when you consider that rock fans see a huge difference between the word "heavy" and the word "hard." For example, Led Zeppelin was *heavy.* To this day, the song "In-A-Gadda-Da-Vida" is as heavy as weapons-grade plutonium. Black Sabbath was the heaviest of the heavy (although I always seem to remember them being heavier than they actually were; early Soundgarden records are actually heavier than Sab ever was). Meanwhile, a band like Metallica was *hard* (as they've matured, they've become less hard and more heavy). Skid Row and the early Crüe were pretty hard. Nirvana's first record on Sub Pop was heavy, but *Nevermind* was totally hard, which is undoubtedly why they ended up on MTV's *Headbanger's Ball* (that was the fateful episode where Kurt Cobain wore his dress, thereby providing the final death blow to the metal ideology).

Clearly, the "hard vs. heavy" argument is an abstract categorization. To some people it's stupidly obvious, and to other people it's just stupid. Here again, I think drugs are the best way to understand the difference. Bands who play "heavy" music are inevitably referred to as "stoner friendly." However, "hard" bands are not. Find some pot smokers and play Faster Pussycat for them—I assure you, they will freak out. It will literally hurt their brain. They'll start squinting (more so), and they'll hunch up their shoulders and cower and whine and kind of wave their hands at no one in particular. I nearly killed my aforementioned drug buddy by playing the Beastie Boys' "Sabotage" when she was trapped in a coughing fit. Her recovery required a box of Nutter Butter cookies and almost four full hours of *Frampton Comes Alive*.

Sociologist and *Teenage Wasteland* author Donna Gaines described the teen metal audience as a suburban, white, alcoholic subculture, and she's completely correct. The only drugs that go with "hard" metal are bottles of booze (and cocaine, if you can afford it, which you probably can't if you spend all your time listening to *Who Made Who*). Conversely, "heavy" metal meshes perfectly with marijuana, especially if you're alone and prone to staring at things (such as Christmas lights, the Discovery channel, or pornography).

It's tempting to suggest that "heavy" metal came from acid rock (like Iron Butterfly), while "hard" metal came from groups who took their influences from punk (that would explain Guns N' Roses). This seems like a logical connection, but it rarely adds up. A better point of schism is side one of the first Van Halen album, released seven years before we all heard "Jump" on our clock radios.

Every so often, guitar magazines come out with a list that's usually titled something like "The 100 Greatest Axe Gods—Ever!" Sometimes Edward Van Halen is number one on the list, and sometimes he's number two behind Jimi Hendrix. The Eddie-Jimi battle goes back and forth from poll to poll. Ironically, Eddie always seems to fall back to number two anytime Van Halen releases a new record. This is because almost every new Van Halen album is horrifically disappointing. But Eddie still scores very well whenever people are *waiting* for a new Van Halen LP, because it makes all those young guitar hopefuls hearken back to "Eruption." (And for those of you who actually care which of these people *is* the better player, the answer is Hendrix. Van Halen remains the most influential guitar player of all time, but only because nobody can figure out how to rip Hendrix off.)

In a now-ancient MTV special about hair bands, Kurt Loder credits Van Halen with introducing a "faster, less heavy" version of metal that pulled it out of the underground. On this issue, Kurt is absolutely correct. Edward's pyrotechnic fret hammering splintered the stereotype of who listened to heavy metal. He gave hard rock musical credibility. He made college girls like it, because you could certainly shake your ass to all the good Van Halen songs (there's never been better summer music than "Dance the Night Away"). But it was still *metal.* It was still long-haired, drunken, show-us-your-tits rock 'n' roll.

However, Van Halen's philosophy did sacrifice one element of the classic metal equation: the sludge. For reasons no one will ever understand, Van Halen took the majority of their influences from Grand Funk Railroad. This is not to say that Grand Funk wasn't a decent group; it merely means they didn't seem to influence *anybody* else (with the possible exception of Autograph, who covered the Railroad's "We're an American Band"). And—apparently—this is too bad, because there are about a kajillion horrible bands who claim they were influenced by Aerosmith and Led Zeppelin. Maybe Grand Funk Railroad knew something everyone else missed (although Autograph completely sucked, so I guess nothing is certain in this world).

Over the past two decades, Eddie Van Halen has taken to citing Eric Clapton as the man who made him want to become a guitar player. This is probably true. Of course, it's almost impossible to hear Clapton's influence in Van Halen's music. I've searched for it, and it's not there. On "House of Pain," the last cut on *1984*, Eddie opens with a delicious guitar intro, and at the very end (just before the lyrics start), there is a certain bluesy quality to how he finishes the riff. That's about as Claptonesque as Van Halen gets.

This, of course, is a good thing. Eddie and Eric are certainly among the greatest rock guitarists who ever lived, but for totally different reasons. Listening to Clapton is like getting a sensual massage from a woman you've loved for the past ten years; listening to Van Halen is like having the best sex of your life with three foxy nursing students you met at a Tastee Freez. This is why rock historians and intellectuals feel comfortable lionizing Eric Clapton, even though every credible guy in the world will play Van Halen tapes when his wife isn't around.

A lot of that credit must go to David Lee Roth. Roth is not exactly a "musician," but he always understood the bottom line: If Eddie had decided to become Pete Townshend, David Lee Roth would never have become David Lee Roth. And—as is so often the case—one man's selfishness ultimately worked to the benefit of everybody. Roth demanded that Van Halen had to be about a lifestyle, specifically *his* lifestyle (or even more specifically, a lifestyle where you tried to have sex with anything in heels). Philosophically, his sophomoric antics limited Eddie; Mr. Van Halen really couldn't develop his classical virtuosity when his frontman was trying to hump the mic stand and scream like Tarzan. But in tangible terms, it made Eddie better. Instead of being an artist trying to make art, Eddie was forced to become an artist trying to make noise—and the end result was stunning. Within the stark simplicity of "Jamie's Cryin'," you can hear the shackled complexity of a genius. It has more artistic power than anything he could have done consciously. And that was obvious to just about everyone, including drug-addled teenagers. It's no coincidence that the *Circus* magazine readers' poll cited Van Halen as "Disappointment of the Year" in 1985, '86, '87, and '88 (the four years following Roth's departure).

So there you have it: a hard rock band that wasn't ponderous and trippy (like Vanilla Fudge) or poppy and sloppy (like the Ramones). Instead of the Hammer of Thor, it was an assault from a thousand guerrilla warriors, all consumed with getting laid. Though the term wasn't yet applicable, those first two Van Halen albums created a future where metal would be "glamorous," both visually and musically. Marc Bolan knew how glam rock was supposed to look, but Eddie Van Halen invented how it was supposed to sound.

December 31, 1984

Def Leppard drummer Rick Allen
loses his left arm in a car accident.

Speaking of Marc Bolan, aren't car accidents weird? I mean, they're obviously *bad*, but every car accident I've experienced has been more memorable for how totally bizarre it seemed.

Like all North Dakota farm kids, I started driving in fifth grade. People from urban (or even semiurban) areas are always amazed—and sometimes terrified—when I tell them this, but it still seems perfectly normal to me. North Dakota farm kids are expected to work like adults, so they start driving trucks and tractors long before junior high (I was driving *to school* in eighth grade). And even though I was a majestically appalling farmhand who spent most of his youth trying to avoid dirt at all costs, I was still granted the obligatory opportunity to start driving at the age of eleven: My dad put me in a Chevy Silverado 4x4 and told me to drive across an empty field of recently harvested barley. I must have done okay, because I was driving on actual roads six weeks later. Of course, ten months after that I put our Silverado in the ditch for the first time, thereby starting a long career of absolutely catastrophic highway destruction.

This may sound trite, but things really do slow down when you're about to have an auto wreck. There's that little moment of clarity where you remain spookily calm and find yourself thinking something ridiculously understated, such as, "Gosh, this is going to be problematic." But as soon as your paws instinctively clutch the steering wheel with nature's biological death grip, every-thing kicks into overdrive: The vehicle suddenly moves in three different directions at once, there is a horrific metallic sound coming from *somewhere*, and every fabric of your existence is pushing the brake pedal into the floorboard. The impact happens in half a moment. And then—just as suddenly—everything stops. And *then* you freak out. That's when it feels like your heart is going to explode, and you feel your hand shake as you inexplicably turn off the radio (which, for some reason, is always the first thing I do whenever I crash). The scariest part of any car accident is the first thirty seconds (when you realize you're not dead).

However, I'm guessing this might not be true if the seat belt lops off your arm at the shoulder, which is what happened when Def Lep skinbeater Rick Allen rolled his black Corvette Stingray on New Year's Eve in 1984. I'm guessing he probably just went into shock, which would explain why he was found wandering around the Sheffield countryside, searching for the severed appendage that had once pumped out the fills for "Rock of Ages."

At this point, I am tempted to say something highly stylized and sensational, such as "News of Allen's tragic mishap crossed the Atlantic with supersonic immediacy." However, that would not be accurate. Oh, I suppose it *technically* did (I'm sure I could locate an Allen snippet on the AP wire from 1-1-85 if I looked hard enough), but this incident never seemed like "breaking news" to anyone I knew—and I knew *a lot* of Def Leppard fans. It was more like a weird rumor that was almost crazy enough to be true, and—of course—it was.

To be honest, I remember a lot more conversation about the wreck Vince Neil had caused three weeks earlier, which killed Hanoi Rocks drummer Razzle Dingley (I'll discuss that fiasco at length when we get to 1991, and—I assure you—my decision to place this event six years in the future will make sense when we get there). I suppose Allen's situation made me wonder what would happen with Def Lep's next release, although the concept of Allen staying in the group never seemed remotely possible. And the fact that he eventually *did* overcome such overwhelming, unbelievable adversity should have blown my mind; it should have made me think that Def Leppard was the greatest fucking band in the world. However, this did not happen. What I mostly remember about Allen's stunning recovery is that I immediately started to hate Def Leppard, because I felt they had quit making heavy metal.

I'm guessing that most readers are now asking some fairly reasonable questions: "Huh? Wazzuh?" This leads to a whole new battery of abstract inquiries: Here again, what exactly are we referring to when I say "heavy" metal? Moreover, what qualifies a band as metallic? What makes a metal band "glam"? Can a "glam metal" band also be a "speed metal" band? Is a "death metal" band always a "speed metal" band? And—perhaps most importantly—is there a difference between being a "rock" band and being a "metal" band (because musicians certainly seem to think so)?

Few people understand the magnitude of these debates. Back in little old Wyndmere, there were four hot-button issues that could never be settled without someone getting shoved: Chevy vs. Ford, Case-IH vs. John Deere (that's right, an argument about *tractors*, if you can fucking believe it), whether or not the Minnesota Vikings sucked, and whether or not Def Leppard was a "metal" band or a "rock" band (the latter term being an insult). Looking back, the answer seems completely obvious: *Of course* Def Leppard was a metal band. If an alien landed on earth tomorrow and asked me what heavy metal sounded like, I'd probably play "Let It Go" off *High N' Dry*. "Let It Go" is not my favorite song (or even my favorite track off that album), but the main riff has the indisputable (yet completely intangible) "feel" of what *heavy metal* is. Moreover, Joe Elliott's voice epitomizes the strain of melodic arena rock, which is probably the best synonym for prototypical heavy metal.

Still, Def Lep was constantly under suspicion of being "poseurs," the ultimate attack leveled by any metal maniac.

Here's the opening line from a letter to the magazine *Hit Parader* from March of 1985: "I would like to know why so many people are so obsessed with groups like Duran Duran, Culture Club, the Thompson Twins and Def Leppard," asks a reader from Denham Springs, Louisiana. What we were too dumb to realize was that the guys in Def Leppard hated the term "heavy metal," and any member of the band would have given his right arm to avoid the label (except for Rick Allen, I suppose).

But before we try to explain why Def Leppard wanted to avoid the metal label, let's try to understand why some of my friends were unwilling to grant them the title (and—as ashamed as I am to admit this—*I was part of the anti-Def Leppard contingent!*). We didn't think Def Lep was worthy of respect for lots of reasons, all of which were about as sensible as the reasons for believing in the existence of the Loch Ness Monster. But here were two of them:

- *Def Leppard made a great album, and then they made a bad one that was even more popular.* Everyone loved *Pyromania*, including antimetal people. It was the single biggest reason metal sales jumped from 8 percent of the market in 1983 to 20 percent in 1984. At the time, the only bigger album in the universe was Michael Jackson's *Thriller*. *Pyromania* was one of the cornerstones of the genre. But then Def Lep released *Hysteria*. Ultimately, *Hysteria* would sell even more units, but success wasn't the problem. The problem was that *Pyromania* seemed like a metal record that crossed into a lot of other demographics because it was so damn good. However, *Hysteria* seemed like it had been specifically made for nonmetal fans. "Pour Some Sugar On Me" sounded like a paint-by-number portrait of what producer Mutt Lange assumed would pass for heavy metal. Even worse, the rest of the record was one long power ballad, which points directly to the main reason Def Leppard couldn't be trusted.
- *Girls liked it way, way too much.* With the possible exception of Floridian porn rap, no genre of music was ever more obsessed

with getting snatch than '80s glam metal. The Los Angeles scene (Mötley Crüe, W.A.S.P., Faster Pussycat, et al.) was particularly pedantic about this pursuit. And since teenage glam audiences were almost entirely composed of horny teenage males, it made for an effective marriage of ideas. The painfully obvious irony is that fans only liked the *image* of women in the scope of metal. Feminists would say the young males were "threatened" by the idea of girls digging hard rock, but—in reality—that had almost nothing to do with it. The distaste came from what a female audience reflected. Since no one could agree on what metal was (or which bands qualified), the only gauge was to look around and see who was standing next to you at a concert. That became your peer group; for all practical purposes, you were the people standing next to you. The metal genre is fundamentally about its audience and always has been. So when girls named Danielle who wore Esprit tank tops suddenly embodied the Def Leppard Lifestyle, it clearly indicated that Def Leppard no longer represented the people who had comprised the core audience for *On Through the Night*. As a shooting guard on our high school basketball team, I recall traveling to an away game and listening to our vapid cheerleaders sing at the front of the bus; they were singing "Armageddon It" and "Love Bites." That alone was indisputable proof that *Hysteria* sucked.

By virtue of this criteria, it would seem that heavy metal was a completely definable entity. And when I was a younger man, those guidelines did indeed seem totally clear. But as an adult, it's damn near impossible for me to make a comprehensive list of every '80s glam band that ever existed, because I've come to realize that metallurgy isn't an exact science. Nonetheless, zine editor Matt Worley did a pretty decent job in a 1995 issue of his publication *Lies* (which may or may not have taken its name from the 1988 Guns N' Roses EP). Here's his hit list: Bang Tango, Love/Hate, Smashed Gladys, Bon Jovi, Mother Love Bone, Poison, D'Molls, Cinderella, Dangerous Toys, Guns N' Roses, Tora Tora,

L.A. Guns, White Lion, Whitesnake, Great White, Little Caesar, Roxx Gang, Enuff Z'Nuff, Child's Play, Danger Danger, Snake Island, Spread Eagle, Kix, Shotgun Messiah, Warrant, Extreme, Vain, Dirty Looks, Dogs D'Amour, Faster Pussycat, D.A.D., Rock City Angels, Dokken, Skid Row, Royal Court of China, liquid jesus, Circus of Power, Katmandu, Kill For Thrills, Bulletboys, Junkyard, Kiss, Lord Tracy, Sleeze Beez, and, oh yeah, Mötley Crüe.

Well, Mr. Worley obviously forgot Helix. But he still did an admirable job of hitting most of the bands everyone else has forgotten. He only missed a handful of major notables: Ratt, Britny Fox, W.A.S.P., Lita Ford, Twisted Sister, Frehley's Comet, Vinnie Vincent Invasion, Winger, Hanoi Rocks, King Kobra, Fastway, Slaughter, the Sea Hags, Tuff, Tiger Tailz, Accept, Quiet Riot, Europe, Zebra, Helloween, Loudness, Autograph, Heavens Edge, Vixen, Tesla, Badlands, Stryper, EZO, Pretty Boy Floyd, Y & T, and Hurricane. I will grant that some of these additions are debatable; I'm sure a lot of these bands would vehemently insist that they were "just a rock 'n' roll band" and shouldn't be included under the amorphous parameters of metal. I read an interview Nikki Sixx gave after the release of the unremarkable Crüe reunion LP *Generation Swine*, and he was bemoaning the fact that a magazine listed Mötley Crüe, W.A.S.P., and Twisted Sister in the same sentence. He seems to think Mötley Crüe was far better and far different than those other groups, which is absolutely insane. Oh, they were better, but they certainly weren't different. Mötley, W.A.S.P., and Ratt were often discussed as a leather-clad trinity of L.A. metal excellence (Twisted Sister hailed from New York). In fact, Sixx personally thanked W.A.S.P.'s Blackie Lawless in the liner notes of *Shout at the Devil*. At one point, I'm pretty sure they were even in the same band (that group was called London, which remains best known for having all its most talented members quit in order to become rock stars with better bands).

Sixx's attitude is an unfortunate (and all too common) denial of his roots. Part of the reason '80s hard rock will never get respect—even kitschy respect—is because so many of the major players have retroactively tried to disassociate themselves from all their peers. Disco didn't wrestle with this kind of shame: Even after it had been flogged like a dead horse, former discotheque superstars were still proud to be part of the phenomenon they built. Subsequently, it's become acceptable to play disco albums at parties. Nikki Sixx could learn a lot from Donna Summer.

The reason so many metal groups hate being lumped into the same category is that writers often turn the phrase "heavy metal" into "glam metal," which is used interchangeably with "hair metal," a term that purposefully ignores musical ability and classifies a band by its follicle volume. By the mid 1980s, it had actually become a savvy business move for some bands to pitch themselves as having no visual appeal whatsoever, because those groups fostered their own niche audience. Somehow, there was a working-class credibility in ugliness. The Scorpions were never dismissed as glammy, and neither were the equally unattractive guys in Krokus or the blues-loving idiots in Great White. AC/DC wasn't either. By lacking visual flair, they were granted street cred.

Even today, I don't consider Def Leppard a "glam" metal band, primarily for two reasons (neither of which is homeliness). The first is that they were already somewhat famous when makeup and hairspray became in vogue, so Lep kind of predates this period (when they released *On Through the Night* in 1980, they were a remarkably young teen quartet; in a lot of ways, they were pop metal's Silverchair). However, the main reason I don't call them glam is that I can barely remember how they dressed or how they looked. I once interviewed Theodore Gracyk, the author of an incredibly well researched and painfully dull book titled *Rhythm and Noise: An Aesthetics of Rock*. The only insightful point he made during our entire discussion was when he flippantly referred to Def Leppard as "the most imageless band who ever lived." Def Lep was actually just a harder-rockin' version of faceless AOR bands like Journey and Boston. You never saw them, except on MTV—and then you really only saw Joe Elliott. The other four guys blended together and were essentially interchangeable (except for Phil Collen, who sort of resembled an underfed frat boy). In and of itself, that wasn't too uncommon; 90 percent of metal nonvocalists all looked like the same guy. The difference was that Def Lep was incredibly popular—way too popular to be anonymous. There's no explanation as to why they were so nondescript. Prior to working on this book, I don't even know if *I* could have matched all five names to all five faces (or all seven faces, if you count the guy they kicked out for boozing and the guy who drank himself to death).

Clearly, the definition of heavy metal is a purely semantic issue. That being the case, let's get as semantic as possible.

Metal is a visceral word. Standing alone, it doesn't really have a consistent connotation. If you're trying to protect something, keeping it in a "metal box" is good; if your tap water tastes "metallic," that's bad. It's completely situational, but we can safely assume it's usually masculine, uncomfortable, and—by its very nature—manufactured.

In the opening pages of his book *Running with the Devil: Power, Gender and Madness in Heavy Metal Music*, Robert Walser talks about the dictionary definition of metal, and he prefers to portray metal music as a metaphor for power (in fact, the manuscript's first line is a quote from Rob Halford stating "metal is power"). That's a valuable insight, but it doesn't really get us any closer to understanding what makes a band a "metal band." Walser's statement would indicate that either (a) metal bands are *always* about power, or (b) powerful bands *are* metal bands.

Certainly, we know the second statement is false. Patti Smith was pretty goddamn powerful, and no one's going to say Smith was her generation's Lita Ford. The same goes for Madonna and Liz Phair. Bruce Springsteen is a powerful character, as was John Lennon. So being a "powerful" artist obviously doesn't automatically make you a "metal artist."

However, the first statement is a little more debatable. It does seem like performing heavy metal often illustrates the possession of power. Mötley Crüe and W.A.S.P. literally wore metal on their bodies, almost like the way Hannibal dressed up his war elephants before kicking ass in the Alps. Keel's signature song was "The Right to Rock," and its opening lyrics were akin to Mel Gibson's rah-rah speech from *Braveheart*: "All our life we've been fighting / For the right to take a stand." And Halford's thesis that "metal is power" was completely true for his band, Judas Priest: Both lyrically and musically, Priest was *only* about power. Insipid PMRC spokesmodel Tipper Gore hated Priest, specifically for one song that had a lyric that even disturbed me: "I'm going to force you at gun point to eat me alive." Even to me, that clearly seemed like a song about violence against women, and—as we all learned from *St. Elsewhere*—rape is not a "sex crime," it's a "power crime." Of course, Halford recently revealed that he's homosexual and always has been, so the song takes on a new, mind-blowing dimension. I suppose it actually validates Halford's longtime argument that the tune was purely a metaphor, but it's more intriguing to imagine thousands of homophobic teens singing along with a narrative about Halford demanding a blow job from another guy.

ANYWAY, I suppose it all comes down to what you define as "power" (which means we have to mosh through another wall of semantic bullshit). For example: Was Ratt about "power"? You could argue they were. The first cut off their hugely successful debut LP *Out of the Cellar* was "Wanted Man," which implied that vocalist Stephen Pearcy was some kind of dangerous cowboy; according to my friend Greg's father, most tracks off *Invasion of Your Privacy* glorified prostitution. Yet Ratt never came across as threatening. They had the usual songs about sex and girls, but—if anything—Ratt seemed to be involved in relationships that didn't work, and there wasn't much they could do about it. "What comes around goes around," crooned Pearcy. Well, yeah—I guess that's true. But what the fuck does that have to do with power? On "Back for More," a girl is warned that if she keeps hanging around with her boyfriend, he'll screw her over . . . but she's obviously not dating anyone from Ratt. It's almost whiny; Pearcy's like a nerd telling the prom queen she shouldn't date the quarterback because he likes to beat up freshmen. Philosophically, "Back for More" belongs on a Weezer record. My all-time favorite Ratt song is "You Think You're Tough," but that was a sentiment the band members wouldn't have even applied to one another.

"[The term] *heavy metal* has become such a wide label," Ratt bassist Juan Croucier said as early as 1985. "I remember when Blue Oyster Cult used that term in 1976, and I thought, 'Okay, BOC is heavy metal and heavy metal is just the really hard stuff.' I would consider Ratt, more or less, to be fashion rock, FM-oriented, yet it's not as hard as Iron Maiden or Saxon . . . we feel that there could be more fashion in rock, outside of spikes and the dark leather look. I don't want to say that it should be more *GQ*, but it could be more colorful and up to date."

Sometimes the power issue is elastic, even within the same group. KISS has always been driven by two forces, Paul Stanley and Gene Simmons. Whenever they're caked in face paint, Paul's character is the Star Child (sometimes referred to as the Lover), while Gene is the Demon. In real life, Simmons has slept with literally thousands of women and consumed vaginas like they were Pop-Tarts; meanwhile, Stanley spent two decades searching for Miss Right and had his heart broken by Donna Dixon, a costar from the sitcom *Bosom Buddies*. Granted, Paul physically interviewed every other candidate along the way, but it always seemed like his heart was in the right place.

Their songwriting style followed suit. Stanley sings songs like "Strutter," "I Want You," "Anything for My Baby," and "Shandi"— all tunes where he longs to be with a woman he can't necessarily have. Certainly, this is not a hard and fast rule ("I Stole Your Love" is an almost comical example of a sex harvest), but as a general precept, Paul Stanley pursues women through song and loses at least half the time.

Simmons is the exact opposite. In "Calling Dr. Love," Gene sings, "Baby, I know what your problem is." And we all know what her problem is too: She wants Gene to fuck her. In fact, she *needs* Gene to fuck her (and evidently for medical reasons). In the context KISS uses these terms, it's all a cartoon, but—if you're looking for tangible examples of domination imagery in pop culture—it's a good place to start. Sometimes it's completely unveiled; on the mega-macho record *Creatures of the Night*, Simmons sings a song titled "War Machine," where he claims his intention is to "Strike down the one who leads me / I'm gonna take his place / I'm gonna vindicate the human race."

There's one glaring irony in the Paul-Gene power axis, however. Of all the songs in the KISS catalog, the one that stands out most clearly as a power anthem is "God of Thunder" from 1976's *Destroyer* (it even surpasses "War Machine," because "God of Thunder" is more epic and archetypal). Simmons carried the vocals, and it ultimately defined what his onstage persona was all about; he usually did his infamous blood-spitting routine during the song's introduction. But what's compelling is that it was written by Stanley, who fully intended to sing it. Simmons likes to insist that Paul was deliberately writing a "Gene song" and always knew he would eventually handle the lead, but Stanley says otherwise. "You want to hear the real story, or do you want to believe the rumor?" he told me in a 1997 interview. "That was totally [producer] Bob Ezrin's idea. He thought it came across better with Gene handling the vocals." In other words, Simmons's powerful image was a better fit for the song's powerful imagery; Paul's androgynous Girl Power would not translate into menace. At least in this case, the tenuous connection between heavy metal and power was completely conscious in the minds of the people who made the record.

But sometimes what seems obvious is not, particularly when you're trying to categorize what an artist represents culturally. That certainly seems true with Ozzy Osbourne, who doesn't seem obsessed with power *at all*. In fact, he seems more obsessed with weakness, particularly his own.

As a public character, Osbourne is the wildest of wild men. During the height of his career, he was constantly chomping off the heads of birds, pissing on historical landmarks, and generally acting like the most berserk, fucked-up lunatic in the universe. It's not an act, either; what's unique about Osbourne is that many of the stories about his behavior are at least partially true. But as he's grown older, another side of Ozzy has become more and more obvious: He is an incredibly vulnerable person who plainly lacks confidence. Rock writer Mick Wall talked about this in a VH1 *Behind the Music* special about Osbourne, and Ozzy made oblique references to his insecurities in his autobiographical video documentary *Don't Blame Me*. I hate to resort to pop psychology, but it seems clear that Ozzy desperately needs people to like him, and—for a long time—the only way he knew how to do that was through drugs, alcohol, performing onstage, and acting like a complete idiot in public situations. And even though it probably wasn't intentional, that insecurity always came across in his music.

You can see this way back with his material as vocalist for Black Sabbath. Sonically, the music was very powerful—but those riffs and song structures came from guitarist Tony Iommi, a very authoritarian person (at least within the internal scope of Sabbath). Iommi made all the band's decisions; Osbourne, bassist Geezer Butler, and drummer Bill Ward were flat-out scared of him. The inevitable result was that Ozzy made up lyrics that were intimidating on the surface but completely vulnerable underneath. "I Am Ironman," said Ozzy, but his Ironman was not a classic superhero: He was seeking revenge against the people who didn't appreciate him, and he was a sympathetic (in fact, almost tragic) figure. In the song "Dirty Women," Osbourne insists he's depressed and in need of companionship, but the best he can do is make a deal with a pimp who has "take-away women for sale." On the cryptic acid track "Fairies Wear Boots," Ozzy goes to his doctor because he's having bizarre hallucinations. The physician says he can't be helped "because smoking and tripping is all that you do." Those lyrics were probably supposed to create a persona of over-the-top madness, but that's not how it felt to the listener (at least not to this one). The desperation in Oz's voice made it all seem a little sad. It romanticized the lifestyle, but in a calamitous sense; the song promoted LSD, but it also seemed to indicate that Ozzy knew he was spiraling to destruction. This goes a long way toward explaining why Sabbath's material stands up over time. There is a human quality to the music that other metal bands can't replicate.

Osbourne's solo work generates the same ideas. The title track from *Bark at the Moon* was about losing control of one's personality. It was the kind of subject that demanded a scary guitar riff and it provided Osbourne a convenient opportunity to dress like a hairy monster, so I would guess most casual fans merely thought this was "Ozzy being Ozzy" (i.e., "Ozzy being stupid"). But try to look at the clip the way a film critic would critique a Lon Chaney, Jr., werewolf movie. There is almost always an unintentional metaphor to Osbourne's rock.

On that same LP, there's a ballad titled "So Tired," which is kind of an updated version of the Sab ballad "Changes." "So Tired" is about the end of a romantic relationship, and this time Ozzy loses twice: Not only does he lose the woman, he also loses the ability to break up with dignity. There's no indication that Ozzy will overcome this, or that he never really needed her to begin with, or even that she'll eventually regret her decision. The final reality is that Osbourne is simply too damn tired to talk her out of leaving. He has tried, and he has failed. She has shattered his heart, so he's just going to fold. He's completely and utterly powerless, and it won't matter how many bats he eats.

This kind of self-loathing is even more obvious on recent Osbourne offerings like "The Road to Nowhere." In the song's most telling (and most shamelessly literal) line, Ozzy sings, "The wreckage of my past keeps haunting me / It just won't leave me alone." In fact, he was already expressing these confused, powerless thoughts on the first cut of his first solo record, *Blizzard of Ozz*: "Don't look to me for answers / Don't ask me / *I don't know*" [italics mine]. These are not the words of a man who thinks he's going to dominate anything (or anyone).

Now, this is not to say Rob Halford was 100 percent wrong; quite often, '80s metal *was* about power. But sometimes it was about wishing you had some.

June 6, 1985

Axl Rose fires guitarist Tracii Guns
and joins forces with Slash,
finalizing the Guns N' Roses lineup
that would record *Appetite for Destruction*.

It might seem odd to list the mere origin of Guns N' Roses as one of metal's most significant dates, mostly because I have no memory of this event whatsoever. Virtually no one does. In fact, I would almost guarantee there isn't one member of GNR who associates this specific anniversary with anything of significance. The date itself might not even be accurate; diehard fans have come to recognize this otherwise unremarkable Thursday as the dawn of Guns N' Roses in a studio apartment on the Sunset Strip, but I suspect the June 6 designation is more akin to the way early Christians decided December 25 was the day Jesus was born.

But if the June 6 date is indeed correct, GNR was created the day after my thirteenth birthday. I would have been at basketball camp, sleeping in a dorm room on the campus of North Dakota State, totally oblivious to the fact that I would one day think W. Axl Rose was the coolest motherfucker on the planet.

One of my best friends is a gay rock writer named Ross Raihala, and Ross once told me he always suspected straight midwestern teens looked at Axl Rose the same way closeted gay teens looked at Morrissey, the British vocalist who fronted the intellectually penetrating and eternally melancholy band the Smiths. When

Raihala first mentioned this, I did not really understand what he meant (or if it was supposed to be a compliment or an insult). But the more I thought about it, the more it made sense. Rose *did* mean something more than his glam peers, especially for people who lived in the middle of nowhere. For rural kids who were too smart for where they were, but still very much a reflection of rural culture—a "redneck intellectual," if you will—Axl wasn't just another cool guy in a cooler-than-average band. He was an iconoclast (in the truest sense of the word). He didn't speak for us, but he sort of represented us. And in a weird way, Rose slowly evolved into the first artist of my generation who showed glimpses of an (ahem) "alternative" to the larger-than-life fairy tale of poofy-haired metal that was the template for all my favorite bands (including Guns N' Roses—at least initially). In a few years, flannel-clad grungers would turn that alternative into an art form, and Rose would subsequently become a ridiculous recluse. Nobody got fucked by the Age of Irony as much as Axl.

The term "redneck intellectual" might seem troublesome to some people, and I can understand why. Is it positive? Is it negative? Is it an oxymoron? I would answer all of these questions by saying "no." It doesn't have a connotation. It describes a person who tries to think critically at an age (and in a place) where critical thinking is almost impossible. And I would guess this scenario occurs almost everywhere in America.

Where I grew up, there were not a lot of people. In fact, there are currently more people in my apartment complex than there were in my hometown. There were no black people, no Hispanic people, no Asian people, no openly gay people, and everyone thought the same way about everything (the major exception being that "Ford vs. Chevy" thing). Now, this does not mean rural North Dakotans are not smart; in fact, the opposite is true. I generally find that midwesterners have far more practical sensibility than people from metropolitan areas; they seem to have a better sense of themselves, and the general education level is higher (this is mostly due to the fact that virtually no one ever drops out of school in a small town and cutting class is almost impossible, so even the least-educated people have spent twelve years at a desk). In a lot of ways, I loved growing up in Wyndmere. But what the culture lacked (and still lacks) is an emphasis on *ideas*—especially ideas that don't serve a practical, tangible purpose. In North Dakota, life is about work. Everything is based on working hard, regardless of what it earns you. If you're spending a lot of time mulling over the state of the universe (or even the state of your own life), you're obviously not working. You probably need to get back to work. And when that work is over, you will either watch network TV or you will get drunk (or both). Even in moments of freedom, you're never dealing with ideas.

Growing up in this kind of atmosphere is incredibly frustrating for anyone who's interested in anything stretching beyond the conversation at the local Cenex convenience store. If you want to consciously be absurd (which is what I wanted to do *all the time*), there simply aren't too many like-minded people to talk to. The big-city stereotype surrounding redneck intellectuals is that they eventually go to college and are amazed by all the different people they meet. I actually had the opposite experience; I was shocked to find people who *were* like me.

Still, we are all products of our environment, even if we like to pretend otherwise. So let's say you *are* the smartest sixteen-year-old in town; let's assume you're creative and introspective and philosophical. You still have a finite number of social tools to work with. You're only going to apply those espoused intellectual qualities to the redneck paradigm that already exists. You may indeed be having "deep thoughts," but they're only deeper versions of the same ideas that are available to everyone else.

This is where Axl Rose fits into the equation. Musically and visually, Axl stayed within the conventional metal zone. He had a Jagger strut and a Plant howl, long hair and leather pants, and he got quoted in *Kerrang!* As a musician, Rose appealed to the same contingency that was rooted in *Toys in the Attic, British Steel,* and *Theatre of Pain.* Axl existed within the one artistic paradigm that a midwestern white boy was going to consume: For lack of a better term, he "rocked."

But Rose was also the most compelling figure within the metal mix. If the thoughts of the redneck intellectual only gravitate along one linear path (and I'm arguing that they did, at least for me), Rose resided on that path's most cognitive extreme. This wasn't because he was necessarily smarter; it's just because he offered a little more to think about.

In the controversial documentary *Kurt and Courtney*, there's footage of a seventeen-ish Kurt Cobain attending a birthday party with an old girlfriend. When I saw that scene, I was shocked by how much he resembled the *GNR Lies*-era Rose. It's well-documented that these two icons desperately hated each other, and—as the two biggest groups of the early '90s—they were often pitted as rivals. The British music weekly *New Music Express* once called Nirvana "the Guns N' Roses it's okay to like" (apparently, *NME* perceives every popular American band exactly the same). The groups even got into a minor shoving match at the 1992 MTV Music Awards, although that altercation can probably be blamed on Courtney Love's hypocritical idiocy.

Axl initially loved Nirvana (he wore a Nirvana baseball cap in the "Don't Cry" video and wanted Nirvana to serve as the opener for the ill-fated '92 Metallica/Guns tour), but Cobain essentially thought Rose was a doofus, so Axl decided Kurt was a queer (or a poseur, or a pretentious asshole, or some damn thing that he probably would never say now that Cobain is dead). But these two guys share a lot of similarities—certainly more than either was ever willing to recognize. Besides strikingly similar facial features and an overlapping audience, they both offered an image that specifically appealed to lost kids with inexplicable rage. Axl did this first, and his tools were hostility and confusion. Cobain came a few years later, and he used personal angst and sexual tolerance (ultimately, Kurt's methods proved to be more effective).⊛ Comparing the two men is kind of like comparing a

⊛Of course, Cobain's victory as an icon does not necessarily mean he made better music; at least technically, *Appetite for Destruction* is a stronger album than *Nevermind*. They're weirdly similar, actually: Both open with songs that

black-and-white photo with its negative: They are totally opposite, yet they're completely the same.

What they shared is a human element; they seemed real.
There was a certain depth to their character. Granted, this is partially due to their popularity; when the media covers a rock
band, they really only cover the vocalist, so singers from the
most popular bands always have more opportunities to seem
interesting (the third person to follow in this lineage was Eddie
Vedder, and for many of the same reasons). But this process
works both ways. During their first months in the spotlight,
there was something about Rose and Cobain (and, to a lesser
extent, Vedder and Trent Reznor) that made me want to know
more about them. It was an undefined fascination that I did not
feel for people like Tom Keifer or Dave Pirner; though I liked
Cinderella and Soul Asylum very much, my interest did not go
too far beyond the musical product. Almost instantaneously,
Axl Rose came across darker, more dangerous, and more credible
than his peers. That's partially to his credit and partially due to
my own naivete. He put himself in a position where I could
comfortably lionize him. Rose was hard rock's equivalent to
U2's Bono.

If you're the type who thinks comparing Rose to Cobain is off-
putting, the comparison to Bono might seem downright insulting. Serious U2 fans tend to be completely humorless (at least
when they talk about early U2 records), and they award Bono an
almost religious respect. This is because they feel Bono "stands

---

defined each band's aethetic; both track 2s are about testosterone-driven
males (Nirvana hates 'em, GNR represents 'em), both track 5s are about drugs
(one prescription, one illegal), and both albums conclude with alienated,
spacey finales. The difference is that *Appetite* . . . always comes across as a tour
de force and a classic rock masterpiece, while *Nevermind* will forever be
remembered as a vehicle for "Smells Like Teen Spirit" and its subversive affect
on mainstream culture. It's periodically brilliant, but half the material on *Nevermind* is filler. There's no doubt about which of these records is more socially
important, but there's also no question about which one gets played in my
apartment when I want to hear something badass.

for something." Even when U2 decided to become the '90s version of KISS and evolved into a bloated commercial monster, U2 fans insisted this was "camp." To rational outsiders, it seemed like U2 was ripping off the blind old fans who refused to judge them as a mortal rock band. And maybe they were. But—if that was truly the case—I give Bono well-deserved kudos for his ability to sell himself as a messianic figure during the 1980s and then reap the capitalistic rewards for that performance ten years later. He's a cagey charlatan.

Bono was able to morph himself into whatever his fans needed him to be: He could be angry, brooding, vulnerable, or romantic—and sometimes all at the same moment. Rose is the same kind of shape-shifter, but for a different, less stable audience. His style is even more schizophrenic. He swings from being openly violent and misogynistic (like on the song "It's So Easy") to acting utterly helpless (such as the brilliant closing two and a half minutes of "Rocket Queen," my vote for the finest 171 seconds of '80s rock). In the video for "Don't Cry," emotional juxtaposition is pretty much all Axl does. But unlike Bono, Guns N' Roses never played "college rock." It was never specifically directed at smart people. GNR wrote for a younger audience—the kind of people who still slammed bedroom doors and huffed gas in the garage.

When Ross Raihala first tried to explain what Morrissey meant to him as a teenager, I didn't get it; whenever I listen to the Smiths, I can sense homosexual overtones, but that's mostly because I now actively look for them. It doesn't seem "obvious" at all. But that says more about me than it does about the Smiths. My favorite Smiths songs are "Half a Person" and "Ask," and—since I apply them to myself—I don't see any indisputable gay imagery in either of those songs. Raihala thinks that assertion is ridiculous and he's almost insulted by the suggestion. The reason he takes it as an insult is because it attacks the validity of the connection between Morrissey and the gay community. As a person, Morrissey has never publicly said "I'm gay," nor has he written any songs that empirically state his sexual preference—

yet he (apparently) drops hints constantly. It's easy to understand why closeted gay teens could relate to that: Like Morrissey, they couldn't say who they were, but a big part of them wanted people to figure it out.

Morrissey was "their voice"—a person who spoke from their minority perspective and was able to inject his feelings and ideas into the mainstream culture. If you were recognized as a Morrissey fan, it said something about who you were: To guys like Raihala, it meant either (a) you *were* gay, or (b) you were certainly comfortable with the gay lifestyle. I would guess there are many members of the gay community who buy Morrissey albums even though they don't especially care for the music, just because it seems like the proper thing to do. His music and social posture built a persona, and that persona ultimately stretched far beyond his albums. But since he's still a mere pop singer, his disciples can only connect with him through the appreciation of his records. Raihala now owns thousands of CDs and listens to new music every day, but he says he can still sing along to all seven Smiths studio records in their absolute entirety.

Interestingly enough, *Appetite for Destruction* is probably the only record I could karaoke from beginning to end. Part of that is because I've listened to it so much—but the larger explanation for why I did is probably similar to Raihala's adoration of Morrissey. My motivation wasn't as specific—it did not derive from a singular issue—but it was reflective of my personality in the same way.

I don't think it would be accurate to call Axl Rose "my voice" or even "our voice," because Guns N' Roses was way too popular. While Morrissey was famous, he was never famous the way Axl was; total sales from all those Smiths LPs would not equal the 15 million-plus copies of *Appetite* that sold worldwide. It's unrealistic to think any rock singer can represent an audience of that size. But Rose did represent his core audience, which were people who came from the same place. The fact that he was a rural kid (born in Lafayette, Indiana) was a huge factor, particularly because he always seemed to weave it into the music. All those *Appetite* songs made L.A. seem (quite literally) like a "jungle" the band had parachuted into. GNR rhythm guitarist Izzy Stradlin was also from Indiana, and he once said, "Nobody goes to Los Angeles. L.A. is where you *end up*." So that was how we came to view Axl: He was the guy who took our small-town paradigm and applied it to the real world—a world that had once seemed glamorous and now seemed like a twisted, sinister paradise city.

Of all the L.A. metal bands, Guns N' Roses talked about Hollywood the most (even more than Junkyard, a band whose first single was specifically titled "Hollywood"). Mötley Crüe had a song called "Danger" that described the seedy underside of Los Angeles, but they always seemed like a band who *belonged* in southern California. Vince Neil looked like a surfer (he was kind of like a belligerent version of David Lee Roth), and Nikki Sixx had bounced around that scene for years.

L.A. Guns was actually named for its place of origin, but that was yet another accentuation of Axl's obsession. You see, Rose was the original singer for L.A. Guns, and he briefly stole that group's guitarist (Tracii Guns) to form an early incarnation of Guns N' Roses (one can assume the name was an abbreviated version of "Mr. Guns and Mr. Rose"). Izzy Stradlin promptly joined this group after brief stints with Shire and London and another GNR precursor called Hollywood Rose (who were sometimes known as the Hollywood Roses and briefly included Axl as the frontman). While in Hollywood Rose, Izzy, and Axl quit working with Tracii to hook up with Slash (who—at the time— was auditioning for Poison). Somehow, Axl managed to keep Tracii's stage name for *his* band. It's all very confusing and incestuous, and it barely matters today. But accept this as true: Axl clearly loved the concept of Los Angeles, even if he constantly sang about how disgusting it was. Like a new student in a new school, he was always trying to prove he belonged there. Judging from his performance on *Appetite for Destruction*, Axl thought about Los Angeles the same way I thought about L.A. when I read those *Shout at the Devil* liner notes in the fifth grade.

Axl wasn't a nice person. He beat up camera-wielding fans and treated women like shit. It seems like most of the women he slept with eventually accused him of being a violent lover (ex-wife Erin Everly and ex-girlfriend Stephanie Seymour both filed abuse charges against him). And generally, this sinister weakness made him *more* alluring to redneck intellectuals. There has never been a time in my life when I supported violence against women, and I can't think of many things that I find more repelling. But there was a weird legitimacy to this kind of image. Let's face it: Sadness and evil are always more believable than happiness and love. When a movie reviewer calls a film "realistic," everyone knows what that means—it means the movie has an unhappy ending. We associate happy endings with fairy tales, and Guns N' Roses was no fairy tale.

I once did a human interest story on two guys from West Fargo named Mark Rudel and Gregg Lura. *(Reader's note: For those of you wondering where West Fargo is . . . well, that should be self-explanatory.)* These two fellows were essentially male groupies; they loved to meet metal stars and had all sorts of tricks to get backstage. They were damn good at it, too: They met virtually every major hair band from the '80s. When I asked them about meeting Guns N' Roses outside of a Fargo hotel at 4:00 A.M. during GNR's '93 tour, this was what Rudel told me: "I tried to get an autograph from Slash, but he just hobbled past me. It was exactly like a video—you couldn't see his eyes, he had his top hat on, and he was stumbling around. One of the roadies said he'd had a long night. Of all the bands we've met, Guns N' Roses appeared to live their life the most like their image."

I'm kind of ashamed to admit it, but hearing that made me very happy. In some ways, I suppose that proves I'm just another stupid fan. I wanted Guns N' Roses to be the band I imagined they were. When Rudel talked about meeting the guys from Cinderella, the conversation focused on how normal they seemed (he specifically said Tom Keifer looked sleepy and "really pale"). Guns N' Roses had always seemed more real than other groups, and I honestly think they might have been. Instead of mirroring the rock 'n' roll lifestyle, Guns N' Roses adopted it for real—almost like they couldn't tell it was supposed to be a gimmick to sell records. They were as fucked up as advertised.

At least I hope they were.

December 12, 1985

While listening to Judas Priest's
Stained Class LP, eighteen-year-old
Raymond Belknap blows off his head with
a shotgun. His twenty-one-year-old friend
James Vance tries to do the same and—
somehow—manages to fail.

I don't know why two guys from Nevada would think that a gay British metal singer was telling them to kill themselves. I honestly have no clue whatsoever, and I can't even speculate. Sure, they were drinking a few afternoon beers and smoking some low-grade dope, but that's hardly an excuse for getting *that* confused about anything. In 1985, I listened to *Stained Class* at a friend's house, and that didn't even convince me to buy the goddamn record.

Moreover, I've never understood why European heavy metal is so appealing to kids who like shooting themselves in the head, but they obviously love it. Oh, I understand the superficial connection and the conventional explanation: Downtrodden people dig downtrodden rock, so it would stand to reason that the darkest kinds of hard rock would fit that criteria perfectly. But these self-destructive obsessions are intertwined in a way that goes far deeper than pop psychology. Teen suicides in 1984, 1986, and 1988 were all blamed on Ozzy Osbourne, and I assume all three accusations are at least partially accurate. I'm also certain that Eric Harris and Dylan Klebold were rocking out to Rammstein when they decided to fill the Columbine High library with teenage corpses.

Now, don't get me wrong: I am not suggesting that the music *made* these people go violently insane. But it's equally as stupid to argue that there's no connection at all. Every year, billions of dollars are spent in the advertising industry. This is done on the premise that information can influence the behavior of consumers, and it obviously does. If kids are affected by Sprite commercials and Ronald McDonald, why *wouldn't* they be affected by Rob Halford?

The difference, of course, is that Halford never specifically told anyone to kill themselves. To me, that's always the weirdest part of all rock suicides: None of these kids were listening to music that actually instructed them to shoot themselves. Parents and lawyers point to the Ozzy song "Suicide Solution," which (granted) is a pretty misleading title for a supposed antisuicide song; Metallica's "Fade to Black" is another example that pushes the envelope. But if you actually listen to the words, you will see that these songs don't say suicide is a good move. And one would assume that any kid so obsessed with a record *that he's going to fucking kill himself over it* would take the time to listen to the lyrics (or at least read the liner notes!).

This paradox is what I find so perplexing about the way young males perceive verbal messages in heavy metal. I'll never understand why music that only made me want long hair is the same product that made some kids want to die. Normal people don't care what Ozzy has to say about *anything*; however, it seems the handful of people who *do care* inevitably get confused and kill themselves. And since the mood of the music tends to be more persuasive than the actual lyrics—and since the words to most rock songs are almost impossible to understand—kids are forced to interpret heavy metal in any way they can. This is a substantial problem, because the kind of kids who truly love heavy metal evidently suck at artistic interpretation.

My favorite professor from college was a guy named Scott Lowe, a very thin man who owns a large collection of cardigan sweaters and briefly dabbled in a 1970s California cult that was led by a false prophet named Franklin Jones. He grew up in Florida with his boyhood friend Jimmy Buffett (which may or may not be true) and is one of the only rational environmentalists I have ever met (the other being a guy named Zinda who admired Glenn Danzig). Scott taught religious studies. This academic program had virtually nothing to do with my major (or even my minor), but his upper-level classes always seemed to involve the wackiest lectures on campus. I can recall at least two discussions that briefly touched on the practice of drinking caribou urine in order to get stoned.

ANYWAY, Scott spent his teenage days as a guitarist in a Kinks-influenced garage band, so we would occasionally chat about pop music. Since these conversations would sometimes occur in the middle of a lecture on, say, the Spanish Inquisition, it was not completely uncommon to connect the topics of Christianity and rock, thereby segueing into a verbal treatise on the value (or lack thereof) of "Christian rock." And it was during one of these conversations that I decided my favorite Christian rock band was Rush.

Most people (or—more accurately—*all* people except me) do not consider Rush a Christian rock band. However, this fact is virtually indisputable. Aren't pretty much all their songs about Jesus? It certainly seems like it. At the very least, Rush albums promote some sort of bass-heavy Christian value system. "He's trying to save the day for the Old World man," proclaim the soaring vocals of Canadian spiritualist Geddy Lee. "He's trying to pave the way for the Third World man." Isn't that the entire New Testament encapsulated in two lines? Didn't Jesus teach us to bid "A Farewell to Kings" and to watch the humble "Working Man" inherit the earth? And I'm sure God likes "Trees" and hates racism at least as much as Neil Peart does.

Nobody ever believes me when I start talking about Rush's hard-line Christian stance, but every time I hear their music it becomes more and more clear. Listen to the song "Freewill": I have a hard time understanding *exactly* what Lee is talking about here, but I can tell it has something to do with being a good person (or with being an honest person, or a stoic person, or holding some vague personality trait that God would probably support). "Freewill" also implies something about agnostics going to hell, but that's just par for the course when it comes to Rush. I even have some suspicions about the metaphorical significance of "The Spirit of Radio," and that goes double for the cover art on *Grace Under Pressure, Fly by Night* (a fucking owl?), and—most notably—the homoerotic purgatory imagery on the sleeve for *Hemispheres*. Who is in the Temple of Syrinx? Perhaps it's Jesus.

The reason I bring this up is because I think it says a lot about perception, which is the tool we all use to build the context for our lives. Even if my thinking is flawed (and I assume it is), it does indicate that—somehow—Rush has purposefully or accidentally put themselves in a position where virtually anybody can make an oblique argument about what they represent. This is a common problem for hard rock bands, and especially for Rush; everyone wants to categorize them, but no one wants to claim them. As bassist Lee once said, "It's funny. When you talk to metal people about Rush, eight out of ten will tell you we're not a metal band. But if you talk to anyone outside of metal, eight out of ten will tell you we are a metal band." And Geddy's totally right. In high school, I would never have classified Rush as a metal band. I barely thought they were a hard rock group; now I'm mentioning Rush in this book

So what does that mean? Well, on one level it simply proves that attempts to categorize anything (rock groups and otherwise) have more to do with personal perception than with reality. Of course—as anyone who has spent too many hours studying communication theory will tell you—perception is reality. And it's within that construct of perception-driven reality where we start to see the relationship between heavy metal and the people who listened to it (and maybe even the people who use metal as a soundtrack for suicide).

Here again, I feel forced to use self-destructive drug abuse as the clearest metaphor for life. Regardless of how someone describes their drug use—as a "habit," as a "problem," as a "recreation," whatever—they are really just trying to find a euphemism for their *lifestyle*. Even if the actual ingestion of narcotics consumes only a fraction of their free time, it's never a minor personality quirk. For one thing, it's illegal; for another, it freaks out a good chunk of the population. Drug use is really a lifestyle choice. Though drugs do not necessarily change your life, taking drugs will change the way people look at you (and the way you will look at yourself). Those who have no personal experience with drugs will assume that you're throwing your life away; certain people will not date you. Employers will be more willing to accept a DUI conviction than the mere rumor that you have a drug problem. Consequently, drug users will absorb these perceptions and recognize that they are now in a different societal class: They have a secret that makes them both vulnerable and dangerous—and it probably makes their lives a lot more interesting (at least for a while).

Talk to people who do a lot of drugs (or regularly drink to excess), and they will tell you they love it for at least two reasons. One is the physical effect of getting fucked up. The other is the actual process. It's not just fun to be high; it's fun *to smoke pot.* It's fun to score dope and put ice cubes in the bong and put on boring reggae records and talk with other stoners about idiotic stoner topics. It's fun to browse through liquor stores and mix drinks on the coffee table and tell memorable puke stories. There is an appeal to the Abuse Lifestyle that exists outside of the product.

Glam metal had the same kind of appeal: It was all about an unspoken lifestyle. It's a feeling that can't be quantified or easily explained, but it absolutely exists.

One of the interesting things about '80s metal is that it was the first dominant pop genre to exist in a readily available multimedia context. What that means is that you could copiously consume heavy metal without listening to heavy metal albums. Pop metal was a mainstay of album-oriented FM outlets, so metal could be heard over the populist medium of radio; unlike punk or late '60s psychedelia, it was not trapped underground. There were also the wide array of tours and concerts, so you might be able to see a few big acts every summer (assuming you lived near a big enough community and your parents felt you were old enough to go to rock concerts).

But just as importantly, the 1980s saw the dawn of what I call the Golden Age of Periodicals. Suddenly, young metal fans could choose from a glut of easy-to-find metal magazines. There was a time when reading about rock 'n' roll was limited to reading *Rolling Stone* or maybe *Creem,* and its distribution was sketchy (unless you lived in New York, or San Francisco, or some kind of a collegiate culture). By 1985, that problem no longer existed. In fact, you did not even need to purchase rock literature; I can fondly remember loitering at the magazine racks in supermarkets while my mom shopped for groceries, paging through *Hit Parader* and *Circus* and *Kerrang!* and *Metal Edge.* And by this point, *Rolling Stone* was so mainstream that it was in my high school library.

And this new explosion in rock journalism wasn't teen idol coverage either. *Hit Parader* and *Circus* were driven by interviews and considered to be "news" publications (at least to its readership). The interviews were always horrible and the information was often fabricated, but these updates were still the main objects of interest. I always felt magazines that primarily delivered posters or pinups were rip-offs.

A third component came in 1981 with the introduction of MTV. Its significance was obvious (especially in retrospect), but people tend to forget that it came with an undercurrent. It would take several years before MTV became a cultural universal. A well-known irony about the network is that it was not broadcast in the city limits of New York until 1983—even though that's where it was produced. Moreover, few rural communities had access to any cable channels. I did not watch two consecutive hours of MTV until August of 1990.

However, videos still had a massive effect, especially on people born after 1970. For (ahem) "Generation X" kids, videos were not seen as promotional gimmicks or special treats: Videos were expected. Since I was a farm kid, I couldn't spend six hours a night staring at Martha Quinn and MTV—but I *could* spend ninety minutes a week watching *Friday Night Videos*, NBC's attempt at a knockoff. Meanwhile, my friends who lived in town could watch *Night Tracks* on one of the seven cable networks that serviced Wyndmere proper (and by 1985, the richer kids could even capture these clips on VHS tape!). Moreover, we knew that people in Fargo were seeing this stuff 24/7. That was the magic of Music Television: You did not have to see MTV to be affected by it: *You only had to know it was out there.* One way or another, the images would all slip into everyone's collective consciousness. Case in point: I never saw the full video for Mötley Crüe's *Looks That Kill* until college—but I already knew what it looked like in 1986. I saw a clip of it on an episode of ABC's *20/20* that examined the rising fear of teen satanism (I suppose the argument could be made that this kind of sensationalistic media coverage provided still another tier for metal appreciation: public discourse).

What this all means is that glam metal was a layered construction. This phenomenon is completely common today—in fact, it's virtually the *only* way rock exists in contemporary terms, and now it includes the especially elastic medium of cyberspace. But it was new in the 1980s. In fact, it was so new that its first consumers never even realized it.

As I mentioned earlier, I never watched MTV until 1990, when I had already graduated from high school and happened to be visiting my eldest sister in Atlanta. However, I hated MTV when I was in junior high; I completely and totally despised everything it represented. I even wrote an essay about it in tenth grade, and I got an A.

The obvious question here is, "Why?" Or, perhaps more accurately, "How?" I had no exposure to MTV, so how could I hate it? The answer came from those "news" magazines I mentioned several paragraphs ago. In *Hit Parader*, all the bands expressed one unifying opinion: MTV sucked. MTV didn't play metal videos. MTV was afraid of heavy rock bands. And most importantly, MTV made metal groups compromise what they truly wanted to do: "Give the kids the fucking rock they fucking deserve!"

My friends and I hated MTV for these very reasons. In and of itself, that's crazy. But what's even crazier is that we would have *loved* MTV if we had ever actually seen it. During all the years I despised MTV, metal was pretty much all they played. Watching my sister's TV that summer made this incredibly clear; I saw Mötley Crüe's "Girl Don't Go Away Mad," Poison's "Unskinny Bop," and Faith No More's "Epic" almost constantly; the only other artists who shared a fraction of the air time were the rap group Bel Biv Devoe and Billy Idol (who almost could have passed for a metal guy himself). The metal world's contempt for MTV was an utter lie; it was unabashed underdog posturing that further illustrates the hypocrisy of corporate shock rock.

But it also makes total sense, considering the state of the world.

I'm hesitant to draw too close a connection between heavy metal and socio-economic policy, and I'm almost as hesitant to say one even reflected the other. It's too easy to do, and it seems like the kind of clever intellectual connection that's almost always irrelevant. But consider this: What were the fundamental messages of Reagan-era politics? It was driven by capitalism (i.e., "the greedy '80s"), saber-rattling (i.e., "the Evil Empire"), and a vaguely hypocritical emphasis on gritty, commonsense values (remember those campaign commercials where Reagan chopped wood?). And what were the fundamental ideals of glam rock? Philosophical capitalism (everyone was a superstar), philosophical saber-rattling (like Nikki Sixx declaring that metal was at war with commercial forces trying to shackle his "identity"), and omnipresent reminders that all these bands came from the lowest tier of society (in song, Axl Rose described himself as "just a small-town white boy" who moved to L.A. and became "just an urchin livin' under the street"—and the operative watchword in both statements is the inclusion of the modifier "just").

There are a few parallels here that belie sarcasm. It's a weird paradox; while rock in the late 1960s and early '70s seemed to exist as a political reaction to Richard Nixon's administration, glam metal latently adopted the Republican persona of the 1980s. And that was a wise move: This was an incredibly popular way of thinking, especially (and surprisingly) among young males. One of the most popular sitcoms of the era was *Family Ties*, and the character that everyone loved was Alex P. Keaton, the savvy young Republican portrayed by Michael J. Fox. Alex was a "cool" conservative—in other words, he wasn't some unlikeable guy who whined about social morality. He was all about making money and out-flanking naive idealists; it seemed that Alex didn't so much hate liberals as he hated *hippies*. And it has always been fun to hate hippies. By the mid-1980s, flower children had inherited the establishment; that alone would have been enough to make teens bristle, but ex-hippies added an even more repulsive element: They constantly insisted that they were the most important generation that ever existed. *They* stopped the war; *they* had things they believed in; *they* changed the world. There is nothing more repulsive or condescending than a nostalgic Baby Boomer. The fact that Alex P. Keaton ridiculed their impractical, antiquated value system was reason enough to support the GOP. Sometimes I think people want to forget how cool it was to cop a conservative persona in 1988. I mean, that's pretty much what being "preppie" was all about: It was supposed to show that you were smart —or at least smart enough not to look stupid.

As this point, one can start to see (or maybe project) the cultural impact of the metal years. Something was going on here: People were using culture as a way to view themselves, just as they always had—but we were dealing with a new kind of iconography.

If you ask someone what's the first thing they remember about (or associate with) '80s metal bands, the answer is almost always "hair." As I've mentioned, "hair metal" quickly became a pejorative term for heavy metal. The derivation of that trend mirrors the derivation of the music: A heavy rock god like Robert Plant had long hair, while a poofy glitter-pop guy like Marc Bolan worried about how his hair looked. Fused together, you had the pop metal persona: Loud glam bands with miles of follicles and a desire to do something with it. And there's only so much you can do with long hair, assuming you're not a Rastafarian—you can braid it, or you can poof it up. Willie Nelson went one way, and Cinderella went the other.

In fact, as I type this very sentence, I am looking at the cover of Cinderella's *Night Songs* LP. Vocalist Tom Keifer is pointing at me with both his index fingers, and his outfit features somewhere between three and five scarves. It's all pretty groovy, but I am nonetheless drawn to his head. It appears perfectly spherical; his hair is a uniform length, and it is standing at attention. It's like a lion's mane. Grrr.

In an old MTV interview, Keifer once bemoaned the fact that he kept seeing reviews of *Night Songs* where writers talked exclusively about the group's hair (guitarist Jeff LaBar had an even more obnoxious coif than Keifer). Truth be told, it was a semivalid complaint; Cinderella consistently wrote better pop metal than their peers (now that I've had a decade to think it over, I would still place *Night Songs* among the ten best albums of 1986, metal or otherwise). But I can totally understand why journalists had a hard time getting over the band's appearance. Though Cindy's music did stretch beyond the glam metal formula (albeit only slightly), their look defined it. I'm sure the group regrets the *Night Songs* album cover. From a cultural perspective, it's a wonderfully telling period piece, but it makes the band seem idiotic. It's like watching episodes of *American Bandstand* from the early 1960s and realizing these people are not actors. You've got to force yourself to remember that *Night Songs* is not satire. In fact, you could not do satire this effectively on purpose.

But—at the same time—I'm also taking an all-too-easy cheap shot. This sardonic commentary comes long after the point of impact, and it didn't seem so stupid at the time. Cinderella's hair may have been a bit outlandish (or at least outlandish enough to be noticed by record reviewers), but that was the style of the day. Conventional pop artists accentuated that even more; a band like A Flock of Seagulls is *only* remembered for its hair (and one catchy single). And there *was* a reason for all this.

Whenever you hear Gene Simmons or Alice Cooper refer to the early '70s New York glam scene, they always talk about "getting noticed." They use that phrase in the context of live performance; if someone like the New York Dolls had played a club on Friday, Saturday's audience would have a certain expectation, and it often had nothing to do with the music.

A new paradigm for musical success had been created. For someone like Brian Wilson, success had meant writing songs that were competitive with the Beatles. For someone like Jimmy Page, success would always be associated by record sales that dwarfed the commercial performance of other artists, including the Rolling Stones. But this generation of glam groups had a different set of priorities. Their two descriptions of success were (a) creating a buzz, and (b) getting paid. The musical product was secondary to being able to get gigs where you would be seen (and hopefully seen again). Style was beating substance, and this time it was on purpose.

"The New York Dolls were media darlings," Cooper told me in 1998, "but—at the time—they were purely a joke to everybody who saw them. They were like Sha Na Na. They certainly didn't sell records. It was only after they broke up that they somehow became important."

Max's Kansas City in 1972 was a microcosm of the whole world in 1985. With the proliferation of pop bands and—more importantly—the proliferation of media, the need for attention became paramount. All of America was now a singular club scene. You could see a band perform through videos, and you could effectively "hang out" with the guys in the group by reading magazine articles. The only key for the artist was entering the public consciousness. You needed to be able to *stop* people—to stop them from flipping channels, and to stop them from turning the page. The means for earning this attention couldn't be too high concept either; accelerated culture does not respond well to the nonobvious. Consequently, bands took the most blatant avenue: Make everything larger. Including your head.

So here we have the first metaphorical example of metal's influence on the teen mind-set of the 1980s—the hunger for what can probably be called "obvious success." Around this same period, African-Americans began proliferating the phrase "living large," the modern incarnation of an old jazz term. This is probably just coincidental—but it still seems strange how fervently the idea of size (both literal and figurative) reemerged as a key indicator of how good something was. As always, it goes back to the idea of a cultural pendulum. The late 1970s had felt the crunch of the oil shortage; our too-nice-to-be-effective president Jimmy Carter even urged Americans to wear sweaters instead of burning dinosaur bones. By 1985, those days were over. America was back, and so was the sweet pleasure of gluttony. The explosion in hair (and fashion, and volume) was the other side of consumerism.

Tom Keifer didn't wake up one morning with that hairdo (although at times it may have looked like he did). That doesn't prove he was necessarily making a conscious *statement*, either. But within all that Aqua Net, there was a message—maybe not his, but someone's. I'm certain no one ever killed themselves listening to *Long Cold Winter*, but Tom was still talking about life and death. Judas Priest supposedly made kids point guns at their heads; Cinderella made me do the same thing with a hair dryer.

It's all too easy to get attention by making yourself dead. I was trying to get attention by being alive in a really obvious way.

Summer, 1986

Poison.

The concept of rock music being tied to glamour is incredibly predictable and—in some respects—essential. Except for those Sarah McLachlan-esque idiots who insist they "need" to make music, it's really the only reason anyone gets into rock 'n' roll.

However, there's an important difference between "altruistic glamour" and "constructed glamour." Some people are going to be perceived as glamorous even if they don't try. Look at some of those old shots of Jane Fonda when she's in the jungles of Vietnam: It was impossible for her not to be sexy, even when she was covered in swamp shit. The same goes for gun-toting Patty Hearst and tennis superfox Monica Seles—it's not just that they manage to look good in unflattering circumstances, they look *famous* in unflattering circumstances. They sweat like they're in Nike commercials. Young Jim Morrison had this quality, as does his modern-day doppelgänger Eddie Vedder. So does Michael Jordan. Altruistic glamour is something that goes beyond the temporary schemata of society and rests squarely on the truth that some people have an undeniable visual charisma.

Like just about everyone else, I am attracted to altruistic glamour. But I'm not interested in it at all.

Constructed glamour is far more intriguing. It's almost as attractive, but not in a visceral sense. Constructed glamour requires an intellectual element. Take heroin chic, the "look" that dominated modeling runways in the mid 1990s. Heroin chic was a weird middle ground between altruistic and constructed glamour; it was *constructed* to make females seem *altruistically* glamorous under the *construction* of a situation that should have been *altruistically* damaging (i.e., seventeen-year-old girls with hollow eyes who shoot smack all day and stay alive by eating unsalted popcorn). To find these models sexy, you have to know they were *trying* to look like they were dying. As always, that's the singular key to appearing ridiculous; as long as everyone knows you're doing it, it's completely cool.

That brings us to the early days of glam rock, which cultural revisionists have started to call glitter rock, mainly to downplay its evolution into glam metal (I've never heard anyone use the term "glitter metal"). Glam rock is the ultimate personification of constructed glamour. It takes an idea and turns it into fashion, and the fashion evolves into a philosophy. The idea is that in order to be a rock star *you have to be a rock star.* You are not a normal person. Even if you don't possess altruistic glamour, you can be glamorous. Quite honestly, it's the same kind of thinking that drives drag queen culture (this will come as no surprise to people who remember Dee Snider).

I no longer think there's any question about whether or not pop culture swings on a pendulum between style and substance—it does. The late '60s had freedom rock, so the reaction was '70s art rock. Since no one could relate to ELP and Jethro Tull, the world was subjected to punk by '77, which burned itself out before anyone got rich. Punk was perfect for lazy people, because anyone could do it—you didn't even need to know how to play your instrument, assuming you knew how to plug it in. There was really no difference between Sid Vicious and anyone in London who owned a bass. But people still wanted to act famous (don't they always?), so that opened the door to glam metal in '83. And as we all know, glam was shattered by '92 grunge, a musical genre that seemed to exist for the sole purpose of making metal commercially unpopular.

Anyone who's taken an entry-level sociology class (in fact, pretty much anyone who has ever used the word "sociology" in its proper context) can explain why Seattle power pop was so effective. The unspoken statement made by '90s alternative music was "We're all the same, man. I play this guitar and you know who I am, and I will never know who you are, but I am still a normal person. I am *not* a rock star. In fact, I am going to make records for a label called Kill Rock Stars. If you recognize me in public, I will hate you. That will prove that I love you, because we are all the same." But there was never anything real about those sentiments. It's an illusion that lasts as long as its audience is willing to believe it. The ultimate goal for Bob Dylan, the Beatles, Foghat, Uriah Heep, the Clash, Bon Jovi, and Sonic Youth was all ultimately the same: *They wanted to make music that other people wanted to hear.* That's really the only reason for going into a recording studio. What music "means" is almost completely dependent on the people who sell it and the people who buy it, not the people who make it. Our greatest artists are the ones who understand how they can be interesting and unique within those limitations.

What happened to music in the 1990s was not bad; it was extremely important for at least three reasons. One was that it better reflected the era; another was that we got a handful of truly great personalities and a few dozen wonderful songs. But the third (and perhaps more disturbing) quality was that the "imageless" Seattle music scene finally achieved what constructed glamour had always intended: It made *everybody* into a rock star, because it no longer mattered what you looked like or how you acted. And eventually, all these superstars were completely interchangeable (which proved to be a painful downside for everybody). This wasn't so much the work of the artists as the spin of the modern media—had the original class of '77 punks existed in the accelerated culture of 1992, I'm sure they would have become just as homogenized. I have no doubt whatsoever that we would have heard Muzak versions of "God Save the Queen."

I was twenty when the grunginess of Nirvana exploded, and—looking back—it *was* a pretty amazing period to be a rock fan in a collegiate setting. Everything about popular music was being analyzed as it happened; everything was so clear. There was never a "vague undercurrent" that the pop world was changing, because all those social changes were being publicly dissected the moment they occurred. I was told why *Exile in Guyville* was "groundbreaking" the very same day I discovered the record existed. In fact, the first time it hit me that all the Seattle bands wore flannel shirts was when I read a news story about how this fashion trend was "changing the self-image of Generation X." Prior to seeing that article, I had barely noticed what the fuck those guys were wearing.

Obviously, the goal (and the effect) of glam rock had been precisely the opposite—you couldn't *not* notice the visual side to the music, even if it supposedly meant nothing and the media didn't give a damn. The metal bands I liked were an extension of an altogether different aesthetic: They created characters, and they did so consciously. If dressing like a lumberjack speaks to an entire demographic of young people, dressing like a transvestite speaks only to the dude who's wearing the heels. Glam is a struggle *against* normalcy.

Ground zero for the glam movement can be traced back to one singular guy—David Bowie. Yet Bowie does not play a role in this discussion, and here's why: He did not directly influence metal (at least not '80s metal). At best, he's at least one full cultural generation removed. Over the past five years, it's become very chic for hard rockers to credit Bowie as a major influence, and it would be cool if he had been—but most of these bands are lying. All that adoration is coming retrospectively. When hairspray bands were developing in 1983, Bowie was putting out records like "Let's Dance" and dressing like a waiter from the Olive Garden. At the time, it was certainly not cool for any self-respecting metal dude to emulate David Bowie (even the old Bowie).

The paradox is that metal bands ended up taking their cues from all the guys who had been able to make a living by *ripping off* Bowie. Even though a third of T. Rex's catalog is folkie unicorn shit and another third is shamelessly gorgeous pop, Marc Bolan was a major influence for countless metal bands. The New York Dolls were also a factor, although not as much as rock critics tend to imply. Music critics consistently make the mistake of thinking that the "dissonant" (read: "tuneless") albums they appreciate are somehow influencing culture. No normal listener gives a hoot about any goddamn song the New York Dolls ever made. The only people who have even listened to their material are (a) rock journalists, and (b) the people who read books written by rock journalists (and half of those people are lying). *But those shoes!* The album cover from the Dolls' debut record is more important than any song they ever wrote. It's the purest, sexiest example of constructed glamour in the history of the world.

And—more importantly—the Dolls were outlandish enough to influence KISS. Time is slowly proving that KISS is the second-most influential rock band of all time. The Beatles will always be number one, because they were the first, the greatest, the smartest, and the origin for everything that would come next. The Rolling Stones introduced the attitude rock guys were supposed to have (no one will ever be cooler), and Led Zeppelin acted the way rock bands were supposed to act (there will never be a group as archetypal as Zep). But KISS were *rock stars*. The guys in KISS were walking metaphors for most of what had come before them and everything that would come after.

Gene Simmons has said that KISS selected its look by accident; since they were big macho guys (or at least he was) playing big macho songs, KISS couldn't be glammy the way the Dolls or Bolan or Bowie were glammy. Instead, they went with the colors black and white, and the attire bordered on the sadomasochistic.

This straightforward template did not last long. By 1975, Paul Stanley had the hair, lips, and stage moves of the hairiest supermodel in pop history. Ace Frehley was trying to look "futuristic" (or at least making his best drunken guess as to how the future would appear—I suppose he did predict the advent of moon boots). As for Peter "Cat Man" Criss . . . well, Peter didn't try too hard. When he left the band, Eric Carr replaced him as "The Fox," which—for all practical purposes—is just a meaner type of cat. (*Reader's note: The author is not a zoologist.*) Gene Simmons's appearance and behavior also evolved over time; between

Rock and Roll Over and *Dynasty,* he went through a long phase where he tried to look and act like a robot. This era officially ended with *(Music from) The Elder,* when the band decided it would be cool to wear capes and headbands. Of course, the crowning moment in KISStory was Vinnie Vincent's "Egyptian Warrior" regalia he donned as the replacement for Frehley. This was a stunningly original character. It paid homage to all the famous Egyptian soldiers renowned for their military prowess . . . of which there are exactly zero. Sometimes Vinnie's persona is referred to as "The Pharaoh," which would seem to indicate that he was a rock 'n' roll slave owner. Oh well.

ANYWAY, it's difficult to overestimate the significance of the KISS makeup. Without the greasepaint, they would have probably made only three albums that would have all sold horribly (although I have the sinking suspicion that if that had been the case all the rock critics who currently hate them would now call them a "raw, seminal influence that predates New York punk"). As it is, KISS made a few million kids want to pick up guitars and pretend to be someone they're not. And that *is* rock 'n' roll, 99 percent of the time.

That predilection was self-perpetuating. Exactly one decade after KISS made *Destroyer,* the world was introduced to Poison, a quartet of lovely ladies who were actually three guys from Pennsylvania and a dope fiend from Brooklyn. We in the Midwest first heard them in the spring of 1987 on AOR stations like Fargo's Q-98; the song was "Talk Dirty to Me," which—if my memory serves me correctly—was the greatest song anyone had ever recorded up to that point in history. It peaked at No. 9 on the *Billboard* charts in May of '87, but its significance was exponentially greater. It was *the* song of the summer, which is the highest honor any single can achieve (regardless of its genre).

I am tempted to claim that listening to Poison in the summer of 1987 remains one of the most vivid memories of my adolescence. However, that would only be a half-truth, mostly because I *swear* the year this song was popular was 1985. This is one of those embarrassing situations where I'm so goddamn positive

I'm correct that I refuse to listen to any opposing arguments, even if the main argument is historical record.

Here's why I'm so adamant about this: 1985 was the year Wyndmere celebrated its centennial. This was a *huge* deal; without question, it was the biggest community event that ever happened to my hometown. The weekend of the centennial, the population of Wyndmere went from just under five hundred to just over ten thousand. And on Friday night of that weekend, there was a "teen dance" on the town's freshly built tennis court, located across the street from the Catholic church. I was about to enter eighth grade, and I had a gut-wrenching crush on a tenth-grade girl named Janet Veit. What was so weird about this particular infatuation was that it actually seemed like Janet kind of liked *me* (although I have never been able to verify this). Earlier that spring, we would occasionally hang around during track practice, which was about as close to dating as I ever got during the first nineteen years of my life. If nothing else, I am certain that Janet thought I was mildly amusing, and she always seemed touched that I was *impressed* that she was a 4.0 student. And I suppose Janet, like any young woman, was a little flattered by my desire to talk to her at every possible opportunity and for any reason whatsoever (I once begged her to proofread a science-fiction novel I was supposedly writing, even though I had only completed its title—*Bud Moe, the Man in the Lighthouse*). I assume all of these factors played a role in our nonexisting relationship, which was punctuated by the event that transpired during "Talk Dirty to Me" on the fateful night of the Centennial Teen Dance.

At this point, savvy readers are undoubtedly trying to guess what this "event" will be. A first kiss? A first snuggle? A first *anything*? I'm sure if Janet Veit is reading this, she's asking these particular questions with exasperated anticipation (or maybe she's trying to remember if she actually talked to me during track practice that year). However, the answer may ultimately seem anticlimactic: We were merely the first people who walked out on that tennis court and danced. The song (obviously) was

"Talk Dirty to Me," a track I requested from the DJ even though Janet told me to request "Danger Zone" or some other fucking song off the *Top Gun* soundtrack. But to be honest, I find this "event" far more memorable than either my first kiss or my first sexual encounter. Why? Because those were both things I *wanted* to do. However, I did not want to dance that night, and I certainly did not want to dance in public. I have always tried to live by a simple principle: If I am sober enough to drive, I am too sober to dance. But this 1985 encounter with Janet Veit and Poison made me realize another principle I would live by, and this one has never been within my control: If I really like a girl, I will do absolutely anything, as long as I think it will make her like me. Oh, I might manipulate the situation to fit my espoused persona (i.e., replacing Kenny Loggins with C. C. DeVille), but it will always be a faint-hearted compromise. As I bounced around the tennis court that night, I thought about how cool it would be to meet Janet at the drive-in or behind the bushes or down the basement (lock the cellar door!). But I knew my life as a man was over, and I was only fourteen.

Now, it *is* entirely possible that this happened exactly the way I remember it. Maybe this whole encounter happened at an altogether different teen dance (although I honestly can't remember going to any others). But I still can't ignore the contradictions of the timing: How could I request a song that hadn't even been recorded? And didn't *Top Gun* come out in 1986? To this day, I am still hounded by the incongruity. Could all this have happened to an entirely different song? Am I actually thinking of "Photograph"? Have I unintentionally fabricated the most telling moment of my teenage experience? If so, I guess that qualifies me as a jackass (or at least a fiction writer). However, I take solace in the fact that by the time school started in fall of '86, it was already totally uncool to like Poison. And I know this *for a fact*.

Poison had taken glam metal to its ultimate (and I suppose logical) conclusion, and it was kind of disturbing. Poison's drummer, Rikki Rockett, had been a hairdresser before the band got famous; I don't think anyone knew that at the time, but it sure seems obvious in retrospect. It wasn't just that Poison looked like girls—they looked like *pretty* girls. Structurally, the cover shot for *Look What the Cat Dragged In* was similar to *Shout at the Devil*, but it caused a far different reaction. It wasn't scary or confrontational or satanic; I think the phrase that probably describes it best is "unintentionally subversive." Here was this cool record with all these cool songs—but by buying it, I would have to admit that *this* was what I *liked*.

In ultra-rural North Dakota in 1987, Poison almost seemed like some sort of gay propaganda. It didn't matter that every song they wrote was about girls or that singer Bret Michaels had sex with Pamela Anderson—*just look at them!* They looked like a bunch of baby-stealing gypsies.

The dumb kids in my school didn't care about that (which I suppose means they were actually the smart kids). They bought Poison cassettes and didn't wonder if they "represented" anything, and they certainly didn't care if they did. The only people who cared were the people who were "into" rock, which in my school meant the metalheads. What made it even tougher was that some of the older kids who were *really* "into" rock had just discovered Metallica, Megadeth, and Slayer. Hardcore fans suddenly insisted that "real" metal bands wore jeans (which I suppose is no more or less ridiculous than any other criteria for liking a group). Even though metal was poised to be popular for five more years, the backlash was already starting. And nobody got hit harder than Poison.

Consequently, I spent the rest of my high school years telling everyone I hated Poison and that they were the most pathetic band in the world, secretly wrestling with the suspicion that they were better than just about every other band within the metal genre. *Open Up and Say . . . Ahh!* was even sexier than their debut, but I refused to possess even a dubbed copy of the cassette in my tape collection. "Nothin' but a Good Time" became (and probably remains) my generation's "Rock and Roll All Nite," but I swore the song sucked. "It's shallow," I would say as I popped a Y & T cassette into my car stereo.

If Black Sabbath can be called the Heaviest of the Heavy (and I already called them that, so it must be all right), then Poison was the Glammiest of the Glammy. And they *sounded* glammy, although that description obviously makes no sense in real terms. It was a constructed sound, and it didn't have soul (at least not in the way somebody like Eric Clapton or James Brown has "soul"). Sometimes people compare the best blues-based rock—like Rod Stewart's Faces and the early '70s Stones—to a sonic metaphor for slow, passionate love-making. Following that line of thinking, the first two Poison records were the sonic equivalent to the best masturbation imaginable.

I guess what I'm saying is that Poison perfected glam metal. They weren't the era's best band and they didn't make the best music, and—quite frankly—they probably have no business being called a "heavy metal" band (there's nothing *heavy* or *metallic* about anything they ever recorded, and as I relisten to their material I'm reminded more of ABBA than I am of Iron Maiden). But they provided an identity for this period of music. As I mentioned earlier, Led Zeppelin was the archetypical construction of a rock band (particularly an arena rock band). Poison embodied the archetypical *philosophy* of a rock band (particularly a hairspray rock band). If I sit in a quiet room and try to imagine what heavy metal sounds like, I find myself making up a song that replicates Motorhead's "Ace of Spades" or Ozzy's "Crazy Train." But whenever anyone asks me to *describe* heavy metal in unspecific terms, I inevitably find myself unconsciously describing a hypothetical band that looks, acts, and sounds a lot like Poison.

September 13, 1986

Bon Jovi's keyboard-saturated *Slippery
When Wet* quietly enters the *Billboard* chart
at No. 45 and goes on to sell 12 million copies.
The following summer, Bon Jovi headlines
the Donnington Rock Festival over "serious"
metal acts like W.A.S.P., Metallica,
and Anthrax.

In an old interview for *Metal Mania* magazine, Anthrax drummer Charlie Benante was asked if Anthrax would ever consider using a keyboard in one of their songs. Benante replied, "That is gay. The only band that ever used keyboards that was good was UFO."

Benante's commentary undoubtedly sounded like a throwaway quote when he first said it, but a decade later it speaks volumes. In those fifteen words, three different ideals within the metal lifestyle are portrayed, and all of them were virtually universal.

First of all, Benante used "gay" as a negative term, but not really in a homophobic sense. He's not so much attacking gays as he is speaking the lexicon of the time, which—in this case—is actually an opinion on the authenticity of rock music. Late '80s metal artists were the penultimate generation of musicians to use "gay" as a colloquial term; only rappers were still doing this by the mid '90s, and almost no one does today. But the result is that ex-metalheads will be the last generation of people who won't immediately recoil at words like "faggot." It's akin to the way the generation that preceded mine is not as affected by the word "nigger" (or at least the Caucasian portion of that generation). Though they completely recognize its degrading connotation and explosive offensiveness, they can still remember a time when saying "nigger" wasn't a complete and utter faux pas. It was part of urban street language, Blaxploitation was omnipresent, and people just assumed you had to accept a little racism now and then. But if you were born after 1970, there was never a moment in your life when "nigger" wasn't among the most volatile, most despised words in the lexicon. For people born after 1980, the same social rules will apply to the word "faggot." But that has only become the case over the past ten years. When we heard that the seminal rap/metal act the Beastie Boys wanted to title their 1986 debut record *Don't Be a Faggot*, it seemed edgy—but not necessarily unreasonable and even a little funny. Today, that title seems totally unreasonable and completely humorless, unless it was being used self-reflexively by Pansy Division or some other "ironic" gay band. The only places where homophobic language is still used without a specific meaning are in areas that are rural and seriously impoverished (for example, I have a close friend named Mr. Pancake who teaches eighth-grade life science on an Indian reservation in Arizona, and he says junior high students still use "faggot" as a way to taunt teachers, even though it really has nothing to do with attacks on their sexual orientation—they're basically just uncreative).

One could easily argue that the use of antigay language in the metal realm was another clear example of its obsession with power, and the argument could probably be sound. But there's another way to read this. It's a little less obvious, but it might shed a bit more light on the music's popularity.

Rock 'n' roll has always tried to appeal to the outcast teenager. It is the voice of alienation (or at least intends to be), and it usually suggests that being weird is okay. When you listen to artists like the Who, Lou Reed, R.E.M., and the Cure, there is usually a vague message of support. Whenever I talk to adults who profess a love for these kinds of bands during their teen years, they inevitably remember dealing with a specific set of feelings: They were different from their classmates, and most often it was because they felt more intelligent and less cool. And these bands always indicated that this was okay. Intellectual introspection was painted as positive, and the social uncomfortability that came with it was the consequence of being wise beyond your years. There was an unspoken cultural compliment to listening to *Fables of the Reconstruction.* The record seemed to indicate that you recognized the reality of your teenage life. You were going through the same things that Michael Stipe did, and it was helping you become a more advanced human.

Some social pundits are eager to suggest that heavy metal was the same kind of medium, merely designed for a less intellectual class of people. I disagree with that assertion. I think '80s hard rock served the same purpose, but it worked in the opposite way. Instead of telling an alienated kid that it was okay to be different, metal seemed to say, *"You're not different at all."* In fact, you're hyper-normal. In fact, you're extremely popular and totally cool. Instead of validating the sad reality of your teenage life, it created a different reality altogether.

You say you don't have a girlfriend? Well, that's because you can't limit yourself to one woman; you're "too fast for love." You're not part of the popular clique in the lunchroom? Well, those kids aren't *really* popular. You are. You are part of the KISS Army, a unified force that is larger and more powerful than they could ever imagine. In the 1987 song "Crazy, Crazy Nights," Paul Stanley explained the war you were fighting against the establishment: "They try to tell us that we don't belong, but that's all right, 'cause we're a million strong . . . and nobody's gonna change me, 'cause that's who I am . . . ugh." Those lyrics are an extension of the same inspirational clichés Stanley was saying in almost every interview he gave during the 1980s. "Even if you can't look like us, you can feel like us," he told *Circus* magazine. "There's a lot of people doing straight jobs where the only thing that gets them by is thinking they're really hip anyway. We just look the way they feel. We make our own rules, we live our own life, and you can follow us but we won't follow anybody else. KISS is a way of life."

Heavy metal was not sympathetic music, and its audience didn't want it to be. Executives at record labels may have marketed it toward the unpopular freaks, but the artists never gave that impression. It told the unpopular that they were better than the other kids, and perhaps even at war with them. So when Charlie Benante said a band with keyboards was *gay*, he wasn't so much saying the group was feminine or weak; he was saying they were *weird*. They were a band for the people who weren't with us. Metal told its audience that they were not different—even if they felt that way most of the time. When the stereo was on, you were among friends . . . at least in theory.

Now, I realize I'm ignoring the fact that some of these metal bands *were* legitimately homophobic, and Anthrax might have been one of them. Skid Row's Sebastian Bach was photographed in 1989 wearing a T-shirt that said "AIDS Kills Fags Dead," which isn't very subtle (although it should probably be noted Bach did apologize for this, cleverly mentioning that his grandmother had just died from cancer and he would have been really offended by anyone wearing a "Cancer Kills Grandmas Dead" shirt). Maybe I'm trying to make these guys seem more symbolic—and less unlikeable—by turning their gay-bashing language into a metaphor for inclusion. So instead of extending that argument, I'm going to break down the second point of Benante's aforementioned quote: The merits (or lack thereof) of keyboards.

I sometimes wonder how many hours of my life I have wasted bitching about keyboards. The use of keyboards and synthesizers is the *Roe v. Wade* of '80s metal. It was—without question—the lamest instrument a band could use. The instrument made a lame sound, and it didn't seem heavy (even when it was making heavy sounds). Kajagoogoo used keyboards. The Thompson Twins and Human League used keyboards. Hell, our high school stage band used keyboards. And the worst part was that the inclusion of a keyboard player could only mean one thing: This band intended to build its success around a power ballad. Quite simply, a keyboardist could not rock.

Of course, most bands *did* use keyboards (although often surreptitiously). Anthrax didn't, but any group that got on the radio probably did. Tommy Lee played "piano" on Mötley Crüe's "Home Sweet Home," but it was really just a keyboard. When touring, Warrant hid their keyboard player off-stage, but he played on most of their songs. And the keyboardist was always the third-most important guy in Bon Jovi (after Jon and Richie), although no one ever seems to remember who he was.

Most importantly, Van Halen proved that cool bands could use synthesizers (at least once in a while). That's pretty much all "Jump" was: a synthesizer, crashing cymbals, some stupid vocals, and one obligatory guitar solo to keep diehards from killing themselves. But this decision did not come easy. It took Van Halen five years before they threw caution to the wind and admitted they were a borderline keyboard band. Eddie Van Halen insists "Jump" could have been made in the late 1970s, but David Lee Roth refused to cooperate. Why? Because synthetic music was not hard rock. The crazy thing was that Van Halen was already using synthesizers on 1982's *Diver Down*. Keyboards explain those weird, warped noises at the beginning of "Little Guitars." The reason Roth was comfortable with "Little Guitars" was because those effects still *sounded* like a guitar. I suppose the wildly misleading song title also helped.

On paper, this debate seems like complete nonsense. But it's a crystal-clear example of why every true metal fan in the world took Roth's side when he split with the rest of Van Halen. Dave didn't think like a musician; he thought like a rock guy. He understood the vile depravity of keyboard metal.

This, however, causes a problem.

I cannot remember what this vile depravity was.

Oh, I assure you: I *used* to know. If I could be fifteen again, I could have written this entire book on why keyboards are gay (and I wouldn't have needed Charlie Benante's philosophical support). But today, I can't think of even one justification for why I (or—for that matter—"we") hated keyboards, besides the fact that they didn't "rock."

And that says a lot about metal culture.

The Keyboard Issue was like a secret handshake. People took it seriously (and sometimes to unjustified extremes), but disliking the concept of keyboards wasn't really about the bands or the music. It was actually about the fans. It was a sign of credibility for someone in the metal subculture. It separated "metal fans" from people who were along for the ride. Keyboards strayed outside the metal ethic, just as long hair and self-indulgent guitar soloing were unacceptable in the punk and hardcore scene.

What's especially strange is that—at least metaphorically—synthesizers made perfect sense as glam instruments. Glam was about a false reality, and synthesizers epitomize a false instrument (they can mimic any sound the musician wants). In theory, the keyboard should have been the premier machine of the glam age. But the problem was that it defied hard rock tradition. Weird as it seems, hairspray metal was a staunchly traditional genre. Nothing was really new. Both visually and musically, glam metal was always an extension of what had come before it. Therefore, only three instruments were acceptable: guitar, bass, drums. Dogmatically, the combination of those three sounds is how you make heavy metal music.

Proof of that traditional thesis can be spotted in the last part of Benante's statement: After blasting the use of keyboards in rock, Charlie feels obligated to make UFO a specific exception to this rule. Though the bread and butter of metal was an anti-authority message, there was a bizarre, undying respect for old-school heroes. UFO is best known for their 1977 LP *Lights Out*. Outside of metal circles, UFO is completely forgotten; even most '80s metal fans weren't familiar with the band's work. But the drummer from Anthrax felt they were important enough to mention in a statement that—quite frankly—had absolutely nothing to do with the rest of the interview.

This is the third thing we learn from Benante's off-the-cuff quote: It was important to recognize where you came from. Here again, we see a principle that goes against the way teen culture is usually described. We usually assume kids want to tear down the past and kill old idols; sometimes that seemed to be the *only* force driving punk. But metal always suggested otherwise, even if its fans didn't care. Personally, I didn't give a damn about Zep or Sabbath or the Stones when I was in junior high. It wasn't my music, and it sounded painfully archaic (far, far more than it does now). But I would never have said that to anyone I hung around with. We had an unspoken respect for all those groups, even though we never listened to any of them. Those cues were mostly aped from the artists we liked (such as Helix). In the 1980s, you did not see bands attack their influences.

Perhaps that was what made Guns N' Roses seem so fresh. GNR was the first metal band that didn't seem to care about the past. It wasn't so much that they attacked people either—they just seemed like a band who fell out of a hole in the sky (or at least they did initially—over time, they would evolve into the world's most expensive cover band, and Axl would credit every artist who existed, including the Skyliners).

To use a sports analogy, it's kind of like the behavior of Allen Iverson, a guard for the Philadelphia 76ers. Iverson, a boundlessly talented gangsta playmaker, was constantly discredited in his rookie season for not "showing respect" to the veteran players (and—by association—the entire game of basketball). The irony is that Iverson never overtly criticized anyone; he never suggested he was a more explosive scorer than Michael Jordan, and he never declared that he could have made Oscar Robertson his bitch. But his demeanor and posture was deliciously transparent: You could tell he did not care about the past establishment. He felt no obligation to pay homage to anyone; their achievements did not apply to him. And this made him seem very, very dangerous. A sportswriter for *Sports Illustrated* once asked Iverson why he wore cornrows in his hair, and Iverson said he did it to scare white people.

That statement reminded me of almost everything Axl Rose ever did.

"Police and niggers, get out of my way," sneered Rose on 1988's "One In a Million," a song that still seems mildly shocking twelve years later. Though never released as a single, it's one of Guns N' Roses' best-known songs—but for uncomfortable reasons. The lyrics attacked blacks, gays, and foreigners, and the ensuing controversy helped Rose and his bandmates become the biggest group in the world, a position they held for almost five years.

Lyrically, the track was like a gritty, acoustic B-side to "Welcome to the Jungle," GNR's breakthrough single from their '87 debut *Appetite for Destruction*. "One In a Million" explains Rose's experience as an ignorant kid from middle America who takes a bus to Hollywood; his initial encounters with diversity are not positive: Rose blames "immigrants and faggots" for taking over neighborhoods and spreading the AIDS virus. A few pages ago, I mentioned how no one uses the word "faggot" anymore. This song marked the end of that era.

Yet for all its unmasked prejudice, "One In a Million" was actually intended to upset the white establishment, not the minorities it ostracized. If anything, Rose should be criticized for using special interest groups as pawns for annoying knee-jerk liberals and social conservatives.

Though one can never be certain about another man's motivations, it's unlikely that Rose was truly advocating the ideas in the song. For one thing, Rose's then bandmate Slash *is* half black (however, it should be noted that Slash halfheartedly criticized the song's inclusion on *GNR Lies*, later saying, "That song was taken exactly how I thought it would be"—in fact, there's reason to believe Slash didn't even play guitar when the song was recorded). If Axl had any sincere distaste for gays, he certainly picks strange heroes; he adores Elton John and Freddie Mercury and was briefly obsessed with the Pet Shop Boys, even sending them flowers after a concert. And—according to the *Lies* liner notes—Rose's main problem with foreigners is that they get jobs in convenience stores without a proper grasp of the English language. That complaint almost seems justified. (It should also be noted that Rose has come to conclude that the constant misinterpretation of "One In a Million" isn't worth the trouble; on future pressing of *GNR Lies*, it will not be included on the disc. This is a shame and a mistake, but I guess it's his song and his life.)

Despite the controversy it caused (or perhaps because of it), side two of *GNR Lies* is modern heavy metal's watershed moment. For the band itself, it was a mark of separation from the rest of the genre; from this point forward, GNR could no longer be called glam, nor could they ever be connected with Krokus or Kix or Keel. But *GNR Lies* is more important for its symbolic value to a certain class of fan. In fact, it unconsciously destroyed everything metal had been about for the past ten years, dooming that style's future in the coming decade.

For those who are unfamiliar with the work, *GNR Lies* came out in December of 1988, right when the hysteria over 1987's *Appetite for Destruction* was in full force. The original title was supposed to be *Guns N' Roses: The Sex, the Drugs, the Violence, the Shocking Truth!* It was technically an EP, but it was almost as long as a full-length album. The aforementioned side two of *Lies* was four new acoustic tracks, including the immensely popular ballad "Patience." Side one was supposedly material GNR had released independently in 1986 under the title *Live ?!*@ Like A Suicide*.

I use the word "supposedly" because there are serious questions about the legitimacy of that claim. In his 1991 book about Guns N' Roses, Mick Wall indicates that this re-release story is legitimate and that ten thousand copies of *Lies* were printed in December of 1986 (some of which even made it to Europe). Apparently, the original EP included two more live songs (a cover of "Knockin' On Heaven's Door" and an original called "Shadow of Your Love"). However, it's now well-established that the EP was actually a Geffen marketing ploy. Guns N' Roses *did* record an early project prior to *Appetite*, but it was not a live, independent recording—in fact, the songs that ultimately made it onto *Lies* might have been versions that were recorded in a studio only weeks before the EP's '88 release. Geffen paid for everything. The crowd noise is obviously fake, a fact that the band has basically admitted.

Today, this kind of practice is completely common; alternative bands are always trying to earn their so-called street cred, so major distributors create vanity labels that make the band seem like an indie (for example, the first Smashing Pumpkins album was "officially" released on the independent label Caroline, even though the band was already under contract with Virgin). But back in 1988, this kind of chicanery was an altogether new idea, and it worked beautifully.

Regardless of their genuineness, these first four songs fall somewhere between "a little above average" and "pretty damn good." Two of them are covers (Rose Tattoo's "Nice Boys" and "Mama Kin" by Aerosmith) and two are originals in the *Appetite* vein ("Reckless Life" and "Move to the City," yet another song about a character who leaves home for the mean streets of Cali). But it's the material on the record's flip side that really matters. Omnipresent metal critic Chuck Eddy said the acoustic tracks on *Lies* might comprise the best music of its generation. Though I disagree with the totality of that assessment, it's not too far off the mark.

"Patience" was (and is) a very good heavy metal love tune, which I suppose makes it a "power ballad." It doesn't seem like that term fits the song though. Whenever someone says the words "power ballad," I think of the Scorpions and White Lion. "Patience" was far better, or at least far different, than most of the songs that seem to define the power ballad concept. It was followed by "Used to Love Her," the EP's second-most controversial track. Taken literally (and—to be honest—there's really no other way to take it), "Used to Love Her" is about a guy who kills his girlfriend for talking too much, and then he buries her in the backyard. It's a wonderfully constructed tune that uses an effective (and I suppose ancient) songwriting gimmick: It places negative ideas against a happy melody. In that respect, it's almost like the Carpenters' "Good-bye to Love." The melodic sweetness makes the lyrical horror all the more striking.

The third cut was a reworked version of "You're Crazy," which was one of the weaker electric songs on *Appetite for Destruction*. Now slower and meaner, it is most recognized for the over-the-top vulgarity that dominates the song's conclusion. The closing profanity of "You're Crazy" segues into the six-minute "One In a Million." Lyrically, it was a politically incorrect train wreck—but to make it even more dangerous, "One In a Million" was a brilliant example of songwriting. People who loved emotional musicianship noticed the song as much as the people who hated the lyrics.

There's something highly compelling about these four songs, especially when considered as components of one another. Though "Patience" was an overplayed radio favorite and "One In a Million" is often singled out as an autonomous monstrosity, I prefer to look at the four songs as they were consumed by the hardcore GNR audience—that is to say, as a twenty-minute listening experience.

I started substantially reevaluating *GNR Lies* while I was watching the PBS mini series *From Jesus to Christ: The Early Christians*, an eight-hour documentary from the producers of *Frontline*. My favorite segment of *Jesus to Christ* was on the gospels, particularly the analysis of how their differences reflect when and where they were written, and—more importantly—who the audience would be. (*Reader's note: I realize this undoubtedly seems superfluous at the moment, but bear with me—consider the next four paragraphs as a hidden bonus track at the end of an album, available only on the Japanese import.*)

The first three gospels—Matthew, Mark, and Luke—are commonly referred to as the synoptic gospels. They tell a (relatively) similar story and are clearly built upon one another. Meanwhile, the Gospel of John is a wild card. It was written much later (probably after 95 A.D., a couple of decades after the Gospel of Mark had been composed) and is intended for a more mature phase of the early Christian movement.

John Dominic Crossan, Professor Emeritus of Religious Studies at DePaul University, used an interesting example to illustrate
key differences in these four tomes. He brought up the scenario
of the tense evening prior to Christ's arrest by the Romans. In
this day and age, we always refer to this event under the general
term "The Agony in the Garden," but Crossan points out a
fairly important reality: In the Book of Mark there is no garden,
and in the Book of John there is no agony. In fact, the two narratives paint the personality of Jesus in two wholly different
ways. This is because each gospel writer catered his story to suit
the specific class of people who were going to read it. But two
thousand years later, our singular image of Jesus (and his life) is
formed through an unconscious combination of these four separate books. Like unknowing Gestaltists, we construct the sum of
Christ's parts without even trying.

How does this relate to Guns N' Roses? Obviously, the content
does not. But the construction does. The four acoustic songs on
Lies can be seen as the four components that tell us who Axl
Rose is, and it works in the same way that the gospels painted the
portrait of Jesus. Those first three songs are the synoptic tracks,
and "One In a Million" is an autonomous cut that simultaneously works with (and against) the other material. It's akin to the
"Agony in the Garden" paradox: In "Patience," there is no sex,
drugs, or violence; in "One In a Million," there is no shocking
truth. But when placed in context with each other (and with the
two tunes in the middle), the EP's original title suddenly
becomes disturbingly perfect.

There is, of course, an obvious problem with this analogy.
Unlike the Book of John, "One In a Million" wasn't written
dozens of years after the other three tracks. Time, place, and
prospective audience is not a justifiable explanation. However,
there is a marked difference in philosophy. Consciously or unconsciously, "One In a Million" serves a different purpose than the rest
of the record. It's Axl's unabashed attempt at personal iconology,
and it appeals to a very specific audience. Rose was trying to speak
to the kind of kid he used to be (and—in a lot of ways—still was).

February 1, 1987

My mom makes stew for supper.

This is a story I had totally forgotten about, but my sister just reminded me: A few members of my family were sitting around the dinner table in the middle of winter—it was me, my mom, my sister Rachel (who's three years older than me and used to like Culture Club), my brother Bill (who's seventeen years older than me and used to like Three Dog Night), and my dad. At some point in the conversation, my father started talking about a local farmer who owned an especially unattractive herd of cattle. It seems this farmer was sort of a slacker and did not properly feed his livestock during the winter months. Moreover, his stockyard was populated by a rag-tag collection of cattle comprised of several different breeds (a few Herefords, a few Angus, possibly even a couple Holsteins). This is a very bush-league move in the world of ranching. Predictably, my dad was disgusted. "What a motley crew that is," my father said of the cows. At that point, Rachel and Bill began laughing like hyenas, and I just sort of stared into my stew. I can only imagine what my dad suspected everyone was howling about.

This kind of memory would bother some people. It would make them feel alienated, or detached from their paternal life force, or depressed that their male parent had absolutely no interest in something they loved. But I don't feel that way at all. When I recall this incident, I simply find it reassuring to know my father obviously never entered my bedroom the entire time I lived in his house.

April 18, 1987

MTV premieres
Headbanger's Ball at 11 P.M.

Watching random rock videos from 1987 is not nearly as nostalgic as you'd expect it to be. You'd think the old images would cause hard rock memories to come rushing back into your consciousness, but that doesn't really happen. In fact, you're struck more by what you *don't* remember.

This is a relatively unique sensation, especially when compared to other modern forms of mass media. It's certainly not true for conventional TV, the most recycled form of entertainment that's ever been created. I see *The Wonder Years* more often today than I did when it was broadcast originally; I still catch *Happy Days* constantly, and I had already seen virtually every episode of that series (via syndication) before I entered sixth grade. Cable has made television less memorable by making it eternally contemporary. There really isn't any era (or genre) of TV that I can't find whenever I want. The VCR and Blockbuster Video have done the same thing with the film industry—it's easy to reexperience *St. Elmo's Fire*, *Urban Cowboy*, and *I Am a Fugitive from a Chain Gang* in the scope of a single evening.

Music is also easy to recapture (at least in a sonic sense). When people buy records and cassettes, they usually hold on to them—and if they don't, it's almost guaranteed that the songs have been transferred to CD. I still possess 98 percent of the

81

music I've purchased (or dubbed) over the past fifteen years. However, I probably have access to less than 2 percent of the videos I've seen in that same period, and it's likely I'll never see most of them again.

Music fans attack MTV constantly, and usually for two reasons: (a) it doesn't play enough videos, or (b) it plays the same video over and over and over again. Both criticisms are valid. And as a result, there is a vast library of videos that are played briefly and never seen again. While Nick at Nite will replay the entire run of a situation comedy, very few videos have a life outside their fleeting window of popularity. This even applies to most tracks from major artists. Oh, you'll see "Hungry Like the Wolf" twice a year for the rest of your life—but when's the last time you caught the vid for "New Moon on Monday" or "Skin Trade"? There's an elite percentage of videos that will always surface in countdowns and retrospectives ("Sledgehammer," "Billie Jean," "Smells Like Teen Spirit," etc.), but most clips do not survive the passing of time. For example, the Black Crowes video for "Remedy" was on ultraheavy MTV rotation in the summer of 1992, and I saw it every single day (often twice or thrice) for three straight months. The image of Chris Robinson dancing barefoot has been forever tattooed into my optic membrane. However, I haven't seen "Remedy" in the past three years. It's entirely plausible that I may never see it again.

This is why I was literally ecstatic after my discovery of *Mike's Videos #1* and *Mike's Videos #2*. For a pseudo-scientist studying the video art of '80s hair metal, this was the equivalent to finding the Dead Sea Scrolls in my parents' basement.

Who's "Mike," you ask? Mike was a guy I went to college with (although once he turned nineteen, he started calling himself "Rex," which was a nickname I had given him simply to avoid confusion with another guy named "Mike"). As a junior and senior in high school, he liked to tape rock videos—but not off MTV. In Mike's hometown, you couldn't get MTV unless you had a satellite dish. Instead, he watched *Night Tracks* on TBS, which was actually better, because they played videos that MTV banned (like L.A. Guns' "One More Reason"). Mike exclusively taped metal videos, along with a handful of nonmetal clips he evidently thought were cool enough to make the cut—Bad English, DJ Jazzy Jeff and the Fresh Prince, UB40, Rod Stewart, and a few other inexplicable additions.

As sophomores at the University of North Dakota, we would periodically watch these tapes when we were drinking vodka in our residence halls, mostly because cable services were not yet available in individual dorm rooms. When fall semester ended in December of 1992, we all prepared to go home for a month-long Christmas break. I was going back to my farm in Wyndmere, where I didn't even have any friends anymore (much less cable services). I had no idea how I was possibly going to entertain myself for the next four weeks. When I mentioned this concern to Rex (a.k.a. The Artist Formerly Known As Mike), he loaned me two videotapes (labeled with Scotch tape). I didn't remember to take them back to school with me in January, and Rex never missed them. Who would have? By May, I had completely forgotten that these tapes even existed. They ended up getting thrown into a box with about fifty other videotapes, most of which had been used by Mom to tape *Falcon Crest*.

Seven years later, I was home visiting my parents in 1999. Once again, I was unspeakably bored (I guess that's one thing that hadn't changed). I found a box full of videotapes in the spare bedroom, and I started randomly throwing them into our VCR. Along with the 1988 NCAA Final Four, a PBS special on serial killers and a shitload of Jane Wyman footage, I came across these two gems. I almost started to cry. For a guy writing a book on heavy metal, it was the find of the century.

The eleven-plus hours of raw footage (taped on SLP) are rough; many videos are partially cut off, and all of *Mike's Videos #2* has static and a vertical shake. Some were taped in stereo, some in mono, and a few were somehow taped in both. But it's still a miraculous collection of glam rock's video age. Since Mike was dubbing any big-haired band that happened to stumble across the screen, the tapes captured bands that no modern videographer would have possibly thought to include—Giant, EZO, King Diamond, and other such trashy flashy easy action. This kind of random sampling provides a staunchly realistic representation of what early metal videos were truly like. Mainstream reality is always founded on commercial obscurity.

Predictably, most of what's on *Mike's Videos #1* and *#2* is primitive. But that's no reflection on how watchable the material is. Many of the cheapest, cheesiest clips from a 1989 installment of *Night Tracks* were superior to videos made today, mostly because modern videos have adopted an enforced artistic agenda that's counterproductive to entertainment. Perhaps the smartest statement ever made about the video medium was written by Rob Sheffield in *SPIN*'s ten-year anniversary issue: "Van Halen's 1984 'Jump' was a self-directed, relatively low-budget video. Van Halen's 1991 'Right Now' was a tasteful, clever, sterile montage of special graphics that looked exactly the same when it became a soft-drink commercial. 'Jump' lives in the soul of everybody who has seen it, while 'Right Now' represents MTV's idealized vision of itself as a serious art medium."

At first glance, this might seem more like a shot at Sammy Hagar than a thesis statement on the video age, but it makes an important point. As the emphasis of video-making moved away from its original objective—the unconditional goal of pushing albums—the videos became more interesting, but less effective. "Jump" is fundamentally a commercial for *1984*, and most hard rock videos from that era were built on the same premise. The goal of the record label was to (a) let people see the band, and (b) convince them to *hear* a song that listeners might normally ignore. In "Right Now," the band is hardly ever on the screen—and the accompanying music is supposed to make people *read!*

This is not to say that "Right Now" is a bad video. It's very good. I honestly don't know if "Jump" necessarily "lives in my soul" any more than "Right Now" does, nor do I understand what's so horribly bad about selling Pepsi. But Sheffield's general premise is dead-on accurate. The video for "Right Now" couldn't possibly make viewers like Van Halen any more than they already did, and it probably made some of them like Van Halen less (if they thought it was boring or pretentious, or if they really hated Pepsi). But "Jump" made me *love* Van Halen. It was like going to a club and stumbling across the coolest band in town: You saw the group's personality, you had something to look at while the catchy hook was latently hardwired into your brain, and you got *the idea.* And what was "the idea"? The easy answer is "nothing"— but the real answer is everything that was ever perfect about Van Halen and rock 'n' roll. I could never explain why so many people like Van Halen, but anyone who has seen "Jump" can figure it out.

"Right Now" is an endless string of important ideas that are supposed to remind us about what "really matters." In that regard, it fails. I don't think about my life one iota differently because of that video; the aggregate of hundreds of concepts ultimately equates to nothing. Meanwhile, "Jump" was an endless string of . . . well, of "jumping." The goal was to make people think Van Halen was a pretty cool rock band. Obviously, it worked. Granted, the motivation for the latter pales in comparison to the goals of the former—but "Jump" is half of something, while "Right Now" is all of nothing.

Sheffield's implication is that the "Right Now" video was too much like a television commercial from the day it was created, and his proof is that it was nicely converted into a soda advertisement without much editing. In a strict conventional sense, I suppose that's true, but the argument really doesn't stand up when you look at the application. The original video didn't make me want to buy *For Unlawful Carnage Knowledge,* and the accompanying commercial didn't make me want to buy a twelve-pack of pop. Meanwhile, "Jump" sold Van Halen. "Jump" was more mercenary than any other video Van Halen ever made, because *all it did* was pitch the product. It was nothing *but* a commercial. Of course, adopting that philosophy always seems to be the best thing that can ever happen to pop music, anyway.

Videos like "Jump" were the cornerstone of the metal video genre. It's a specific type of creation I call the "live without an audience" video. Every band who made at least two videos made at least one of these: It's the group, performing a prototypical stage show, with no one else in the building (except, I suppose, the camera crew—and in the case of Autograph's "Loud and Clear," an exclusive audience of Ozzy Osbourne, Vince Neil, and a bunch of foxy whores). The intention is to present the band as a living entity, but there's no attempt to fool anyone into thinking this is actually a "live" event; often, band members change clothes several times during the clip, and the wardrobe switches are all edited into one seamless track. Smoke machines were often utilized, and the three obligatory shots were (a) a vocalist running with the microphone stand, (b) a guitar player sliding on his knees during a solo, and (c) the drummer pointing at the camera with his drumstick and smiling (or snarling, if the band happened to be pretending they worship Satan).

To break up the concert footage, most videos would insert random, unrelated scenes that made the piece "unique." Common items were girls in tight dresses, shots of the band laughing (or sleeping) on the tour bus, sneaky men wearing trench coats, birds (particularly doves and crows), girls dancing in cages, and/or a horse walking through fog. For the song "All We Are," the female-fronted German band Warlock blew up cars, much like Wendy O. Williams did.

Sometimes the director simply had the group perform in a weird place, like a church or an open field. The best location was for Raging Slab's "Don't Dog Me," where the country-fried metalheads rocked out on a flatbed trailer, pulled by a monster truck. You still see this kind of move from modern hard rock videos; a 1998 clip for the Deftones, "My Own Summer (Shove It)," had the band performing on top of shark tanks, interspliced with images of *Carcharodon carcharias* yapping at the camera.

From a promotional perspective, the "live without an audience" vid was especially suited for pointing out which member of the group was supposed to be the star. About 90 percent of the time, this meant the vocalist. However, there were some notable exceptions. The potential for "isolation footage" was perfect for egocentric band leaders who wanted to make sure everyone knew who was writing the songs (and thereby paying the bills). In the Badlands video "Dreams in the Dark," the focus is on guitarist Jake E. Lee; Lee had built a name for himself as Ozzy Osbourne's third axe player, and he was Badlands' creator and best-known commodity. Jimmy Page tried to reintroduce himself as a metal god with his *Outrider* album, and the accompanying performance video for "Wasting My Name" was centered around Page awkwardly re-creating his stage moves from *The Song Remains the Same*. Meanwhile, the vid for Bonham's "Wait for You" promotes that outfit's drummer more than any other video I've ever seen; this is obviously because the drummer was Jason Bonham, the group's namesake and the son of deceased Led Zep percussionist John Bonham.

Part of the allure of "live without an audience" videos is that they capture the universal teen experience of lip-synching songs in front of the bedroom mirror. A fabricated performance allows the camera crew to get tight shots of the artists, so the viewer is assaulted with a sense of hyper-reality. You could be sitting in the front row of a Warrant concert, and you'd still never be as close to Jani Lane as you are in the video for "Down Boys." Since everything is shot (and reshot) a hundred times, everything is perfect; every stage move can be choreographed and accentuated. The director can also play with size and scale: In Ratt's "Round and Round" video, all five members of the band are squeezed into the main shot. It's like a portrait of the group, and it makes the audience perceive them as a gritty, focused unit. It was just as easy to create the opposite perception. In "You Give Love a Bad Name," the members of Bon Jovi are spread all over a mammoth concourse (which even included a fake audience!), and it immediately made them seem like a supergroup; it also provided opportunities to isolate the singular star power of its singer.

Probably the strangest entry in this genre was Stryper, the self-proclaimed "Yellow and Black Attack." The fact that Stryper had two platinum albums might be the ultimate testament to metal's popularity: When you consider the stereotype of what kind of people listened to hard rock, it's amazing that Stryper was even cast in a position to compete as a major act. In their performance video for "Always There for You," the band is referring to Jesus, and vocalist Michael Sweet constantly points to the heavens; to combat the demonic power of Iron Maiden, their faux stage is decorated with the digits 777. Stryper also made copious references to the biblical passage Isaiah 53:5. When I eventually looked this up in the Old Testament, I expected to see something like, "And the Lord said unto them, you shall all bow before the power and majesty of rock." However, it actually gives a prophetic description of how the Messiah would be beaten and wounded for all of mankind's sins. Stryper was not exactly a party band.

The growth of MTV's artistic significance is often credited to the competitive and insular nature of Hollywood. During the 1970s (and particularly because of Vietnam), it slowly became standard for absolutely everyone to go to college, particularly if they had no desire to get a real job. One of the results was a massive population of film school students, most of whom became waiters and valets in the 1980s. Since the vast majority of these Kubrick wannabes couldn't crack the motion picture industry, they saw opportunities to make minimovies in the world of rock 'n' roll. The idea was that cinematically compelling videos could catapult an artist into feature films, and—occasionally—it worked. The best example is probably David Fincher, who went on to make amazing movies like *Se7en* and *Fight Club* after a prolific career as a video director for everyone from Madonna to Loverboy.

However, it soon became very obvious that you did not need a skilled filmmaker to tweak the appearance of a fairly straightforward rock video. Escalating technology made the addition of video effects incredibly easy, if not necessarily sparkling. In Vixen's "Edge of a Broken Heart," a glove-covered hand (presumably lead singer Janet Gardner's) reaches up and appears to "turn the page" of the TV screen, advancing between color shots of the girls jamming and black-and-white clips of the girls putting on lipstick, shopping in strip malls, and hanging out with their friends in Poison. When watched today, it seems painfully simplistic. But "Edge of a Broken Heart" is a perfect illustration of the "live without an audience" abstraction: You see the musicians performing, you briefly see them frolicking, and it's more than a moving picture. There is fantasy, as well as a few fleeting grains of reality. Through both production and presentation, we actually feel like we've *learned* something about these people.

The "live without an audience" video was an especially cagey move for upstart bands (like Vixen) since they didn't necessarily have an audience, anyway (again, like Vixen). It would not be very cool for any band to shoot a video with fourteen people in the audience, except for maybe Belle and Sebastian.

However, there was a larger plan: If your "live without an audience" clip was wicked cool, maybe you'd get people to come and see you for real. And if enough kids showed up for at least one show, you could make the "live *with* an audience" video. These projects are among the most memorable shards of the metal legacy; when you close your eyes and try to imagine the biggest hard rock bands of the 1980s, the most fluent image tends to be the marquee shot of a long-locked vocalist communicating with twenty thousand screaming kids. These are the videos that show which groups hit the big time—they are proof that a given group graduated to the class of *rock stars*.

Once again, the early template for this creation comes from Van Halen. The video for "Panama" opened with a massive shot of VH playing before the kind of crowd only they could draw; it clearly outlined who was the biggest band in the land (this kind of distinction was always a serious concern for Van Halen—in the early 1980s, they always wanted to make sure they had larger amps than KISS, and Alex Van Halen always wanted a larger drum kit than Eric Carr). The onstage action in "Panama" focused on the band members hanging from cables and swinging across the stage, capturing the wild (but still boyishly playful) Van Halen image. The band had actually made a primitive live video for "Unchained" in 1981, but "Panama" was a far better representation of the band's rambunctious personality.

The strength of "Panama" is that the concert footage is not overused; in fact, it's underused. The problem with most performance videos is that they're usually less than five minutes long, but they still get boring. "Panama" does not, and that's due to the non-live footage that creates a goofy, non sequitur story line.

Director Pete Angelus had a good grasp on what made David Lee Roth appealing. He understood that Roth was a clown, but not necessarily a joke; Dave might do something stupid, but he didn't do stuff that was dorky. The most memorable shot from "Panama" is Roth getting dragged out of a hotel by police, wearing only handcuffs and a towel. The offense is never explained, but it's obviously illegal and it obviously involved nudity. Seconds later, Roth is back drinking Budweiser with the posse and doing karate kicks in public. That kind of paradox was '84 Van Halen personified: One minute you're arrested for snorting coke off a hooker's ass; the next minute you're hoisted on a bungee cord in front of twenty-two thousand people.

When a band makes a video like "Panama," the members often claim the clip is a "tribute" to their fans. Usually, this is a lie; it's akin to how groups regurgitate studio tracks onto a live album and swear it captures the true feeling of what a band is "really about," even though it's just a way to sell the material to the same audience twice. Still, there may be some sincerity to the suggestion that a live video credits the audience as a group's unofficial "fifth member" (or as the unofficial "sixth" member, if you have a five-person group—or the unofficial "ninth member," if you're in Guns N' Roses). Take Mötley Crüe's "Home Sweet Home." It's a love song that's about touring, and the video translates that idea with an abundant degree of clarity (much more so than the actual lyrics). The slow-motion footage in "Home Sweet Home" is particularly effective; it makes the image of sweat flying off Vince Neil's hair seem *dramatic*. It's amazing how simple any movement can be glamorized by elementary slow-motion photography; Neil becomes as momentarily captivating as Walter Payton's icy breath in an NFL Films production.

The video for "Home Sweet Home" was the most important career decision Mötley Crüe ever made. When *Theatre of Pain* was released, a lot of diehard Crüe fans were less than over-joyed—after the dark, hardcore style of *Shout at the Devil*, the glitter rock on *Theatre of Pain* seemed awfully swishy. I remember being especially disappointed the first time I played "Home Sweet Home," because it came across as the epitome of a sell-out chick ballad geared toward a nonmetal crowd. In a nonvideo age, Mötley Crüe might have lost its core audience. But "Home Sweet Home" briefly became one of the most popular videos in the history of MTV. It was the channel's most requested video at a time when MTV was rapidly switching from a cultural anomaly to a cultural linchpin. By virtue of a well-shot, well-timed video, Mötley Crüe climbed into the next tier of rock popularity. It sud-denly became clear that the Crüe was going to hang around for a while, even if devout metal fans quit playing the records. And since Mötley was clearly the "most metal" of that year's major pop acts, kids like me supported *Theatre of Pain* out of virtual obligation. My thirteen-year-old logic knew that any lame Crüe ballad was still better than Starship's "We Built This City" or Jan Hammer's "Miami Vice Theme," so "Home Sweet Home" became a classic by default. When the Crüe made this kind of video a second time (for the song "Same Ol' Situation" off *Dr. Feelgood*), it was slicker and sexier—but it would never be as defining as "Home Sweet Home."

Def Leppard's "Pour Some Sugar On Me" was another concert video that helped cement a band's image for all time. Whenever I think of Joe Elliott, I picture him wearing shredded jeans. "Pour Some Sugar" also provides a snapshot of a commercial jug-gernaut flexing its muscles during its period of greatest prosper-ity (according to writer Mick Wall, beneath the mammoth stage used in this video was a harem of totally naked women waiting to get fucked—a legend that's probably exaggerated, but certainly possible). Guns N' Roses' "Paradise City" might be an even bet-ter example: Even though he probably only wore it once, Axl Rose's white leather suit is a permanent piece of his historical benefaction. In fact, the entire "Paradise City" clip is almost perfect. It was mainly shot at two locations: Giants Stadium in the Meadowlands (where Guns was opening for Aerosmith) and at the 1988 Donnington Rock Festival in England (an event infamously remembered for the deaths of two fans during GNR's set). Filmed in black and white, the live images show the band in full force—but the offstage footage accentuates each band member's identity in a surprisingly unforced fashion (serious fans may recall a casual shot of Steven Adler on a boat, and another of Slash signing an autograph while he takes a piss). More than any other video, "Paradise City" re-creates the larger experience of an emotive live event.

However, the Jedi Masters of this concept will always be Bon Jovi. From a creative standpoint, no other band could rival their sincere appreciation for the audience. Watching a Bon Jovi video made you want to see them for real, even if you didn't like their songs. And why? Because they seemed legitimately *honored* to be performing for their fans.

Bon Jovi took at least one substantial influence from Mercury label mate KISS: They believed that anyone who bought a ticket for the show temporarily became their employer. They worked for the people and gave them whatever they wanted. The video for "Lay Your Hands On Me" was actually a lot like "Pour Some Sugar On Me" (which was a lot like "Livin' On a Prayer"), and this similarity made sense; both groups particularly appealed to women and not-so-serious metalheads, so one would expect them to be marketed in the same way. But Bon Jovi seemed *happier* about it. In fact, they seemed so happy that they made "Bad Medicine," a simple idea that spoke volumes about the entire metal genre.

For the "Bad Medicine" shoot, Bon Jovi scheduled an intimate club show and gave every member of the audience an eight-millimeter camera. The agreement (or at least the espoused agreement) was that everyone could keep the camera, as long as they gave the band whatever they had filmed during the performance (this technique has since been copied by lots of just-married couples who put disposable cameras on all the supper tables during the wedding reception).

Video producers spliced together a grainy hodgepodge of Bon Jovi being cute and frisky, along with several bonus shots of really hot girls crouching like the amateur photographers they are. Most of the footage looks like it was directed by B-minus film students from UCLA. From a critical standpoint, it gets a little boring.

However, this was the kind of well-intended gimmick that showed where Bon Jovi was coming from. This was not a band who was going to look at the people who made them wealthy and say, "We're only doing this for ourselves." Jon Bon Jovi recognized that half the value of his art was derived from the people who received it. "Bad Medicine" pushes that idea to its extreme.

A widely held opinion in the aesthetic community insists an artist is more credible if he doesn't consider his audience during the creative process; the philosophy suggests that a true artist *has* to make his art for personal reasons, regardless of whether or not people like it (or even want it). That's plainly stupid, and Bon Jovi knew it. Art is not intrinsic to the universe; art is a human construction. If you killed off all the world's people, you would kill off all the art. *The only thing important about art is how it affects people.* It only needs to affect one person to be *interesting*, but it has to affect many people to be *important*.

Like virtually everything else in life, it all comes down to simple mathematics: The more people who are affected by a piece of art, the more important it is. The video for "Bad Medicine" multiplies that principle by making the audience both sides of the equation. They are the creators of the art, and they are also the receivers. Guys like Richie Sambora merely acted as the conduit.

For a fan, performance videos were appreciated as surrogates; they were the way to see a band when you could not see them for real. Warrant's video for "Heaven" was the closest thing to seeing them in concert. However, it still could not compete with a really well-done conceptual video, even though those were few and far between.

Concept videos change the way a song is consumed by the audience, and some artists have become very good at it. Just about every Radiohead video makes me like that band a little more. R.E.M. has excelled at this art from the beginning. Electronica bands seem particularly suited for this kind of creative medium; world-class hipster Spike Jonze (now better known for directing *Being John Malkovich*) has created some brilliant concept videos for the Chemical Brothers, Daft Punk, and Fatboy Slim.

On the whole, metal bands are less successful at this venture, and that was especially obvious in the middle 1980s. This entire video genre had improved drastically (for everybody) by the end of the decade, but the early half of the period was not too stellar.

For a group like Cinderella, the failures were all too obvious. The video for "Nobody's Fool" has the band performing amid bright pastel lighting (one assumes this is supposed to seem surreal), but the subplot revolves around a girl who runs home and takes a nap. If this is supposed to indicate why she is not a fool, I don't get it. The clip for "You Don't Know What You Got (Till It's Gone)" has the group playing instruments around a lake (or possibly a loch); the majority of the footage frames Tom Keifer plunking away at a piano while the sun sets behind him, and it ends up looking like a promotional clip for a travel agent.

Even worse was "Coming Home," a minifilm about a mysterious man (probably an aspiring soap opera actor) who rides a motorcycle to "come home" to his blond love interest. Judging from the terrain and the copious windmills, the lonely blonde vixen evidently lives in Kansas. The narrative of the video is a rote replication of the lyrics, a technique that almost never works. Poison's "Fallen Angel" tried the same approach, and it failed just as horribly.

In "Fallen Angel," a teenage girl makes an announcement at supper: "I've decided to move [*dramatic pause*] . . . to California [*longer dramatic pause*] . . . and I want to leave on Friday." A few seconds later, she gets off a bus in L.A. and immediately becomes a whore. Bret Michael explains that she's just a small-town girl with her whole life packed in a suitcase by her knees, and she's rolling the dice with her life. At the conclusion of the video, another small-town girl gets off at the same bus stop, and one assumes she is destined for the same slutty future. Actually, this video may have been a form of subliminal marketing for the band. It seemed to be delivering a peculiar rock message: "Stay with your parents! Never go anywhere! Stay in your bedroom and listen to more Poison tapes!" It's kind of like the ending of *The Wizard of Oz*.

However, Poison did make one wonderful concept video, even though its greatness might have happened by accident. When Poison released "Every Rose Has Its Thorn" to MTV audiences, the goal was to show their fans what "life on the road" was like. A decade later, the result is kind of spooky, especially when viewed against Poison's ultimate collapse. Today, "Every Rose Has Its Thorn" seems like a sobering examination of Poison's alcoholism, and it deserves a compliment few rock videos can be granted—*it looks real*. There is a shot of bassist Bobby Dahl being carried off the stage by a roadie, and there is no question about the validity of his intoxication. Retrospectively (and perhaps unintentionally), "Every Rose Has Its Thorn" has become a conceptual artifact of the glamorous, pathetic existence of a metal band embracing the height of its self-indulgence (in other words, the other side of "Pour Some Sugar On Me" and "Paradise City"). The sunken, drunken eyes of Michaels say a lot about rock 'n' roll: The dudes in Poison were famous, but they still lived like jobless guys who never made it out of Pennsylvania. Booze is the greatest of all equalizers. Rich drunks and poor drunks both pass out the same way.

The metal bands who consistently made the best concept videos were the groups that truly understood their audience. As I grow older, it's getting harder for me to remember who and what I could relate to when I was fifteen, but I bet it was Skid Row. Though they did make at least one clip that was a literal depiction of a song ("18 and Life"), two of their other early vids were brilliant examples of the less-is-more philosophy of filmmaking. The core shot in "Youth Gone Wild" was just a kid *running*—you can't see his face and you don't see where he's going, but it seems obvious that he's running *away* from something. "Piece of Me" has the same aggressive aesthetic, and the images go straight for the adrenal gland: It's footage of a particularly violent concert, evidently a riot going on outside a Skid Row venue. I suspect the director staged the whole thing, because I've never been to a rock show policed by storm troopers and attack dogs, but it looks remarkably plausible. There's actually a great deal of creative tension in "Piece of Me."

All three of these videos were shot in black and white, and they provide an amazingly insightful portrait of Skid Row's audience: Even though they had a cute lead singer and a bunch of radio songs, Skid Row was a band for the bad kids. These were not the kinds of fans who spent $80 on leather pants, $11 on hair mousse, and still got a CD player for Christmas; these were the kids who wore denim jackets and wrote "Skid Row" on the back with a black Magic Marker. These were the kids who stole cheap beer and actually got in real trouble. These videos show why Skid Row could release a ballad like "I Remember You" and still tour with Pantera (which they did in 1992). They spoke to the people who felt Skid Row was part of their own identity.

The opposite of the Skid's pseudo-realism were all the postapocalyptic videos that spoke to absolutely no one, but still succeeded on the strength of absurd entertainment value. For whatever the reason, Mel Gibson's 1981 film *The Road Warrior* influenced metal video-making in a major way. Videos from two high-profile releases from '83 (*Shout at the Devil* and *Lick It Up*) constructed fantasy worlds that appeared to be set in postnuclear wastelands where it's always very windy and all the women wear ripped clothes.

Mötley Crüe's "Looks That Kill" stars a Xena-esque female character who emancipates a corral of strippers, much to the chagrin of the Crüe (who were thereby forced to call on the power of Satan by joining fists and creating a fiery pentagram). Mötley's "Too Young to Fall in Love" was more of an Asian kung-fu thriller (best remembered for Tommy Lee spitting out a mouthful of rice), but its *Escape from New York* vibe was very much the same. Meanwhile, KISS sold themselves as warriors who walked the earth for no reason in particular. "Lick It Up," the first video that showed KISS without makeup, suggests that futuristic women will live underground and eat navy rations —but only KISS can help them rock! Its artistic companion, "All Hell's Breaking Loose," evidently takes place at the same time and place but also includes a lot of women fencing.

To be honest, my favorite postapocalyptic video was probably Lita Ford's "Kiss Me Deadly." The entire clip was basically just Lita, writhing in a cavern after the world had been destroyed. Luckily, the holocaust that prefaced "Kiss Me Deadly" did not seem to affect Lita's bosom, which always seemed on the brink of escaping from her leather corset.

The problem with metal concept videos was pretty simple: They didn't have a concept. Very often, a director tried to be inexplicable in the hope that it would seem innovative. Kix's "Don't Close Your Eyes" has lots of shots of trees set against weird, muted lighting, but nothing much happens. White Lion made three videos like this. Winger's "Headed for a Heartbreak" is shot in black and white, but it's mostly images of Kip Winger trying to look forlorn; if they hadn't included a few extraneous shots of some unknown woman's cleavage, "Headed for a Heartbreak" would resemble the opening sequence for a gay porn flick.

But not everybody failed. The Cult beat the odds and got it right. They were always a little more artsy than their contemporaries, and their videos showed it. The action is pretty subdued in "Fire Woman," but it still seemed cool; it opens with a replication of the *Sonic Temple* album cover (smart marketing, boys), and it features Ian Astbury banging a tambourine like Linda McCartney. "Edie (Ciao Baby)" is far more stylized than the vast majority of hard rock vids, almost akin to an INXS video.

Van Halen was another who made this work, this time with "Hot for Teacher," a perfect fantasy with a strangely disturbing sense of humor. However, I must begrudgingly concede that the all-time best concept video was Metallica's "One." It was a big deal when Metallica made this clip, because they had never done a video before and usually implied they never would. "As for a video for MTV, there's no thoughts about it," drummer Lars Ulrich said in the summer of 1988. "Having one is pretty useless anyway. *Headbanger's Ball* is a fucking joke." But when the band finally sold out (read: got smart) and caved into MTV's begging, they made a visual composition that was credible, intelligent, and downright spooky. Using footage from the 1971 movie *Johnny Got His Gun*, Metallica created a seven-minute, twenty-four-second masterpiece that far superseded the original film. The images are now totally familiar to anyone who follows hard rock; a soldier loses his arms, legs, sight, hearing, and voice. What's interesting is that if you have not seen this video, it's almost impossible to understand what "One" (the song) is supposed to be about—but once you *have* seen the video, it doesn't seem like the song could be about anything else.

For a lot of purists, that's exactly what's bad about music videos: They stop people from creating their own perception of what a piece of music means. By now, even the interpretation of sound has become a socialized process. Without a doubt, the video age is the worst thing that ever happened to teenage creativity. But—at least in the example of "One"—it's hard to imagine how any kid could come up with anything better.

October 10, 1987

Whitesnake's "Here I Go Again" is America's No. 1 single, ousting Whitney Houston's "Didn't We Almost Have It All."

Intelligent metal fans always felt a grudging sense of respect for Whitesnake.

Whitesnake was not very cool. This was mostly because they were fronted by the generally unappetizing David Coverdale, the male slut who replaced Ian Gillan in Deep Purple from 1973 to 1976. Coverdale was from a bygone era, and—no matter how hip and popular his band became—that fact was always a little too clear. Whitesnake was overtly constructed, and unabashedly so (especially when axe mercenary Steve Vai joined the group). They had no grit.

Coverdale was always accused of ripping off Robert Plant; Plant himself was particularly willing to rail about this similarity. Indirectly, Jimmy Page made the same comparison when he created Coverdale-Page in 1992, one of the worst experiments in rock history and assumedly just a way to goad Plant into recording *Unledded*. For all practical purposes, Coverdale was always a shameless Plant imitator—but sometimes it worked. "Still of the Night" was the Gen X "Immigrant Song." It was hard to resist a lot of Whitesnake's songs.

Their biggest hit (and their only No. 1 single) was "Here I Go Again." This song is interesting for a couple of reasons, but mostly for its video. Though the lyrics of the song are about forging one's own path and being a loner, the director of the video interpreted the song far differently: He seemed to think this song was about watching a woman trying to fuck a car. Luckily, this was 1987, and Coverdale happened to be dating Tawny Kitaen. Ms. Kitaen isn't a particularly skilled thespian, but she is very, *very* good at humping the hood of a Jaguar. "Here I Go Again" almost immediately became the most popular video on MTV. Coverdale and Kitaen would later split (surprise!), and Tawny claimed that her car-fucking was the primary reason Whitesnake became commercially popular and that she deserved a huge chunk of the back royalties. She may have a decent argument.

That video is kind of a microcosm for the '80s metal mantra— *everything* was about sex, even when it wasn't. It was certainly the genre's most pervasive cliché and its most maligned Achilles' heel. The element of sexuality was what set the glam aesthetic apart from other forms of loud rock 'n' roll. *Rolling Stone* writer Kim Neely had a firsthand look at two styles of hard rock (she first broke both Guns N' Roses and Pearl Jam to mainstream readers), and when I asked her what *really* separated '87 metal from '93 grunge, she said it was basically fashion—but she wasn't referring to clothes. She meant a sort of intellectual fashion: "Every style of music has its own philosophy and ethics. Heavy metal's philosophy was about getting as wasted as possible and walking into a room with a bimbo on both of your arms. All the bands that came out of the Seattle scene wanted the exact opposite of that. But the audience for both kinds of music was basically the same."

Hair metal's relationship with sex is pretty overt (at least on the surface). It continues to this day, at least in certain subcultures. There's still at least one place where '80s metal is thriving—strip clubs. "Girls Girls Girls" will always be in heavy rotation at any nudie bar, just like "Monster Mash" will find its way onto AM radio every Halloween. Both lyrically and sonically, glam metal is the sensible accompaniment for removing one's pants for money.

One of the many negative synonyms for '80s metal was "cock rock," and the term is still thrown around whenever someone wants to attack any masculine genre of music. A few especially impolite artists, like Gene Simmons of KISS, actually embrace that moniker (he claims a good rock guitar player "plays [the instrument] with his dick"). That kind of attitude is mostly unleashed for effect; it basically stares musicologists in the face and says, "Okay, Poindexter—tell me what you think *that* means." It's really more of a sociopolitical argument (albeit a pretty primitive one).

Whenever people try to explain the role of sex in heavy metal, they usually offer the easiest answer; that is to say, they usually conclude that metal caters to teenage boys, and teenage boys like sex. And there probably is a lot of logic to that explanation. I don't know if it actually explains much, though.

If this relationship was the only explanation, the sexual adulation of women would always be part of rock music. But it's not. Lots of popular music does not stress animalistic sexuality, and it's still readily consumed by adolescent males. Electronica, *the* youth music of late 1996/early '97 (at least according to the media at the time) didn't seem to have any sexual elements, beyond that fact that you could dance to it. I realize divas and Mormons love to claim that dancing is the closest thing there is to having sex, but I've never agreed with that assertion; if these two practices are so damn similar, why can't girls ever get their boyfriends to dance (and why can't boys ever get their dance-loving girlfriends to fuck)?

Even though Prodigy's brilliant video "Smack My Bitch Up" had an insane amount of sexual content, there really wasn't anything *sexy* about it. It was more disturbing than arousing. Meanwhile, the Chemical Brothers look like two guys who have never even talked to girls, much less slept with them. Electronica is about thumping, not humping.

And electronica is not alone. The whole "straight-edge" movement doesn't seem to approve of *anything* the rock stars might consider fun—straight-edge kids don't drink, smoke, eat meat, or (presumably) fuck one another. Obviously, the "riot grrl" phenomenon was another genre wholly absent of any kind of debased sensual pleasure, and—truth be told—there were still probably more males buying Bikini Kill, Bratmobile, and Sleater-Kinney records than there were females (boys are simply more willing to spend money on rock music than girls are, even when the songs are specifically intended for a female audience).

The clearest example, of course, is the one that Neely already pointed out: Seattle-based grunge bands went to elaborate lengths to separate themselves from rock sluts. It was a return to the whole punk ethic, reinvented through the burgeoning PC ideology. And it's nothing new. There is an undeniable connection in music circles that will always associate the concept of "sex" with the concept of "dumb."

Oddly, this rule only seems to be applied to loud music. The operative word here is "loud," not "hard" or "heavy." Disco, for example, is considered totally dumb, and that's because it's loud and sexy. Conversely, Marvin Gaye would never be seen as dumb, because he's *soft* and sexy. Soft and sexy is cool. Fugazi is not dumb, even though they're loud and vocally inaudible. This is because Fugazi doesn't sing about sex. Sex is the one subject that automatically erodes a hard rock artist's public IQ.

When critics first attacked Zeppelin, it was for their "dumb" material, like the loud and sexy "Whole Lotta Love." Now that cultural revisionists have declared that Zep was a bunch of geniuses, they point to tunes like "Achilles Last Stand" and "The Song Remains the Same," partially because of the layered song structure but mostly because they don't want to be accused of lionizing cock rock. "The Rain Song" makes for a stronger argument than "Livin' Loving Maid," even though the latter is a better tune.

Heavy metal had no qualms about being shackled with the dumb label, especially in the 1980s. In fact, it actively pursued it. Glam rock carries the mildly unsettling aura of "the lowest common denominator," sort of like the first few questions in any game of *Who Wants to Be a Millionaire*. Without really saying it, metal works under the impression that the world is stupid, and its people are much less complicated than they'd like to admit. It's a philosophy that superseded language and defies deconstruction. Basically, it deconstructs itself.

Here's an easy example: Skid Row was a very good metal outfit. They were a prototypical metal success story: Their eponymous debut record went multiplatinum, their follow-up LP debuted at No. 1, the group made the cover of *Rolling Stone*, and then they fell off the face of the planet (only to be rescued by KISS in the Y2K, who asked them to partially reform and open the KISS Farewell tour). They have two power ballads, "18 and Life" and "I Remember You," that will probably slip into the growing rotations of classic rock radio outlets. Skid Row doesn't define its genre, but they were paradigmatic of what decent metal bands were like. And what that means is that there's not a whole lot to analyze, at least in terms of what their music was "about."

Skid Row's catalog is an example of how metal deconstructs itself: During the height of hard rock's popularity, metal magazines were faced with a unique predicament—kids wanted to hear about the biggest bands on a monthly basis, even if those bands weren't doing anything newsworthy. Skid Row propelled themselves into this class, so *Hit Parader*, *Circus*, and *Metal Edge* were always on the lookout for new ways to feature them. One easy technique was to ask a band member to comment on every song on a record; the article would list the ten or twelve tracks on the given LP, and the artist (usually the singer) would provide insight on what each song "meant."

Even at its greatest depth, this rarely taught the reader much of anything. The quotes were usually vague and could often be applied interchangeably; I recall the most popular description was something along the lines of, "This song is just directed to the people who keep you down and try to tell you how you live your life." Skid Row's vocalist Sebastian Bach was asked to do this kind of blow-by-blow analysis for the band's first record (for multiple publications, if I recall), and he generally played along with the idea and gave all the predictable answers. However, when asked about the song "Big Guns," he didn't try to make up anything clever or unorthodox. He would just say something that essentially translated as, "Well, you know, we like big tits."

Are we to take this analysis at face value? Well, it's pretty hard not to. One assumes this kind of commentary is supposed to be funny (I suppose today we might call it irony), but it has a strange sort of philosophical effectiveness. You have not been given a lack of information (in fact, the question has been answered in its absolute entirety), but there's still no information to process. The question is the same as the answer.

That's kind of the role sex played in metal.

Have you ever wondered what happened to all the beautiful girls who used to be in rock videos? They disappeared about 1993, and I used to wonder where they went. In a strange way, I felt sorry for them; I imagined all these bombshells in the unemployment line, bemoaning the fact that the Bulletboys never call anymore.

However, it turns out that these buxom hip-grinders are, in fact, thriving. They have become part of the "new metal" movement—CMT. Forget about the Deftones and Orgy; the glam metal torch is actually being carried by Alan Jackson and Shania Twain. Flip your TV to the Country Music Television station, turn down the volume, and throw a Trixter cassette into your stereo. Suddenly, it's the summer of 1991.

Back when Ice-T was still relevant (again, the summer of 1991), he used to compare rap with country music. Ice felt both genres shared a common principle: It was guys telling stories about life and love. Granted, Garth Brooks never threatened to pull a Glock on Reba, but his argument did make some sense. I think a similar comparison can be drawn between '90s country and '80s metal—but this particular analogy is more conceptual.

The connection seems to be in attitude. Country songs (and especially the videos) mimic the good times and fast whores of hard rock; many seem to follow the same plotline from Poison's "Nothin' But a Good Time." For those who don't remember the video (and for those who never saw it in the first place), "Nothin' But a Good Time" is basically a performance clip framed by two scenes of a kid washing dishes in a restaurant. He has long hair and a bad job, and his boss screams at him for being such a lazy jackass. But when the fat manager finally gets off his case and leaves the kid alone, our hero kicks open a door. It opens into an empty concert hall, and Poison is rocking inside. Musicologist Robert Walser compares this sequence to Dorothy's arrival in the Land of Oz, and the similarity is indisputable (and probably conscious). The idea is that Poison is a fantasy, and they offer a bridge to a fantasy life. You see this theory in country videos all the time, although (a) the blue-collar labor is usually farm-related, and (b) the bands inevitably own monster trucks.

The ironic thing about "Nothin' But a Good Time" is that its fantasy does not involve even one woman, a real rarity for that group's lifestyle. Poison was one of the era's most pussy-gorged bands, and that sexual appetite was integral to their success. Bret Michaels had the same "male tart" appeal as Rod Stewart, and Poison used his pretty boy looks to make unabashed attempts at wooing a female following.

In *This Is Spinal Tap*, Nigel Tufnel momentarily confuses the words "sexy" and "sexist," oblivious to the fact that the two words so similar in spelling could have totally different meanings. Amazingly, Poison seemed to perceive those words in the same way—but it worked! It's not just that rock chicks weren't offended by the sexist nature of Poison's music; they were actually turned on by it. Compared to bands like Judas Priest, Iron Maiden, and Armored Saint, the guys in Poison seemed harmless and cuddly. In the eyes of hard-rockin' female teens, Bret Michaels was the kind of guy who would take you to a keg party on the back of his motorcycle and act real macho around his friends—but you knew he wasn't going to get drunk and punch anybody. Bret was a lover, not a fighter. And young women were really drawn to that (especially those who had small-town, pseudo-rocker boyfriends who inevitably proved to be the opposite).

Sadly, this persona would ultimately doom Poison to the depths of social disregard. It might sound chauvinistic, but there is a sad reality in rock music: Bands who depend on support from females inevitably crash and burn. There are a few exceptions to that rule, but it's true more often than it's false. When I interviewed Gene Simmons in 1995, he was shockingly (or perhaps predictably) frank about this: "You don't want a large female audience. If you depend on women to buy your records, you end up going the way of New Kids on the Block. Female audiences tend to be unfaithful."

This phenomenon creates a baffling headache for record companies. It's a confusing situation, because female audiences are usually more intense about how much they like a particular artist (this is especially true for the teenage demographic). Girls who love the Backstreet Boys (or Rick Springfield, or Bon Jovi) love them in a way that made my teenage adoration for Mötley Crüe seem pale. I mean, I certainly would never have *screamed* at Vince Neil. But here I am—ten years later—and I'll still be buying every Mötley Crüe album that gets released, fully knowing I will probably only listen to it once. Males have a weird sense of loyalty toward the bands they like; they sometimes view record buying as a responsibility.

As I try to analyze this incongruity, I feel myself swaying between "overthinking" the answer and "underthinking" the answer. One moment, the difference seems complicated; the next, it seems completely obvious. The complexity comes from the assertion that men and women think about the world in a fundamentally different way. The simplicity comes from the fact that just about everyone accepts this premise and always has. But the complexity returns when this assertion is applied to music, and—for whatever the reason—the male ideology somehow comes across as superior (even though it isn't).

Donna Gaines is currently teaching sociology at Barnard College, the all-female branch of Columbia University. She once told me that few of her female students think about culture as a concept, and they're rarely interested in debating the significance of social iconology. Conversely, Patrick Springer is a news reporter in his late thirties who won a Bush Fellowship in 1996. I used to sit next to Pat when we worked in the same newsroom, and he once told me that whenever he talked to college-age males, pop culture was the *only* thing they seem to know anything about. (An interesting side note to this comparison is that both of these individual commentaries were expressed as negative social trends.) And generally, I suspect Gaines and Springer are both right in their respective analyses.

If I had to bust this down into one sentence, I'd probably say the ultimate difference is that guys like pop culture even when it's not there; more specifically, they like music even when they're not listening to it. Young males like rock music—and culture as a whole—both tangibly and intangibly. Young females are more vehement about the former and virtually indifferent about the latter.

I am a little uncomfortable making these statements, because—as I said before—it seems to indicate that guys somehow like music "better" than women. It suggests that a male listener can appreciate the visceral sound of a Van Halen record, but he can also hold a high-minded discussion about why it's aesthetically superior to Aerosmith; meanwhile, a female can only sustain some kind of mindless, fleeting obsession with Celine Dion that has no regard for intellect or taste. It preys upon the classic stereotype that men are fundamentally more analytical and women are fundamentally more emotional.

All of which is true.

So let's just assume I'm right about this. Let's assume that men and women think about music differently, and if they do like a common artist, they like the performer for different reasons. What does this tell us about the role of sexuality and gender in heavy metal?

First of all, the relationship between sex and hard rock is an *idea*, not a tactile reality. Heavy metal is clearly not a conduit for actual intercourse. Though no studies were conducted at the time, it's safe to say that most guys listening to Iron Maiden in the 1980s were not getting laid all that often. It's not like metal was the soundtrack of rampant teenage sex. It was actually the soundtrack from rampant teenage abstinence. If parents *really* wanted to keep their sons from getting the neighbor girl pregnant, the best thing they could have done was buy them several Dio albums and the AD&D *Dungeon Master's Guide*.

Still, society inevitably makes a connection between sex and hard rock: As I stated earlier, metal will always have a home in strip clubs, and that's for two reasons. The first is sonic; glam rock is sleazy and trashy, and the tempo suits the action. But the second reason is a metaphor for how this music illustrates sex. Strippers are fantasy women; I don't think any man who goes to a strip club views the dancers as real people—at least not when the girls are onstage. Personally, I've only been to six strip joints in my entire life (and four of them were in Canada), but I completely understand why some men love them. When I explained this to a former girlfriend, she was very hurt when I told her that guys look at strippers as fantastical objects. "*I* should be your fantasy woman," she insisted. And I was forced to explain that she could never be my fantasy woman, despite the fact that she was doe-eyed and voluptuous and once made me pass out (literally) during a period of physical ecstasy. She could never be my "fantasy woman" because I couldn't avoid the fact that she was real. I had seen this woman vomit. I had seen this woman gorge herself on pancakes. I had been with her when she purchased tampons. Regardless of her unspeakable midwestern sexiness, I would always recognize her as a genuine person. My feelings toward her would be based on fact, not visual fiction. With strippers, the opposite is true.

And that's how it is with the women who were aligned with heavy metal. They were inevitably described in one-dimensional terms. It was once pointed out to me that most of the planets in the *Star Wars* trilogy were described as having only one climate (the "ice world" Hoth, the "desert planet" Tatooine, etc.). I have come to notice a similar trend in hard rock. Women are often described as having a singular characteristic. The aforementioned "Big Guns" from Skid Row is an easy example. "She Goes Down" by Mötley Crüe talks about a girl who (apparently) does nothing but give blow jobs. Winger's "Seventeen" talks about a girl who is seventeen, and that's her whole life story.

Love/Hate's "Rock Queen" worships a highly desirable women, but we know virtually nothing else—except that she has "cookies" (the lyrics keeping pleading, "Let me touch your cookies / Let me eat your cookies"). Maybe Love/Hate's "rock queen" is Betty Crocker.

Still, we somehow managed to use a band's songs and videos—and more importantly, a band's social posture—to get an image of what kind of women they preferred (or appeared to prefer). This goes back to the idea of thinking about pop culture even when it isn't there; with only scraps of information, metal followers were able to construct the sexual appetites of their favorite musicians. Here's a list of what type of girls the premier metal groups liked (or at least *seemed* to like) . . .

GUNS N' ROSES: Bisexual models; submissive women; girls who would buy them booze.

MÖTLEY CRÜE: Strippers; women who have sex in public (particularly elevators); lesbians.

RATT: Hookers with a heart of gold. Or strippers with a heart of gold. Or thirteen-year-olds.

WARRANT: Virgins who exhibited the potential to become nymphomaniacs.

DEF LEPPARD: Drunk girls; female vampires.

THE CULT: Female vampires only.

FASTER PUSSYCAT: GNR rejects.

W.A.S.P. : Magician's assistants; women with rape fantasies; lower primates.

AEROSMITH: Models, but not waifs; high school snobs; more girls who like having sex in elevators.

CINDERELLA: Gypsies.

TESLA: Farm girls; whoever they used to date in junior high.

SKID ROW: Nameless, faceless, top-heavy sex machines (with hearts of gold).

BULLETBOYS: Girls with particularly deep birth canals.

L.A. GUNS: Drug-addled hitchhikers who like rough sex.

BANG TANGO: Faster Pussycat rejects.

VAN HALEN: Party girls; bikini models; the homecoming queen; cast members of *One Day at a Time*.

DAVID LEE ROTH (solo): The same as Van Halen, except with bigger boobs.

BON JOVI: The girl next door.

VINNIE VINCENT INVASION: The dominatrix next door.

SLAUGHTER: Girls who couldn't make the cut as Bon Jovi groupies.

WINGER: Whoever Bon Jovi groupies used to baby-sit.

POISON: Girls who liked to tease; girls from small towns; good girls gone bad.

KISS: Any girl who wasn't dead.

IRON MAIDEN: Dead girls.

JUDAS PRIEST: Boys.

METALLICA: None of the above.

Oh yeah . . . I guess I forgot Whitesnake. As previously stated, they liked girls who fucked cars. But all this analysis only provides us with half of the intercourse equation. We know who all these bands liked to sleep with, but what about the rest of us? If '80s metal was so sexual, what was the best metal song to actually *have sex* to?

This is a complicated question, because most prototypical metal fans never had sex. Thus, we have very little historical precedent to use as a guide. In the film *Less Than Zero*, Andrew McCarthy and Jami Gertz make love gravy to the song "Bump and Grind" off David Lee Roth's first solo album, but this was not a particularly romantic interlude. I went to high school with a secretly sleazy farm girl who once said it was "totally awesome to fuck to Faster Pussycat," and since this girl always had a lot of boyfriends, I assume she knew what she was talking about. But these two examples are pretty much all we have to work with.

Part of this problem is that metal is painfully Caucasian, and most good sex music is made by black guys: Prince, Stevie Wonder, James Brown, etc. Logic would therefore indicate that Living Colour should have been the sexiest metal band of all time.

This was not the case. I recently re-listened to both *Vivid* and *Stain*, and neither made me want to sleep with anybody, except maybe a guy. However, the experience did re-instill my belief that (a) I am not a glamour boy, and (b) I am fierce.

So what makes for a good sex song? That depends on whom you ask. I recall having a heated argument with a woman over what made for better sex music: White Zombie or Yanni. In my mind, "More Human Than Human" is *very* sexy; I actually think it sounds like sex. My female opponent strongly disagreed with that assertion, although I don't think she was so much advocating Yanni as she was attacking White Zombie. But this really isn't the point (especially since when we *did* end up having sex, we were listening to Steely Dan). The point is that just about everyone sees a clear difference between "making love" and "fucking" —even headbangers.

If you want to "make love" to a heavy metal song, you're probably going to lean in the direction of a power ballad. Luckily, there were about 4 million of these made between 1983 and 1991. The origin comes from the big '70s arena bands: Aerosmith ("Dream On"), Nazareth ("Love Hurts"), Lynyrd Skynyrd ("Tuesday's Gone"), Black Sabbath ("Changes"), and KISS ("Beth" and "Hard Luck Woman"). None of these songs were particularly sexy (Skynyrd's was probably the best for slow dancing), but they did set a universal template that a thousand bands copied: You put bittersweet lyrics against an acoustic instrument, and then you steamrolled the refrain with a plutonium-heavy guitar riff. The chorus was the "power," the verse was the "ballad." If you were a guy in the backseat of a car, you went for the bosom during the chorus.

The popularity of the '80s power ballad was mainly due to a radio mentality that carried over from the previous decade. If a rock band wanted to break into the mainstream in 1976, they needed to release a love song that radio stations felt comfortable playing. Since MTV was originally programmed like a Top 40 radio station, they often used the same criteria for breaking metal acts. Extreme's "More Than Words" is a prime example; in fact, when MTV first played that song's video in the summer of 1991, VJs would regularly compare Extreme to KISS (i.e., a hard rock group who used a love song to cross into the mainstream).

"More Than Words" was about as good as power balladeering ever got. On the whole, Extreme was only slightly better than okay, but they were *great* at this kind of prom schlock ("When I First Kissed You" off the same album is also quite capital). Unlike most of their spandex-clad peers, they didn't feel the need to inject their heavy metal roots into the middle of every sweet love song. That proved to be very wise. I'm always a little surprised by how well "More Than Words" stands up over time, but I think I know why it does: It's legitimately romantic. It kind of makes you want to cuddle up to someone, especially during the harmonizing. If you lost your virginity to this song, it might be an embarrassing story to tell people, but—at least when no one else was around— it will still seem special to you.

Unfortunately, there really aren't too many other power ballads that qualify. Warrant's "Heaven" would probably make the cut, as would a song by the band Steelheart that I can't remember. Truth be told, Journey, Boston, and Styx were much better at this sort of thing than groups like Quiet Riot and Trixter.

Faster Pussycat's "House of Pain" was a really wonderful ballad, but it had nothing to do with sex (or even girls). The same goes for the Crüe's "Home Sweet Home" and Slaughter's "Fly to the Angels," which was supposedly not about suicide but certainly seemed like it.

Guns N' Roses' biggest ballad was "Patience," but that was about *not* having sex. "Sweet Child O' Mine" was a little too upbeat in the beginning (and a little too menacing at the end), and "November Rain" was too much of a wedding song (and I thought that *before* I saw the video). The best GNR sex song was actually "Rocket Queen," which isn't a ballad at all, except maybe at the end.

But perhaps you don't want romance. Maybe you want the same thing all those metal dudes claimed they needed: Hot, gooey, uninhibited pelvis banging. Well, you're in luck— there's bushels of material for those purposes too: Def Leppard's "Saturday Night (High N' Dry)," Mötley Crüe's "Sumthin' for Nuthin'," the KISS songs "Lick It Up" and "Fits Like a Glove," Cinderella's "Push Push," Faster Pussycat's "Little Dove," Warrant's "Sure Feels Good to Me," Poison's "You Can Look but You Can't Touch," "F.I.N.E." from Aerosmith, Vinnie Vincent's "Naughty Naughty," and a song by Danger Danger that was *also* titled "Naughty Naughty."

Oh yeah . . . and that Whitesnake song. I forget the title. Something about fucking a car, I think.

April 23, 1988

The 1988 Class B State Speech & Debate
tournament is held in Mandan, North Dakota.
Meanwhile, Lita Ford's "Kiss Me Deadly"
crawls up to No. 59 on the pop charts.

At this point, I find myself driven to inject Lovely Lita Ford into this discussion.

Lita Ford was one of heavy metal's "exceptions." This means ninth-graders constantly used her as a pertinent example whenever they wrote an essay for English class that argued metal was more than just satanic cock rock (in case you're curious, the Christian supergroup Stryper was the other overused "exception" for these arguments). Ford began her career in the seminal all-female band the Runaways, a group that has since become a favorite among rock writers. The other star from the Runaways, Joan Jett, became a successful solo artist, but people rarely considered her version of hard rock to be metal. I'm not completely sure why this is. Part of it was timing; "I Love Rock & Roll," her biggest hit, had come and gone before the modern glam era exploded. More importantly, Jett was always more of a punk rocker than a metalhead. That fact has become even more evident during the past decade; today she's a lesbian icon and the godmother of riot grrls.

However, Lita took a different path. She was metal to the core, even marrying Chris Holmes of W.A.S.P. (that move heightened her "bad girl" credibility, because Holmes had posed in the "For Ladies" section of *Hustler* magazine and evidently has a huge dick). In a lot of ways, she tried to embody the fantasy image created by all those macho male groups. And—at least in 1988—she succeeded.

I discovered Lita as a sophomore in high school. She had released the single "Kiss Me Deadly," which went to No. 12 on the pop charts but pervaded bedrooms and school parking lots far more often than its *Billboard* peak would indicate. "Kiss Me Deadly" was similar to "Talk Dirty to Me" and "Panama"—it was simply a great pop song, and anyone who tries to argue otherwise is ignoring the actual tune and attacking the genre. This is not to say Ford had some special gift for making music; "Kiss Me Deadly" is basically the only better-than-average song she ever made (and she wasn't even the credited songwriter). I can barely remember anything else on the album (*Lita*) it came from: I know she had one song called "Back to the Cave" and another called "Blueberry," plus a semipopular duet with Ozzy Osbourne that seemed to openly promote suicide pacts. This is the extent of Lovely Lita's musical legacy.

However, I really liked *Lita*. Of all the albums I never actually listened to, it was probably my favorite. Lita was crouching on the front of the record, kind of like Daryl Hannah in *Clan of the Cave Bear*. In one of the photos inside, she was wearing one of those Mexican bandoliers across her chest, and she made the bullets look foxy. Lita was ready to go to war . . . and then come home and bang somebody.

My fondest memories of *Lita* focus around a particularly unrocking time in my life. I was fifteen and attending the North Dakota state speech and debate tournament in Mandan, North Dakota, right across the Missouri River from Bismarck. My speech coach (a semihip English teacher named Brenda) drove me and two girls (including Janet Veit!) the four hours to Bismarck, where I was scheduled to compete in extemporaneous speaking. We even stayed in a hotel, which is always strangely exciting during high school.

I spent most of the trip down talking about Lita Ford. The reason I can so clearly remember this is because it was the first time I ever really talked about anything sexual in the presence of women. Prior to this weekend, the only time I had ever discussed a physical attraction to a woman was with other guys (usually in some type of cliché locker room situation). As soon as we got to Bismarck, we went to the local mall and I immediately bought the *Lita* cassette. I didn't have my Walkman with me, and my teacher's car didn't have a cassette player; basically, it was a useless acquisition. The four of us spent about two hours in this mall, and I didn't buy anything else (although I did play three dollars' worth of *Elevator Action* in the arcade). I mostly walked around the shopping center, reading the *Lita* liner notes. I also remember thinking it was very strange that the floor of the Bismarck mall was carpeted. Actually, that still seems strange to me.

For the next two days, I loudly insisted that I wanted to sleep with Lita Ford. And I suppose I did. Why wouldn't I? Lita was the rock chick I had always heard about in other bands' songs. The fact that I couldn't play this cassette didn't matter; in fact, the music might have made me *less* interested, because most of *Lita* turned out to be shit. But at the moment of purchase, I had to assume that every song on the LP was going to be as cool as "Kiss Me Deadly." Talking about the music was more exciting than hearing it (which is still the way I feel about most rock 'n' roll).

In retrospect, it seems clear why Lita Ford was the catalyst for my sudden willingness to talk about sex. She may have been totally unreal, but she was a step closer to reality. I mean, at least Lita Ford was a woman. She wasn't David Lee Roth *talking* about a woman. She wasn't acting as the faceless recipient of Blackie Lawless's penis. Lita was a female entity with a real personality. And since my only exposure to sexuality had been through metal music, I was only going to be comfortable expressing an attraction to a woman who existed in that world. I had never had a girlfriend in my life. I had never even kissed a girl. Even though I was thinking about sex constantly, I had no idea how to process or manage those kinds of thoughts. But I *did* understand hard rock. I understood the glam rock depiction of being in love and being in lust. And I didn't feel awkward having those feelings toward Lita Ford. Somehow, I felt like I knew what I was doing.

Every once in a while, Ford is remembered as a rare role model for female guitar players in the 1980s. She was one of the few women who succeeded in a male-dominated world, and I'm sure some girls did look up to her. But she may have even done more for stupid boys like me. As contradictory as it might seem, Lita Ford made me think about sexy women as *people*—not just as the subject of some long-haired guy's lyrics.

The irony to all this is that by talking about Ford as an exception, I am unconsciously working under the assumption that heavy metal *is* sexist. I'm discussing metal's sexism as if it's an indisputable fact, outlined in the Constitution (or at least in the Articles of Confederation). Sometimes I forget that this may or may not be true. I guess I never consider the alternative.

Certainly, '80s metal was almost always about sex. And—certainly—that sex was almost always described from the perspective of a man. But does this automatically mean it's sexist? Do those elements automatically make anything (or everything) that comes with it a sexist art form?

Probably.

I suppose any opinion that comes almost exclusively from one gender is going to be sexist, although the term "genderist" would technically be more accurate. This is amplified when the subject is physical intercourse; few aggressive opinions can be safely expressed about sex, and never by guys like Sebastian Bach.

I've always been baffled by—and strangely attracted to—feminists. It's hard not to notice their amusing hypocrisies more than their "confrontational" ideas, as is typical of most people who hold strong opinions. Feminists are one of the three kinds of people who express the most outrage over the sexual content of metal music. The other two groups are right-wing Christian conservatives (who express outrage over pretty much anything that's remotely interesting), and pseudo-intellectual male academics (who share my attraction to feminists but actively try to do something about it). I am most interested in the arguments from classic feminists; I use the modifier "classic" to differentiate between prototypical ERA types, like Gloria Steinem, and those so-called neo-conservative feminists like Camille Paglia (neo-conservatives like Paglia tend to *adore* cock rock and seem just as crazy as classic feminists, but in a good way).

I never give any credence to the anti-metal arguments from Christian conservatives or sensitive male feminists. The first group bases its stance on an enforced morality, and the second group holds their argument because they think it somehow makes them seem smart. Neither has any idea what they're talking about. I will, however, listen to antimetal arguments made by classic female feminists (and I have on countless occasions). The problem is that—no matter how intelligent they may be— they inevitably attack the same ideas they typically support. It's kind of like whenever abortion opponents argue in favor of capital punishment, or when ardent pro-choice types talk about the inhumanity of the death penalty. The philosophical inconsistency always overwhelms the potential for logic.

Often, feminists go after the alleged misogyny in metal with a stock argument that's hard to counter: "If I'm offended by it," they say, "then that is proof enough." The thinking is that the only criterion for what is *offensive* is that someone was *offended* by it. In a linguistic sense, the argument makes perfect sense. In reality, it means less than nothing. In fact, this kind of thinking is the worst thing that has happened to language, publishing, and damn near everything else in society over the last twenty years. If you are personally offended by the "Hot for Teacher" video, it might be because the video is sexist. It also might be because you're the kind of person who is easily offended. Or it might even be because you're fucking crazy. But regardless of how you feel, your personal feelings do not constitute an argument over whether something is sexist.

A slightly more compelling argument (the operative word being "slightly") is that metal was sexist for "contextual" reasons.

The suggestion is that it inevitably placed sex in a context that made women objects or victims (or at the very least secondary to the existence of a man). I suppose this is somewhat true. I slip into that argument when I write about Lita Ford. It's hard to imagine rock music done any other way, though. That's the nature of personal art. Liz Phair certainly sings everything through the eyes of a woman, and her narratives sometimes portray men as jerks and manipulators. Chrissie Hynde does that same thing—yet I would never assume the Pretenders were sexist. That's just the way songwriting works. When I try to think of pop songs that objectively paint both sides of a relationship, the only one I can come up with is that tune from the Human League where the girl was working as a waitress in a cocktail bar.

But this much is true: There *is* an undeniable difference between someone like Chrissie Hynde and someone like Jani Lane (despite the fact that they both happen to hail from Akron, Ohio). The difference is simple. Chrissie seems smart, Jani seems stupid. This does not mean that Chrissie *is* smart or that Jani *is* stupid; it merely means that it seems that way. So when Warrant sang about sex, they came across as mindlessly horny musk oxen. The reason they were popular is that they fully recognized this perception and used it to their advantage. Like any smart metal band, they marketed their weakness into a strength.

Just about everyone agrees that sexism is an act of ignorance, or at least that's what people say if they need to make a public retraction about an indisputably sexist statement. For example, if a public figure does (or says) something so obviously sexist that it's indefensible, there's really only one means of spin control: A well-respected ally must come forward and say, "I know [*insert name of sexist jerk*] as a person, and he is not a sexist jerk. He is simply ignorant about this issue" (Public Enemy's Chuck D had to make similar statements on behalf of former bandmate Professor Griff whenever Griff mindlessly declared war against the Jews). It's a necessary form of surrender, but it has a cost; once you're shackled with the perception of ignorance, you can never again comment on anything controversial without getting nailed by everyone who lacks a sense of humor (or wants to punish you for having one).

Since metal was so willing to be dumb, it put itself in a position where it had to absorb the insults of its detractors. Everyone knows there's a difference between "dumb" and "unintelligent." Unfortunately, heavy metal was perceived as both. And that's why Warrant's idea of sex was always going to demand the inclusion of an "ist" at the end. The main explanation for heavy metal's sexism was its conscious willingness to let itself be burdened with that particular cross.

Probably the best argument I've heard about metal's sexism is the least verbal one—*just look at it.* It you're clever enough, you can make a good argument for anything. You can explain why heavy metal isn't sexist a thousand different ways. However, it's hard to stare into the Red Sea and claim it's not wet. To insist that the video for "Cherry Pie" is not (at the very least) somewhat insulting toward females ignores the most obvious reality in the universe. The same goes for David Lee Roth's "California Girls," Y & T's "Summertime Girls," Mötley Crüe's "Girls Girls Girls," or any video that features girls fucking automobiles. Everything can be debated, but that doesn't necessarily mean it's debatable.

Okay, fine. *Heavy metal was sexist.* It's a judgment call, and I'm making the judgment. But that raises yet another question:

What's the big deal?

Here again, I run the risk of insulting most smart people. However, that's not always such a bad idea. There is no reason to assume that something that's generally bad is *always* bad, and it's very possible—in fact, pretty likely—that the sexism in glam rock was perfectly fine.

It seems that people who complain about rock 'n' roll tend to have a problem with consistency. Half the time they bemoan the content of Judas Priest, and half the time they are insisting that it's akin to a bad joke. It really can't be both. If art is stupid, it can't really be harmful. If it's not stupid, then it can't be dismissed as socially irrelevant.

In order to avoid this problem, I'm going to eliminate both scenarios.

Let's start by working under the assumption that metal is stupid. It's a position widely asserted by critics: Of all the popular genres of rock music over the past fifty years, metal is the least regarded and most maligned. So let's assume it has no real social consequence.

If all this is true, how do we perceive AC/DC? They sing songs like "Giving the Dog a Bone" (which is not about dogs), "Inject the Venom" (which is not about venom), and "Big Balls" (which *is* about balls). When they're not beating you over the head with monster guitar riffs (most of which were way too good for any "legitimate" musician to come up with), the boys in AC/DC claimed to be fucking your sister. And her best friend. And maybe your mother. And they're not being real sensitive about it either. In fact, they might even be killing these women when they're finished, but that's not totally clear.

This being the case, we can safely place AC/DC into the "probably sexist" category (and I'm sure they would be very offended if we didn't). There are many who would denounce Australia's loudest band for this not-so-chivalrous attitude. These people would say that their music has a negative effect on both men and women, and it turns sexual intercourse into a violent conquest.

But isn't this what it's supposed to do? I mean, heavy metal is universally assumed to be stupid, right? And AC/DC is one of these stupid metal bands, right? So it seems to me it's almost their *job* to be sexist. It's naive and irrational to expect a world where everyone is enlightened (there cannot be light without darkness), so we always need some definitive heroes and villains. Someone has to wear the white hats and someone has to wear the (back in) black hats. If sexism is dumb—and we all seem to agree it is—one would have to assume that the most sexist bands are going to be the dumbest bands. And according to our premise, this would be the metal bands. And who could be more metal than AC/DC?

As a medium, heavy metal isn't very adept at swaying public opinion. It's not protest rock, and it's not a teaching tool. Tipper Gore hated W.A.S.P.'s "Animal (Fuck Like a Beast)," but she never made a good argument about why it needed to be banned. There's really no argument to be made. She hated hard rock and she thought it was moronic, but it was like she was screaming into a brick wall. Complaining about "Fuck Like a Beast" was like . . . well, like complaining about beasts that fuck. The song was brainless and without motive, and there was no "idea" about what it represented. It didn't affect behavior and it didn't lead to a new way of thinking. Why? Because—as we stated earlier—*metal was stupid*. There was no method behind the madness. It was the cultural equivalent of watching a car wreck, and no fourteen-year-old boy could ever avert his eyes from that. That's as far as it went.

But—just for the sake of argument—let's go back and rethink our original idea.

Let's assume that metal is *not* so terribly stupid (a premise that's probably quite appealing for those of you trying to force your way through a book about heavy metal). Suddenly, we have to rethink the AC/DCs of the world; they are no longer six-foot hormones who don't know any better. If glam metal is intelligent (even mildly so), the sexism is conscious. It's either (a) a marketing ploy, or (b) a negative artistic statement.

Either way, it's still completely defensible.

If these groups were making women into whores for the sole purpose of selling records, they are a *reflection* of society—not the problem that's poisoning it. The nature of capitalism is to feed on desire. A commercial entity will take on whatever characteristics it needs to move the product. For '80s rock, that was misogyny. And if you find that concept "irresponsible," you are naive.

There used to be a clothing store franchise called The Id, which I always felt was a brilliant name for a store (even though I'm sure 75 percent of its clientele had no idea what that name meant). "You want this sweater!" the store's sign seemed to scream at its customers. "Your impulses are telling you to possess more khaki slacks!" For the most part, we don't need culture; we want it. Culture feels good. And I don't fault musicians who take advantage of the lowest common denominator to sell their version of culture to the public.

A band like KISS fed my appetite for sex, but they didn't create it. Gene Simmons's depiction of sex seemed like a joke. By the time I was smart enough to consider what the social consequence would be if he was actually serious, I was also smart enough to realize that this is how marketing works. If someone uses sex to sell you a product, they are not changing your mind. They are taking advantage of your mind's preexisting weakness.

But what if all this was *not* just a way to make money? What if Nikki Sixx is operating under the same motivational construct as Bob Dylan, but he's simply more interested in promoting loveless sex and the quest for power? Is artistic sexism justified?

Certainly.

If we're going to give metal credence as an art form, we have to give it the same benefit of the doubt we'd give *Piss Christ* or Robert Mapplethorpe or anything else that's controversial. We have to live with the (sometimes uncomfortable) idea that it serves a benefit merely by its existence. The music creates discourse. It's an *idea*. And if you're willing to believe that something that's often absurd can be occasionally insightful, there are ideas in the sleaziest trenches of glam metal.

Growing up, I used to have lots of dreams where I lost my teeth. Sometimes they would get knocked out in these dreams, but usually they just fell out. Often, I dreamt that they were ripped out of their sockets while I brushed in front of the mirror. It was basically the only "nightmare" (if you can call it that) I ever had as a teenager.

When I reached my sophomore year of college, I stopped having these dreams. A few months later, I found out that this particular type of dream is pretty common, and dream analysts almost always characterize its symbolic value with the same diagnosis: This is a sign of sexual frustration. And in retrospect, I would say that was frighteningly accurate. It's not just that I didn't have sex until I was twenty—I hadn't even masturbated

(Catholicism is more powerful than any teenage lust). At the age of twenty, I had never had an orgasm while I was awake. The only sexual outlet in my entire life was rock music. And that may explain why I was so drawn to the one-dimensional sexuality of heavy metal. To be honest, even that level of sexual insight was probably a little too deep for me to mentally manage.

There is a value to art that appeals to visceral idiocy; there is an intellectual aspect to negative ideas. The problem is that people who comment on culture always feel an obligation to point out the obvious, lest they might be perceived as unqualified for their job. Pointing out that Mötley Crüe's "Ten Seconds to Love" is a sexist song about a cheap fuck in an elevator proves nothing, beyond the fact that you managed to listen to the lyrics and recognize that some people might find the premise unappealing.

But is there a deeper meaning to "Ten Seconds to Love"?

According to the band, not really. When I asked Crüe guitarist Mick Mars about misogyny in their early music, he said, "Some people probably find it sexist, and that's fine. You can overanalyze anything if you try hard enough." But Mick's argument is weak. Mars is basically doing the same thing that rock critics do: He doesn't want to inject complexity into the Mötley message, so he declares there is no message whatsoever. Music writers don't want a message to be there either; that would latently give a band like Mötley Crüe too much credit. Critics need to show that heavy metal is stupid in order to validate their own intelligence (if you're going to insist that P J Harvey and Yo La Tengo are brilliant, the opposite has to suck). They are expected to perpetuate the herd mentality that drives rock journalism. It's like *The Boys on the Bus*, except the drugs are better and you get free CDs.

The result is that both sides of the equation will insist that "Ten Seconds to Love" means nothing. When the band says that, they mean it in a good way; when pundits say it, it's supposed to be bad. But the reality is that the people in the middle—the 3 million kids who bought the record—don't care. They like it, and it's going to matter to them. They create the meaning, and their creation is absolutely valid.

What's great about rock music (and specifically heavy metal) is that the consumer is more important than the product itself. Billy Corgan of Smashing Pumpkins once said that Van Halen is infinitely better than an "important" band like Sonic Youth because Van Halen's music was for everybody. No one was excluded from the party. When you apply Corgan's philosophy to a song like Van Halen's "Feel Your Love Tonight," it says a lot about what it meant to be a teenager in 1979 (Corgan would try to personally recapture a similar emotion in the song "1979," which—somewhat ironically—sounded a lot like a slowed-down Sonic Youth single). Van Halen's vibe was directed at *everybody*, and a huge chunk of that everybody liked it. It made sense, and it was embraced. The universal acceptance of Van Halen helps us understand the culture that spawned it. Without trying, it has more social and intellectual value than anything Thurston Moore ever tried to teach us.

Those sex-saturated metal anthems of the 1980s were not autonomous creations. They are reflections of the time and place from where they came. Clever people always want to imply that life imitates art, mostly because it makes the artists seem as important as we wish they were. Everyone with common sense knows the opposite is true: Life makes art. Life makes heavy metal. To attack the sexism in the latter is no different from pretending it doesn't exist in the former.

June 18, 1988

For the sixth consecutive week,
George Michael has the No. 1 album in America,
holding off GNR, Poison, Van Halen,
and the Scorpions.

I could lie about my heavy metal past if I wanted to. If I needed a sudden injection of retrospective coolness, I could easily fake myself into coming off as an ex-goth. I know how Bauhaus fans view their youth; I could pretend to smile knowingly whenever I hear "Bela Lugosi's Dead," and I could describe my junior high bedroom as "sepulchral." I could just as easily claim I spent my formative years listening to R.E.M.'s *Document* and all those stupid XTC records, and I could swear that I used to imagine I was Bono at Red Rock whenever I'd see my breath while window-shopping for Christmas presents in the December air of downtown Fargo. I know enough about music to make people think I was one of the smart kids who was thinking about social alienation when everyone else was thinking about fucking.

However, this masquerade would crumble under scrutiny. Inevitably, I would stumble into a contradiction that would ultimately blow my cover. This has happened before. I remember going to a party in 1992 when someone played "Come On Eileen" by Dexy's Midnight Runners, and I thought it was a brand-new song. That was tough to explain.

You see, metal kids did not listen to Top 40 radio. It wasn't

126

allowed. Every morning, my clock radio was set to *buzz*, never to *music*. If your car didn't have a cassette player, you kept a boom box in the backseat. The goal was not just to hate pop singles, but to deny (or at least ignore) that they even existed. I went to amazing lengths to avoid whatever teenage girls supported. It was at least 1995 before I listened to an entire Depeche Mode song.

Still, there were a few bands that—somehow—were not included in the non-metal embargo. There was rarely much explanation for what slipped under (or in this case, *over*) our hard rock radar. Sometimes it was just that one of our respected metal peers would declare that it "rocked," and we'd all inexplicably agree.

The one artist who particularly sticks in my mind was John Cougar Mellencamp. In this case, there was a logical reason for his popularity among North Dakota metalheads. Mellencamp probably does not realize how important his music was to kids who grew up in rural areas. In fact, I didn't even realize how much until I had moved away.

I can clearly remember driving around on abandoned gravel roads in a pickup with two of my friends, drinking rootbeer schnapps and Old Milwaukee. The pickup belonged to my friend Cliff; it was a gray Dodge, but the second lowercase "d" on the hood logo had fallen off. His truck was thereby referred to as the "Doggie." Cliff was the five-foot-eight-inch point guard on our basketball team and had been nicknamed after Metallica bassist Cliff Burton (even though he didn't play bass, didn't resemble Burton in any notable way, and had never been in a catastrophic bus accident). He was just about the toughest kid I've ever met. As a seven-year-old, he had been trampled by a herd of cattle, crushing part of his spine. He only had one kidney, which may have been caused by the cows but might have been caused by God. Five years after the ministampede, he flipped a Honda three-wheeler and needed eighteen pins placed in his left shoulder. His shoulder recovered completely, but it forever carried a two-hundred-ton chip of pure maleficence; to this day, I've never known anyone meaner than Cliff as a sixteen-year-old. He actually kind of scared me, and I admired that.⊛ The other kid in the truck was nicknamed Duke; he had been my best friend since we were five, even though I always got the impression he didn't like me very much. He was probably the best athlete in our school, but (of course) he despised sports. He was also among the smartest, but (of course) he was so remarkably lazy that he barely got Bs. By the time he was a senior, he was so accustomed to being an academic underachiever that people started to actually believe he was legitimately average. He never applied himself to anything, except the act of being charming; mostly, he smoked Basic cigarettes and acted like Paul Newman in *Cool Hand Luke*, even though he'd never seen the movie and probably still hasn't. Obviously, Duke was the most popular kid in our school and would eventually be elected homecoming king.

The three of us were parked in a grove south of town, and we had two cassettes on the dashboard: Bon Jovi's *New Jersey* and Mellencamp's *Scarecrow*. I sort of thought Mellencamp was singing about a place that was like Wyndmere. When I got older, I would come to realize that John's version of a "Small Town" wasn't a fraction as small as our rural village, because we all considered Fargo to be nothing less than a city. It's still disconcerting to me whenever I hear someone describe Omaha or Green Bay as a small town; where we were sitting, it was impossible to imagine what it would have been like if Wyndmere's population doubled to one thousand. The idea of that many people living in our community was unthinkable. But it seemed like John Mellencamp felt the same way about his home in Indiana.

In all likelihood, this is a purely regional anomaly (although I did stumble across a full-page advertisement for *Scarecrow* on

⊛It must be noted that I recently spoke with Cliff for the first time in seven years, and he is no longer an angry young man. In fact, he now wears Hawaiian shirts in public and has become shockingly amicable. Cliff works as a beef inspector for the state of North Dakota (he actually has an office in the capitol building in Bismarck) and recently purchased a pontoon boat for the purposes of "beer drinking and womanizing" on Lake Sakakawea. I suspect he is the only meat inspector in America who talks like Paul Stanley in casual conversation.

the back cover of a 1985 copy of *Circus*, so maybe there was a connection). It's hard to imagine Mötley Crüe fans in Atlanta thinking little Johnny Cougar was the cool shit. But I don't know if we necessarily did either. He wasn't really *cool*. He was *like us*. He was a good guy. We were never worried about nuclear war or global warming; we were, however, nervous that someone was going to foreclose on my parents' farm, even though we weren't exactly certain how that process worked. All we knew is that there were auction sales whenever times got tough, and (at least according to the talk around my dinner table) times were *always* tough (at least after 1976). All that "rain on the scarecrow, blood on the plow" stuff was a little too fucking possible for farm kids; I suppose it was kind of like inner-city kids hearing Notorious B.I.G. songs and wondering if they'd ever get shot.

There were only two kinds of music in rural America during the 1980s: metal and country. Nothing else was culturally relevant. Mellencamp fit into neither category, yet somehow he was both. "Authority Song" was like Judas Priest's "Parental Guidance," only less obvious. "Jack and Diane" was akin to the better Skid Row power ballads, only more applicable (Wyndmere had a Tastee Freez too!). Oh, Mellencamp certainly pumped out some boring crap that made everybody yawn; I still don't understand the allure of "Pink Houses" (is that about a gay community?). "R-O-C-K in the USA" was a little too much like Bryan Adams, and none of us were going to sit around and listen to any tributes to Jackie Onassis. But Mellencamp was definitely one of us. Actually, Duke and Cliff seemed to understand that better than I did. Whenever I punched *New Jersey* back into the tape deck, we never got past "Bad Medicine." To them, "Born to Be My Baby" paled in comparison to bloody plows.

Mellencamp wasn't the only fellow who made the cut, however. Tom Petty did too, and for a lot of the same reasons. While he did not specifically apply his lyrics to rural people, there was clearly a provincial feel to his material; he's definitely the most positive role model for small-town stoners. It seemed that metal kids only allowed metal dudes to act like "rock stars," so we were drawn to pop singers who consciously downplayed the Hollywood image. Petty knew his place. The Heartbreakers were a completely unglamorous rock band; they almost seemed like the Allman Brothers. Their songs had the simple three-riff structure of pop metal. "Running Down a Dream" was the key track, and I remember thinking that Izzy Stradlin would probably write songs like this if he wasn't in a metal band. It turns out I was basically dead-on.

Tone Loc was another semipredictable favorite, although that had nothing to do with the Allman Brothers. Loc was just this cool, unthreatening black guy who rapped about sex and wine, and it was perfectly constructed to bleed into the white American metal scene. Much has been written about how mainstream Caucasian audiences refused to accept rap music until it was delivered by the wonderfully Jewish Beastie Boys, and that's somewhat true—but their whiteness is only part of the equation. The main reason white kids didn't immediately embrace rap is because they didn't understand the music. It came from a different place, and human ears are always drawn to the familiar. We were not ready for James Brown samples (at least not yet). The Beasties overcame that barrier when they met producer Rick Rubin, who introduced them to Led Zep and AC/DC. Rubin made hip-hop user-friendly to farm kids. We all called *Licensed to Ill* a rap album, but even though we didn't know why, it seemed more like classic rock. In 1989, Tone Loc made things even simpler: He abandoned the idea of a riff and offered a *thump-thump-thump*. Listen to "Funky Cold Medina"—there's *nothing* there, beyond a beat. If you liked bass and had a sense of humor, it was impossible not to dig Loc. The fact that he sampled Van Halen and KISS didn't hurt either.

Less understandable was our universal agreement that the Bangles were cool. And as unbelievable as this might sound, it had nothing to do with how they looked, either. We all thought Susanna Hoffs was hot, but so was Kylie Minogue and Tiffany. This had more to do with their attitude: There just seemed to be some kind of understood belief that the Bangles were our kind of people. It might have been their cover of "Hazy Shade of Winter" on the Rubin-produced *Less Than Zero* soundtrack, but I kind of doubt it; I can't recall anyone except me actually buying that album. Maybe everyone else was mixing them up with Vixen.

Though it seems even stranger, the B-52s were another guilty pleasure for many hard-charging headbangers. This was actually one example of metal kids being ahead of the curve. While the standard dumb teenager liked "Love Shack" because he thought it was a neat song, adolescent Ratt fans immediately assumed it was some kind of a joke. We didn't necessarily understand *irony*, per se, but we had enough exposure to rock posturing to know that this was mostly a gag. It may have been a catchy joke, but it certainly wasn't an earnest attempt at rock 'n' roll. The one thing all those metal magazines taught us was how to spot the stereotypes of rock stardom, and the B-52s were clearly representing the opposite ideal on purpose.

After this point, the list gets pretty barren. If your cassette collection had too many other nonmetal artists, you were bordering on being one of those goddamn eclectics who really didn't *love* anything. One of my primary theories as a junior high kid was that people who claimed to like every genre of music were liars and hypocrites; they lacked backbone. I never trusted open-minded people.

Of course, a few pop songs always managed to weasel into the metal stratosphere. Here's a fairly comprehensive list of all the nonmetal singles that a midwestern headbanger could publicly appreciate. The vast majority were released between 1985 and 1990, but there are a few exceptions. I've tried to figure out the unifying quality that made these specific songs *rock* (or what made them *bitchin'* or *heavy* or *wicked* or whatever it was we were saying at the moment), but that appears to be impossible. I like most—but certainly not all—of them, and I've included a key at the bottom of the list that explains how they were introduced into the glam rock subculture. They are listed in the approximate order of their universal popularity within the metal community.

"The Devil Went Down to Georgia," Charlie Daniels Band [a]

"So Alive," Love & Rockets [b]

"Black Cat," Janet Jackson [c]

"The Race Is On," Sawyer Brown (*cover version only*) [a]

"Holiday in the Sun," the Sex Pistols [d]

"Red Red Wine," UB40 [e]

"Blister in the Sun," the Violent Femmes [b]

"Don't Be Cruel," Cheap Trick [a]

"The Warrior," Scandal (*featuring Patty Smyth*) [d]

"Strut," Sheena Easton [c] [d]

"Darling Nikki," Prince [d]

"Flesh for Fantasy," Billy Idol [d]

"Just Like Heaven," the Cure [b]

"Fishin' in the Dark," the Nitty Gritty Dirt Band [a] [c]

"Ice Ice Baby," Vanilla Ice [f]

"Legs," ZZ Top [a] [d] [e]

"You May Be Right," Billy Joel [h]

"She Drives Me Crazy," Fine Young Cannibals [b]

"Invincible," Pat Benatar [g]

"You Spin Me Round (Like a Record)," Dead or Alive [d]

"Who Can It Be Now?," Men at Work [h]

"Goin' Back to Cali," LL Cool J [e]

"Touch Me (I Want Your Body)," Samantha Fox [c]

"Rock Me Amadeus," Falco [f]

"Hippy Hippy Shake," the Georgia Satellites [d]

"She's Got the Look," Roxette [c] [e]

"Centerfield," John Fogerty [a] [c] [d] [f] [h]

KEY

[a]: The guys who bought us beer loved it.
[b]: Introduced by nondescript "cool kid" from neighboring town.
[c]: Local metal chicks liked to dance to it.
[d]: Thought it maybe *was* metal.
[e]: Somebody saw the video and wouldn't shut up about it.
[f]: Too stupid to ignore and/or it seemed pretty cool at the time.
[g]: Prominently featured in the film *The Legend of Billie Jean*.
[h]: Origin unknown.

July 20, 1988

Iron Maiden headlines
the Donnington Rock Festival in front of
107,000 people, two of whom die
during Guns N' Roses' set.

I have never met Satan, but he actually sounds like a pretty cool guy. A bit geeky, perhaps, but I'm sure we could still hang out and play Scrabble or something.

I've never been to Satan's apartment, so I can only guess how it's decorated. However, certain aspects of his personality have been well-established by the media: He obviously likes to play AD&D. He obviously owns a Ouija board. He obviously likes to smoke angel dust. And he obviously has an awesome stereo with kick-ass speakers, and he obviously plays nothing but heavy metal. In fact, he probably has a framed poster of Ronnie James Dio on his living room wall.

To paraphrase the insightful sock puppet stars of *The Sifl & Olly Show*, all the really cool rock bands are from hell. Ever since Lucifer and chain-smoking bluesman Robert Johnson made a deal "down at the crossroads," Satan has been the finest A&R rep who ever existed. The Rolling Stones had sympathy for the devil; the Eagles stayed at his hotel; Van Halen went jogging with him. Styx named their band after a river that flowed *next* to hell, which probably explains how they managed to stay cool for about twelve weeks in 1978.

If you believe *Hammer of the Gods*, Satan's favorite band of all time was Led Zeppelin, a group who only occasionally sang about hell but copiously mentioned Valhalla (which would probably be just as frustrating). During the band's heyday, Jimmy Page lived in a castle near Loch Ness, where he supposedly spent all day sitting in the dark, taking drugs, and dabbling in the occultist works of Aleister Crowley (the estate's former owner). It can safely be argued that this is the most awesome thing anyone has ever done in the history of rock. If I ever get to the point where my daily routine revolves around shooting junk in a rural Sussex castle and talking about black majik, I will know I have made it.

According to a popular legend that I don't think even one person ever believed to be true, three of Led Zep's four components made a deal with the devil in exchange for superstardom. The story goes on to suggest that John Paul Jones was the only one who declined this pact, which is why he remains the third-remaining and fourth-best known member of the band. However, he is also the only Zepster who was never penalized by Satan's power; the other three were all struck by evil (John Bonham choked on his own vomit, Robert Plant tragically lost his son Karac, and Page would go on to collaborate with David Coverdale).

Of course, Page and his Loch Ness monstrosities couldn't hold a ceremonial candle to Black Sabbath, a band so intent on pretending to worship Satan that they actually might have done so by accident. The cover of *Sabbath, Bloody Sabbath* has a skull, the number 666, and a reenactment of the money shot from *Rosemary's Baby*. The record itself includes a song called "Killing Yourself to Live." It may as well be a travel brochure for hell.

Sabbath was always doing weird, spooky shit; from what I can tell, 50 percent of their songs were about the devil, 35 percent were about taking drugs, and (oddly) 15 percent were about traveling through time. Geezer Butler told me the song "N.I.B." was actually about drummer Bill Ward's poorly grown beard, which Butler thought resembled a little "nub," which he pronounced as "nib," which was then inexplicably turned into the acronym

"N.I.B.," which made every kid with an ounce of creativity assume it was supposed to stand for "Nativity in Black" (particularly since the lyrics do not mention facial hair, but they do refer to Lucifer *in the first person*). Boy, how did anyone misinterpret *that?*

Amazingly (or perhaps predictably), this kind of sinister gimmick would ultimately become Sabbath's most recognized influence on rock 'n' roll: fake satanism. "That came from the record company," Butler now insists. "They manufactured the image. We just called ourselves Black Sabbath to match the lyrics; the record company did the rest. We never worshiped the devil. We never even talked about the devil, except to warn people against him."

Part of what Butler says is probably true, but none of it matters. Anyone who saw the album covers were either scared, fascinated, or amused, and all three reactions were connected. In terms of darkness, Sab broke new ground. In his autobiography *Soon to Be a Major Motion Picture*, Abbie Hoffman described a Black Sabbath concert as a microcosm of everything that went wrong at the end of the 1960s. Hoffman was absolutely correct—and for that, I praise Jesus. More than any other rock group, Black Sabbath killed off the hypocritical, self-righteous hippie mentality that was poisoning the planet. Pseudo-political idealism was crushed by pseudo-satanic nihilism, and the world of rock was a far better place.

For me, the occult illusion was always a big part of what I loved about heavy metal. The devil intrigued me more than sex or drugs combined, mostly because I was under the impression that Satan was everywhere. I honestly believed the odds of me encountering Satan were much higher than my chances of meeting a dealer or a whore.

Metal stars who appeal to midwestern kids understand this perception. Take Marilyn Manson, a modern superstar who's not really a metal guy but plays one on TV (more importantly, he was raised with the same sensibilities; the pubescent Manson adored bands like Mötley Crüe and Judas Priest). I've interviewed Manson twice: immediately after *Portrait of an American*

Family was released in 1994 (back when he was a nobody), and again in 1995 (when he was opening for Danzig and starting to raise cultural/social—if not necessarily musical—eyebrows). Over time, his ability to manipulate the press has grown at an exponential rate.

The first time I spoke with Marilyn, he was among the most interesting and insightful musicians I'd ever encountered. When we talked a year later, he was surly and consciously outrageous. In that second conversation, Manson even feigned stupidity—he claimed he didn't know where North Dakota was, and he said he was unfamiliar with the name "Newt Gingrich." By the time he released *Antichrist Superstar* in 1996, Manson was so popular he would only respond to requests from major press outlets; when he did talk to the media, he usually said stuff that was totally insane, sometimes mentioning how he enjoyed cutting into his flesh with razor blades and pouring drugs into the open wounds. Like every shock rocker before him, his weirdness was directly proportional to his fame.

But what's fascinating about Manson is how well he understands what society is afraid of.

Marilyn Manson was born Brian Warner in Canton, Ohio. The community of Canton is a weird little town; before Manson, its only social import was the Pro Football Hall of Fame and the fact that it's the former home of the only U.S. president ever assassinated by a self-described anarchist (William McKinley, for those keeping score at home). Of course, that kind of sweeping statement is exactly what the people of Canton hate to hear. It's difficult to find anyone in town who wants to talk about the musician's local legacy; they're not necessarily ashamed of Manson, but they are really sick of hearing his name. In 1998, I went to his old high school (GlenOak High) and I asked a student who the school's most famous alumnus was. After a ridiculously long pause, the seventeen-year-old girl said, "Well, I *guess* it would probably be Marilyn Manson." Who else was it going to be? It appears that Manson's Ohio connection is a fact that everyone in Canton knows but nobody seems to care about. From what I could tell by chatting with area kids, most of the "urban legends" about the young Brian Warner weren't even passed down through oral tradition—they all came directly from Manson's own autobiography, *The Long Hard Road Out of Hell*.

When he was pushing *Antichrist Superstar*, Manson's shtick was built around satanism. According to his book (which—I must note—is remarkably entertaining), he even met with Church of Satan high priest Anton LaVey in San Francisco (they ate steak and talked about the possibility of fucking Traci Lords). This is a good example of Manson's cleverness; he knows how the media works. Whenever he talked to a reporter, he would mention how true satanism has nothing to do with the devil and how it's actually a way to worship intellect and egoism. And no mater how accurately the reporter represents his quotes, the story's headline will include the words "devil worship" or "*Satanic Bible*" or "Anton LaVey," and parents will freak out. Technically, Manson did nothing that was particularly outrageous—he simply described a philosophy that would probably be classified as merely amoral if it wasn't tied to Satan. But the obvious reality is that weird teens will always associate Manson and his music with the colloquial definition of Satanism—animal sacrifice, perverted sex, and ritualistic occultism that gives supernatural abilities to mortal beings. Intellectuals are forced to give him a few grains of credibility, and the black-hearted masses will always see him as the hard-partying Prince of Darkness.

What's even more fascinating was Manson's personal reinvention for his 1998 album *Mechanical Animals*. The look and sound were both conscious rip-offs of glam-era Bowie, but his new scare tactic was a little more original: The main set piece on his tour was a huge electric sign that screamed **DRUGS,** and the record's best song was titled "I Don't Like the Drugs (But the Drugs Like Me)." During his live performance of the tune "The Speed of Pain," his set was dusted with a blizzard of fake snow that clearly represented cocaine.

The significance of this new gimmick is substantial: Manson slowly realized that American society had grown to fear drugs more than the devil. We have so demonized narcotics that they now seem worse than actual demons. In the eyes of a lot of stupid parents and confused teachers, the concept of a kid experimenting with marijuana is more terrifying than a kid who is intrigued by *worshiping the devil!*

Part of that evolution is due to the ill-conceived rantings of idiots like Nancy Reagan, but a larger factor was the decline of American spirituality throughout the 1980s and '90s. Regardless of how many people still describe themselves as "Christian" in census surveys, we live in a primarily agnostic culture. Intellectually, agnosticism makes more sense. But the downside is that when people lose their convictions about the existence of God and Satan, they are less able to have personal perspectives on what's right and what's wrong. They are more open-minded about old taboos, but they're also less able to see what's obvious (and therefore susceptible to propaganda). It was easy for a vocal minority to turn drugs into the postmodern Lucifer, and savvy rappers like Cypress Hill and House of Pain picked up on that perception immediately. However, Marilyn Manson was the first *metal guy* smart enough to capitalize on a new era in spook rock: In the twenty-first century, Satan can be smoked, snorted, and shot.

Of course, there is a problem with all that metaphorical social deconstruction: It's all speculative. Rock 'n' roll has followed the same path as politics, sports, film, and every other slice of the pop culture hodgepodge—they've all placed a greater reliance on mixed messages in order to cloak selfish motives. One obviously suspects Manson's true quest is to parlay outrageousness into fame, and then sell that fame to consumers. His ultimate aspirations are almost stupidly transparent. However, his *modus operandi* is more sophisticated and non-linear—at least when compared to the guileless metal satanists from the '80s.

My friend Mr. Pancake lived in Nepal for three years; he somehow became involved with one of those wretched Peace Corps programs where we send bright American students to foreign wastelands so that they can stand in flooded ditches and watch people starve. Since he had no access to any American culture except *Baywatch*, I would periodically send him cassette tapes of new alternative music and classic rock standards. (And here's a warning for anyone who ever has a buddy move to Nepal: The mail service over there sucks. I made Mr. Pancake at least sixteen tapes during his stay in Asia, and he received about seven of them. I heavily suspect the rest of my "American Rock and Roll Music" was stolen in customs and is still being used as barter in the Katmandu sex trade.) Every once in a while, I'd throw an Iron Maiden song into the mix, particularly stuff like "The Number of the Beast." Since Pancake was never a metal fan, he always assumed I was just sending tracks off the soundtrack from *This Is Spinal Tap*. But not even Christopher Guest has the skill to write satire as deft as lyrics like, "666—the number of the beast! / 666—the one for you and me!" As far as I'm concerned, Iron Maiden was the funniest band in the entire metal genre. "Sex Farm" and "Big Bottom" are jocular, but I laugh even harder at "Bring Your Daughter . . . to the Slaughter!"

The irony (or at least what I find ironic) is that Iron Maiden was often referred to as "metallectual rockers." They had a very bizarre fan base—a lot of musicians, along with an army of loner outcasts who didn't drink or smile or talk to anyone who was still alive. Maiden never sang about girls (except when they were slaughtering them), opting instead to do musical versions of poems like "The Rime of the Ancient Mariner," which I actually convinced my senior English teacher to play during class. Iron Maiden was fond of "perspective" songs, a songwriting technique that later evolved into a cornerstone for death metal artists. They sang "Hallowed Be Thy Name" from the "perspective" of a man about to be executed; they sang "The Trooper" from the "perspective" of a kamikaze cavalier battling the Russians; they sang "Fear of the Dark" from the "perspective" of a paranoid man who felt he was being followed. This allowed bands to sing about virtually any subject imaginable without personal responsibility for what they said, which was especially important to groups who wanted to specifically address occultism in the first person. For five minutes, the singer became the equivalent of a character in a novel, and the audience was supposed to view his espoused subject matter with the same kind of aesthetic distance.

By disassociating themselves from the content of their lyrics, Iron Maiden could sing about satanism with brazen disregard. The video for their best song, "Can I Play with Madness," was filled with Celtic imagery and Gothic cloud formations; the video's story followed a close-minded schoolteacher who was hunted by Druids after he harassed a young metalhead. It was pretty much the epitome of what made the occult enticing to teenagers: Iron Maiden's music was painted as a conduit to a dark force that empowered the weak. In every interview I've ever seen with mixed-up teenagers who kill classmates after dabbling with the devil, they always (and I mean *always*) mention how they were drawn to the "power" of satanism. "Can I Play with Madness" took that figurative concept and made it literal: The "madness" they're playing with is some kind of religious witchcraft, and the result (at least in the video) is an army of hooded pagans who will fuck with your teacher's life, possibly by erecting a Stonehenge monument in his front yard.

Part of the reason Maiden was tagged for being so intelligent was the guitar work of Dave Murray and Adrian Smith, two classically minded musicians who loved to go for baroque. As stated earlier, they appealed to a specific kind of metal fan—for those who took time to study the genre, Iron Maiden seemed more credible than most of their peers. Of course, they also had no pop sensibility whatsoever. For casual listeners, most of their catalog is boring and self-consciously complex, and the lyrics are more comedic than poetic. But the band was able to get a tremendous amount of mileage out of their unique iconography. Album covers, posters, and T-shirts almost never showed the group members; that role was filled by Eddie, a sinewy cartoon corpse who had (presumably) been inspired to rise from the dead by the awe-inspiring majesty of rock. Any time the PMRC wanted to illustrate the dangers of rock 'n' roll, they would always show the cover art for *Live After Death* or *The Seventh Son of a Seventh*

Son. It's my suspicion that Eddie (or, more accurately, the concept of what a character like Eddie reflected.) was the biggest reason Iron Maiden became an elite metal band. These guys were unattractive, they weren't prototypically cool, and it was impossible to sing along with any of their songs—but Iron Maiden was a *type* of band. They were the type of band who embraced demonic geekiness, and they did it very, very well.

Danzig was another group who fit this motif, although they were less literary. After fronting two musically inept devil bands who mostly sang about killing babies and raping children (the Misfits and Samhain), Glenn Danzig put together a legitimate group in 1988, named it after himself, and had Rick Rubin produce the music. From what I can tell, every song is about committing suicide and partying with Satan. Punkers who liked his early work will swear Mr. Danzig is being sly, but I've never seen anything to support that claim. Much like Iron Maiden, it sure seems like virtually all of his songs are absolute shit, but his diehard fans disagree with a passion that borders on the unfathomable—they don't just think he's good, they think he's fucking *brilliant*.

Danzig's punk roots attracted a different kind of audience than most conventional metal bands (that heritage also allowed him to stealthily convert into the alternative scene during the early '90s). Still, the group's subterfuge was heavy metal satanism in its most traditional form; if you unfolded the liner notes to their second CD, it formed an upside-down cross. In the video from "Mother" (an artistic and consciously unmetal clip shot completely in letter box format), the same kind of upside-down cross is drawn in blood on the body of a nude woman.

I suppose I might be missing the joke here (after all, Danzig's second LP was titled *Lucifuge*, which must be a synthesis of the word "Lucifer" with the word "fudge"), but if this was supposed to be funny, I don't think his adolescent disciples got it either. Basically, Danzig sings about dying and going to hell; some people want that sentiment to be a joke, and some people want that sentiment to be serious. Taken either way, it's mildly amusing but mostly boring.

That leads us back to Ozzy Osbourne, who was rarely boring and usually hilarious. At various times in his career, Ozzy has behaved like a satanic pope. Though a lot of his devilish material from Black Sabbath seems trite today, he was the guy who made this into an artistic template. On the cover of *Blizzard of Ozz*, he brandishes a crucifix as a weapon; on *Diary of a Madman*, he inverts one on the wall. In fact, the *Blizzard . . .* cover even pictures Ozzy with a black cat (apparently, his art director must have been heavily influenced by *Hansel and Gretel*). But— somehow—Osbourne made these clichés seem clever and vaguely plausible. Alice Cooper was more creative, but Ozzy was more sincerely fucked up.

Now, it's important to realize that there is no question about whether or not Osbourne has any allegiances to the devil. He does not. In fact, he seems legitimately bothered that so many people associate him with the occult. Other rockers have denied allegiances to the devil, but none were ever as clear as Ozzy on the song "Rock and Roll Rebel." He uses no metaphors and does not leave any room for interpretation: "I'm just a rock and roll rebel / I tell you no lies / They say I worship the devil / They must be stupid, all right."

I do not question Osbourne's sincerity on this issue. I do, however, question the validity of his indignation. Even if you discount his participation in the Black Sab catalog, his efforts in the 1980s were not exactly gospel hymns. Like Jimmy Page, Osbourne found the work of Aleister Crowley fascinating, and he talks about that fascination in 1981's "Mr. Crowley." If you're trying to convince people that you don't worship the devil, this is not the way to do it. Personally, this kind of songwriting strikes me as very cool, and I can completely understand why Osbourne (or anyone) might find a mountain-climbing freak like Crowley interesting. But there's no way you can express those ideas without justifying people's suspicion that you're a devil worshiper (and biting the heads off birds doesn't help your case much either).

What's even crazier is the growing number of pro-Ozzy apologists who suddenly want to put a different spin on his message.

In his book *Running with the Devil*, Robert Walser insists Ozzy is "mocking" Aleister with "Mr. Crowley." Oh, of course. That makes sense: Osbourne is delivering "satire" about a dead man of whom 90 percent of Ozzy's audience *had never even heard of* prior to the release *of this particular song*. There is no need to make excuses for Ozzy's affinity for the occult. He's not trying to teach people stuff; he's trying to be cool. Ozzy Osbourne is a rock star—*that's his job!*

That's not to say Osbourne is too stupid to understand sarcasm; I suspect he's smarter than most hard rockers, and he's definitely smarter than just about everyone else who dropped acid every single day for two years in the 1970s. There's even a lyric in "Mr. Crowley" where Oz rhetorically asks Aleister if he sent his message "polemically," which is not a word often used in metal songs. Walser's argument also meshes with a song like "Miracle Man" off 1988's *No Rest for the Wicked*, where Oz skewers PTL leader Jim Bakker (who is precisely the kind of self-righteous charlatan who would have wanted Osbourne's music outlawed). Of course, in the video for "Miracle Man," Osbourne pretends to sodomize a pig. That doesn't negate his argument, but it certainly should remind everyone that all of this—and I mean absolutely *all of this*—is simple theatrics. If it wasn't, rock 'n' roll would be as boring as real life.

Ultimately, that's probably what made me so interested in devil rock: I was able to inject my reality with the kind of dark fiction that would have made my poor mother shiver. That's the only explanation I can think of to explain why I slept beneath a pentagram from the age of fourteen to seventeen.

Actually, it might be more accurate to say I slept beneath a Mötley Crüe bumper sticker, but the satanic bottom line was the same. My obviously cool brother-in-law had sent me the sticker through the mail, and since eighth-graders don't have cars (and since my older sister balked at the opportunity to promote the Crüe on her '73 Plymouth Scamp), it was affixed to the headboard of my bed.

I keep trying to picture myself as a fourteen-year-old, nestled in my comforter (which featured raccoons participating in the Lake Placid Winter Olympics), sleeping blissfully beneath this menacing symbol of Satan. This paradox should be symbolic of *something*, and I'm pretty sure it probably is. But I honestly have no idea what that would be.

You hear a lot about how TV and film can desensitize kids to sex and violence. The argument is that fictionalized bloodshed makes actual violence less disturbing; a modern teenager may see a real car wreck and understand that the people inside are *really* dead, but the event doesn't affect him. Heavy metal desensitized me to devil worship in the same way.

A popular trick in my junior high study hall was to steal a kid's notebook and draw a bunch of satanic symbols on the cover (pentagrams, skulls, inverted crosses, the digits 666, and—if the prankster was artistically gifted—the head of a goat). The hope was that the kid's mother would find this notebook and assume her son was going to don a hooded death robe and sacrifice the family beagle. We all found this unspeakably amusing.

The 1980s were generally a good era for faux satanism, especially in the Midwest. At the beginning of all our social studies classes, we always started the hour with "current events," which was a great way to kill time. Students would raise their hands and inform the class about whatever they perceived as a newsworthy "current event." These events could be almost anything; it could be the *Challenger* explosion, or it could be information on prominent athletes from nearby towns who were arrested for open container. Very often, these "current events" would include a new rumor about which North Dakota community was currently shackled by satanism. Bismarck seemed to be the state's most demonic city, because somebody supposedly found a bunch of bones and satanic scrawlings in a series of caves on the city's outskirts. In Maury Terry's book *The Ultimate Evil*, the "Son of Sam" killings can be traced back to cult activity in Minot. Even smaller North Dakota towns, like Oakes (pop. 1,300) and Langdon (pop. 2,000), were periodically mentioned as cultic hotbeds. In fact, parents in Langdon had to have an emergency meeting at the high school to address the risk of Ouija boards randomly possessing local teenagers.

The reality of these rumors is irrelevant. As cloistered kids living somewhere else, we always assumed they were partially true. But we also assumed the tales were ridiculous overreactions. They had to be. There was just an understanding that all adults were confused about Satanism; they saw it as a one-way ticket to hell (and—in the meantime—prison). But we saw it as a cultural accessory. It *was* kind of scary (certainly scary enough to be cool), but it was never outside of our control. Satanism was weird, compelling, and—in extreme cases—deadly. But it could also be taken in doses. You could kind of "experiment" with the occult by buying certain albums. Groups like Damien and Armored Saint provided an opportunity to dabble with sacrilegious dynamite, and there really wasn't any consequence. Here again, heavy metal was an aqueduct for vicarious, harmless evil. Even as an adolescent, I understood that the kind of kid who thought Bruce Dickinson was telling him to worship Satan was the same kind of kid who would have been corrupted by the hum of a refrigerator.

Perhaps the most important thing to remember is that the connection between metal and Satan didn't have that much to do with the music itself. From a purely technical standpoint, "Shout at the Devil" isn't any more clear about its intentions than Pearl Jam's "Satan's Bed," but the latter would never be seen as occult.

Of course, if Ozzy Osbourne sang those same lyrics, "Satan's Bed" would almost certainly be seen as a song about lying down with Lucifer for carnal destruction. This stuff was always about the source. The specter of metal satanism is one genre of communication where the medium really is the message.

October 15, 1988

Heavy metal's finest hour:
The three best-selling records on the planet
are Bon Jovi's *New Jersey*, Guns N' Roses'
Appetite for Destruction, and Def Leppard's
Hysteria.

Every time I invite a hipster over to my house (and this happens far more often than I'd like to admit), I put myself in a precarious position.

At some point in the evening, the visiting hipster is going to look at my CD collection—the single quickest way to assert any individual's coolness quotient. I do the same thing anytime I'm in another person's home. My problem is that (obviously) I am an '80s metal fan, and that devastates my indie rock cred. Since I'm not a musician, I'm not sure why this should matter; it certainly seems ridiculous that private citizens should need indie rock cred. But it always seems important, especially if I'm trying to sleep with the aforementioned hipster. And CD collections don't lie: No matter how many times you mention Matador Records, you cannot consistently explain why Poison is nestled between Pizzicato Five and Polara.

Of course, this situation can be played to one's advantage. You can out-hip a hipster by taking things to the next level—you can promote yourself as an Ironic Contrarian Hipster, the Jedi Knight among trendy rock fans. Being an Ironic Contrarian

Hipster is rather complicated; it forces you to own over a thousand CDs, and you have to hate all of them. In fact, the only things you can openly advocate are artists like the Insane Clown Posse and Britney Spears.

Once you get the reputation as an Ironic Contrarian Hipster, you'll suddenly have a lot of freedom. You can sit around and watch *Roadhouse* and *Footloose* all day, and you can eat at buffet restaurants and wear stupid clothes and smoke pot before work because it's "wacky" to be a "bad employee." Most importantly, you can throw away all your cool records by Stereolab and Built to Spill and listen to stuff that's actually good. This mostly equates to classic rock, new wave groups with female vocalists, Fleetwood Mac, any band from Sweden, and hair metal. If questioned about these choices, you simply scoff and smile condescendingly at your accusers. It also might be a good idea to tell them they need to "think outside the box" (or something like that), but you must say it in a way that indicates you would never actually use that phrase in a real conversation, despite the fact that you always do.

Unfortunately, there will be a point where someone will call your bluff. There will come a day when someone will say, "Hey man, I don't care how far outside the box you think—there is nothing cool about owning Iron Maiden's *Best of the Beast*." And if they are serious and if you are not stoned, you will be forced to host a serious argument about the musical merits of heavy metal.

Arguing for the aesthetics of hair metal probably seems like an impossible task. There are no respected sources to provide support, and you can't simply suggest that the sonics are too complicated for the average listener to understand. There is no high road. You can tell people they just don't "get it," but that's really a self-defeating argument. Opponents will inevitably insist there's nothing to "get," and they're not going to feel any regrets about missing the nothing that you are apparently "getting" and making it into "something." In other words, they will pretty much have you over a barrel, and your only recourse will be insisting that Ani

DiFranco is trying a little too hard to look ugly, which really isn't that compelling of a point in most musical debates.

Usually, the fundamental strategy in prometal arguments hinges on an insistence that most metal *is* horrible. In order to seem rational, the metal advocate is constantly saying things like, "Yeah, I agree that most of those bands did suck, *but . . . ,*" and then they try to build a larger point out of the ashes of a seemingly negative confession. They admit that hair metal did not succeed in a macro sense, but it was sometimes brilliant in a micro sense. This is the only way to seem like a sensible person (it's the same philosophy one uses when trying to support the Libertarian Party).

What's so frustrating is that this kind of statement actually applies to every genre of music (metal included). That's the reality of rock 'n' roll: Just about every band is absolute shit. Listen to the *Sub Pop 200*. Listen to any disco compilation or punk retrospective. Listen to 98 percent of the ska bands that emerged in the mid-1990s (or most of the originals, for that matter). The overwhelming majority of what you'll hear will be wretched. And it generally seems that fans know this, even though they might not feel comfortable admitting it. Few people listen to entire albums, even when they're released by their so-called favorite band. The single biggest force driving the compact disc revolution was not sound quality, nor was it durability: It was the convenience of being able to hear a specific track instantaneously, and then being able to move to another track as soon as the previous one got boring (usually, about two minutes and thirty seconds into a tune). Record reviewers spend way too much time analyzing albums in their entirety; this is because most rock writers have a problem—they like music way too much, often to the point of idiocy. It's very common to see an album panned because "there's not much beyond the single." I don't think that kind of logic matters. For example, *Tubthumping* by Chumbawamba has proven to be a more important album than Bob Dylan's Grammy Award–winning *Time Out of Mind*, simply because Chumbawamba's disc offered one great song that defined the moment of its popularity. I don't think there's any question about which of those two LPs will be more fun to find in a jukebox twenty years from now.

OKAY . . . so we've established that all popular music is basically crap. If your opponent agrees with that assertion, I suppose it essentially makes the rest of the argument moot, but arguments never end this way. You will inevitably keep talking and arguing and loudly scoffing and telling the other person to shut the hell up, and (at some point) you will need to explain what was good about heavy metal in a musical sense. And this *can* be done (sort of). There are a handful of metal records that are simply good—and I challenge anyone who disagrees to fight me!

Still, I've always found it a bit silly whenever someone makes a list of "essential" albums. None of my albums are the least bit essential to *anybody,* myself included. I mean, food is barely essential—most people can go two days without eating before they start gnawing at the flesh of their own grubby paws. Air is essential; water is essential; I suppose defecation is essential, lest you die of your own toxins. However, the Velvet Underground are never "essential." People always ask me questions like, "If you were stranded on a desert island, what five CDs would you want to be trapped with?" My answer: Five of those twenty-six-dollar remastered Pink Floyd discs that are made out of twenty-four-karat gold. The content of the disc is irrelevant; I simply assume gold would be malleable enough to pound into an arrowhead so I could kill myself a wild boar. Gold is also nice and shiny, which is ideal for bartering with the natives (maybe they could trade me a kayak or something). Things that are *essential* are things that keep you alive.

Of course, once we get beyond semantics, I would have to begrudgingly admit that I love my CDs. They give me a lot of pleasure, and they remind me of better days. And that's the criteria for the following list of "Nonessential Hair Metal Records I Really, Really Like."

It's always difficult to set up parameters for this kind of list. First of all, it's basically impossible to find an indisputable definition for what qualifies as "hair metal." I don't want to exclude any good bands simply because they didn't wear mascara, and I don't want to strictly limit this catalog to releases from 1980 to 1989. So instead of specifying what records I *will* consider, I've decided to simply outline the albums I *won't* consider.

Every rock record is eligible for this list, with the following exceptions:

1.) No **Led Zeppelin albums.** Just about every Zeppelin record is better than just about every record on the following buyer's guide, so I don't see any sense in mentioning the obvious. This is the material that created hair metal. There is no value in measuring teachers against pupils.

2.) No **Ozzy-era Black Sabbath albums.** Same justification as Rule No. 1.

3.) None of the **first four Van Halen albums** will be considered. Same justification as Rule No. 2.

4.) No **alternative bands that some people would call heavy metal just because they're loud** (Soundgarden, Alice in Chains, Primus, Nine Inch Nails, etc.). Even though they might display sonic similarities, it comes from an entirely different aesthetic sensibility.

5.) I will not include any **KISS albums from the era with makeup,** nor will I list any **Aerosmith albums from their 1970s drug phase.** Skip back to Rule No. 1 if you're still confused.

6.) No **multi-artist compilation albums** released by Rhino Records after 1995. No multi-artist compilation albums sold on TV, either.

7.) No **"seminal influences."** (For example, I'm not going to throw in the White Album just because "Helter Skelter" is on disc two and it would make me seem like a better student of pop history.)

8.) I will include no **albums that are only noteworthy for having a cool title.** In other words, I am resisting the urge to include *Bangkok Shocks, Saigon Shakes, Hanoi Rocks,* even though it's unspeakably fun to type.

9.) No Alice Cooper concept records, and no **Alice Cooper records that** *seem* **like concept records** (which—as far as I can tell—is the **entire Alice Cooper catalog before he started to suck**).

10.) Finally—and here's a big one—no albums from **groups who have no logical reason to be listed here.** If no reasonably informed person would classify a given artist as a "metal act," I'm not going to put them on this list, even if I could make a semi-entertaining argument as to why they warrant inclusion. For example, the guys in Oasis may have been groupie-shagging coke addicts who could out-rock Trixter eight days a week—but "Acquiesce" ain't metal, and both of us know it.

I'm not listing these records in any real order, except that—at the conclusion of every review—I print the amount of cash someone would have to pay me never to listen to that record again. I call this the "Jack Factor." Personally, I have little love for money (especially after reading *Tuesdays with Morrie*), but bones are the only means our society has to measure stuff. As part of that society, I must do the same. To me, that's always the best way to measure how "essential" something *really* is—if you can't buy it off me, it must be pretty important. You might want to look at it as rock criticism via Ayn Rand.

Now, when I say that I would "never listen to something again" for X amount of dollars, realize that I'm not insane. For example, I'm not going to jump out of a moving car if "Sweet Child O' Mine" comes on the radio. I'm not going to walk out of my sister's wedding reception if the DJ spins *Out of the Cellar.* What it means is that I would remove the CD from my collection, never buy it again, and never actively put myself in a situation where the primary goal would be hearing the music. It may be worth noting that I currently earn an annual salary of $54,400 and my rent is $605 a month. My car is not paid off, and I will be repaying my student loans until 2004.

So, keeping this in mind . . . let's rock shit up, bitch!

*   *   *

Van Halen, *1984* (1984, Warner Bros.): More obligatory than nec-essary, the videos off this album were much better than the songs. It's certainly the least groundbreaking VH record from the David Lee Roth years (in fact, I sometimes think the middle section of *5150* actually has way better songs). However, it's probably the best effort from producer Ted Templeman (the drum sounds on *1984* are particularly stunning). It also provides multiple exam-ples of Van Halen's longtime secret weapon: the backing vocals of bassist Michael Anthony. The all-time single-best illustration of Anthony's wonderful harmonizing is on the "Ooh, baby baby" part from "Dance the Night Away" on *Van Halen II*, but *1984* has a larger bank vault of Anthony larynx-oriented gems.

I've never been informed as to why "House of Pain" was finally included on this LP, since that's one of the oldest songs in the Van Halen catalog (you can hear versions of it on bootlegs from 1976). It's probably just supposed to be a treat for the type of metal trivia fanatics who win bar bets by knowing that Edward Van Halen soaks his guitar strings in honey. **(Jack Factor: $66)**

L.A. Guns, *Cocked and Loaded* (1989, Polydor): In the same way that Mudhoney has become famous for being the guys from Green River who didn't join Pearl Jam, L.A. Guns will always be remembered as the guys who hung out with Axl but didn't become Guns N' Roses. Since they kind of jumped into the fray late (their debut LP was in 1988), they never really had an oppor-tunity to be superstars (in fact, I think a lot of people assumed they called themselves "L.A. Guns" to gravy train off GNR). Nonethe-less, they quickly developed a small-yet-loyal fan base. At the time, there was a minirivalry between Guns N' Roses and Mötley Crüe, and a lot of the Crüe supporters saw L.A. Guns as an espoused rival to Axl's group, prompting them to buy *Cocked and Loaded* as a show of solidarity for Vince Neil.

On the whole, this is a better LP than most people would like to remember. Tracii Guns was a workmanlike virtuoso, and he produced several shards of semi-wicked metal ("Rip and Tear" being the best of the bunch). Of all their efforts, *Cocked and Loaded* has the least amount of throwaways (which is a nice way of saying *Cocked and Loaded* still has a little too much shit on side two, but that's no sin). If you remember this album at all, it's probably for "The Ballad of Jayne." As soon as they got the taste of success, L.A. Guns took the Aerosmith route and pushed a prom song, which will always be a pretty fast way to get famous. **(Jack Factor: $80)**

Scorpions, *World Wide Live* (1985, Mercury): As a general rule, I hate all non-KISS, non-Cheap Trick live albums, but this one demands inclusion (if for no other reason than it seemed to remind all their peers that metal bands were socially obligated to make at least one shitty live record). Considering how much the people of Canada love Rush, one has to assume that Germans literally worship the Scorpions. I mean, what else is there? Kraftwerk? Warlock? I've always wondered if the Scorps somehow represented the German culture (kind of in the same way the Cardigans and Whale seem to reflect Scandinavia). If they do, I will never go there, regardless of how fast I get to drive.

The big-ticket item on *WW Live* is "Rock You Like a Hurricane," the breakthrough hit about rocking like a hurricane. I tend to prefer the studio version off *Love At First Sting*, but maybe that proves I only rock as hard as a tropical storm. I wish they would have included "Love Drive," the best tune this band ever made, but it's not here. In fact, the smart Scorps shopper might be better served by buying the 1989 compilation *Best of Rockers n' Ballads*, which (at least according to the title) should cover both poles of the Scorpions' guitar-charged ineptitude. **(Jack Factor: $92)**

AC/DC, *Back in Black* (1980, Atlantic): Just about everyone in the free world perceives *Back in Black* as AC/DC's ultimate contribution to society, and I suppose I agree, which generally makes me wonder how this band got so popular. But they obviously knew what the fuck they were doing: This record sold 14 million copies, and I suspect it will be recertified platinum every three years until the apocalypse.

Prior to Bon Scott's vomit-gorged death, AC/DC was a legitimately intriguing group, particularly when they were saying "Oi!," whacking girls in the head with billiard cues, and/or inspiring Richard Ramirez to kill people. What's unfortunate (or perhaps admirable) is that this album made all of Scott's catalog obsolete: Unless you're a serial killer, AC/DC will forever be remembered as a buzzsaw guitar band, and that's mostly because Angus Young was so stunningly effective on *Back in Black.* On the strength of two particularly captivating tunes—"You Shook Me All Night Long" and the bone-crushing "Shoot to Thrill"—Young cemented a certain kind of guitar tone that would influence every '80s metal band that wasn't interested in being cute (and eventually Veruca Salt, who actually were). **(Jack Factor: $98)**

Ratt, *Out of the Cellar* (1984, Atlantic): Until *Appetite for Destruction* exploded in '88, this was probably the single-biggest record to rise from the L.A. glam scene. Even though Ratt never seemed as popular as Mötley Crüe, they initially sold better; "Round and Round" was able to score more consistent radio play than "Smokin' In the Boys Room" and "Looks That Kill" combined.

The best songs on *Out of the Cellar* tend to be the "hits," which equate to "Round and Round," "Back for More" and "Wanted Man." To be honest, the rest of the record hasn't aged that well. Ratt struggled with the fact that they had a rote delivery; they seemed a little too musically serious and never had the luxurious sleaze factor of the grittier Sunset Strip groups. They were able to slide by on the strength of an unappetizing band name and smart marketing (the *Out of the Cellar* cover shot was a postapocalyptic image of Tawny Kitaen that made them seem auspicious), but all they really had were a few good songs and Stephen Pearcy's bangs. In 1985, they made a second album (*Invasion of Your Privacy*) that sounded exactly like this one, and it did the same sort of business. I guess I'm still a little bit confused as to why we all loved this band, but I know we did, because I still remember playing every one of these songs over and over and over again. We simply could not resist the awe-inspiring power of Ratt 'n' Roll. (**Jack Factor: $110**)

KISS, *Lick It Up* (1983, PolyGram): This was the first KISS record to feature the band unmasked (which somehow didn't happen on *Unmasked*), and it's the only one where psychopathic axe genius Vinnie Vincent was on board for all the playing and composition. Vincent clearly dominated the songwriting sessions (he gets credit on eight of the ten tracks), and *Lick It Up* sounds vastly unlike all previous KISS records. The other guys in KISS swear he's a jackass, but Vinnie's artistic template ultimately set the direction for the band's next four or five efforts.

When left to his own devices, Vincent plays incredibly fast. Gene Simmons and Paul Stanley forced him to slow down and play behind the beat, which was an attempt to mimic Ace Frehley's style (Simmons refers to this as the "monster plod"). The only song where Vinnie is able to shred maniacally is "Fits Like a Glove," which is (ironically) one of the only two songs he didn't help write.

By and large, *Lick It Up* is a pretty good hard rock record and the catalyst for KISS' recovery as a platinum-selling artist. It's got quite a bit of filler (which was an all-too-common problem on every KISS record from the '80s), but the better stuff —"Fits Like a Glove," "All Hell's Breaking Loose," and the title cut—proved that Paul and Gene could make competitive, contemporary metal music for a second (third?) generation of KISS fans. If *Lick It Up* had tanked, one might speculate that KISS would have folded— or maybe they just would have reunited with Ace and Peter ten years earlier. (**Jack Factor: $125**)

W.A.S.P., *Live . . . in the Raw* (1987, Capitol): After three studio albums, W.A.S.P. had quickly established themselves as the most sexually depraved rock band in America. As far as Tipper Gore and the Parent's Music Resource Center were concerned,

W.A.S.P. was Public Enemy No. 1, mostly because they liked to pretend they were butchering women onstage. Tipper Gore was actually the best thing that ever happened to W.A.S.P.; thanks to the PMRC, the band got famous for a song virtually no one in America had ever heard—"Animal (Fuck Like a Beast)," a track that Capitol refused to release (and was subsequently distributed as an "underground single" on the Music for Nations label).

That song isn't on this record, but most of W.A.S.P.'s better material is. None of their studio albums were spectacular; the best was probably 1985's *The Last Command*, which was recently re-released with a bonus cover of Mountain's "Mississippi Queen." (For reasons that shall forever remain unknown, the entire W.A.S.P. catalog was re-released by Snapper Music in 1998, as if these works were somehow lost musical treasures that demanded further examination.)

W.A.S.P. frontman Blackie Lawless was briefly the tour drummer with the New York Dolls, which basically meant he understood showmanship (if not necessarily musicianship). Almost all of these songs improve when played live, particularly "9.5 Nasty" and "Harder Faster." There's also a nice segue between Humble Pie's "I Don't Need No Doctor" and "L.O.V.E. Machine," two songs about needing medical attention but having sex instead. Lawless described himself as a "Manimal" who slept in a fire and had to ride an intoxicated horse from Long Beach to Los Angeles, much of which I suspect is untrue. Though I can no longer understand what seemed so appealing about buckets of blood and raw meat, these guys definitely had their gooey paws on the metal community's pulse in 1987. If only they had been willing to perform oral sex on each other, I'm sure they could have been Marilyn Manson. (**Jack Factor: $129.99**)

Judas Priest, *British Steel* (1980, CBS Records): I'm a bit disappointed this album didn't make me want to kill myself, but I still enjoy it immensely. It has a sense of credibility that most metal albums lack, although you'd never guess that if your only exposure was the ultra-stupid track "Metal Gods."

Yet for all practical purposes, *British Steel* defines all the stereotypes of the metal genre: screaming, soaring vocals; screaming, soaring guitars; booming bass; machine gun drums. It's impossible to deconstruct a song like "Breaking the Law," nor can you deny the tight, clean perfection of "Living After Midnight." By all accounts, *British Steel* is a cornerstone of late-twentieth-century hard rock, even if a few of the songs manage to be really heavy and really lame at the same time. And I'm still waiting for "United" to become a gay anthem. (**Jack Factor: $160**)

Junkyard, *Junkyard* (1989, Geffen): This L.A.-based band got an incredible amount of mileage from the fact that Axl Rose wore a Junkyard T-shirt to a GNR photo shoot and was subsequently shown promoting the band in about two dozen different photographs in five different metal magazines. Rose might have done that because he liked Junkyard, or he might have done that because Junkyard was on Geffen and somebody in a blue suit told him it would be a fine idea to pretend he was a fan. Either way, it worked—it seemed like everybody had heard of this group before they ever released any records.

My gut tells me Axl probably *did* like Junkyard, mostly because they had the same sort of trashy, hooker-hungry, just-an-urchin-livin'-under-the-street appeal. Vocalist David Roach sounded a lot like Vince Neil (in fact, when I heard "Hollywood" I thought it was Mötley Crüe), and he was especially Axl-esque at combining depression with semidangerous anger. "Hands Off" is maybe the best metal song ever written about having a woman break your heart; when Roach says "God *da-amn*," he may as well be Hank Williams. (**Jack Factor: $172**)

Heavy Metal, Music from the Motion Picture (1981, Elektra): This movie is pretty lousy if you're sober and/or an adult, and the soundtrack should be either glammier or skankier, or maybe both. But it does have the best Sammy Hagar ever recorded ("Heavy Metal"), the only decent post-Oz Sabbath tune ("The Mob Rules"), some foxy witch rock (Stevie Nicks's "Blue

Lamp"), and some nifty math rock (Devo's "Working in a Coal Mine"). Nine of the sixteen tracks have magnificent intros, so the album makes for wonderful car music in the summer. It's also fun to get drunk and cry during "Open Arms," and maybe even call your ex-girlfriend and apologize for things that actually happened in an altogether different relationship with an altogether different person. Just trust me on this one. Steve Perry is a fucking genius. (**Jack Factor: $180**)

Ace Frehley, *Frehley's Comet* (1987, Megaforce): I'm not exactly sure what Ace Frehley did between his 1982 departure from KISS and this '87 debut. I do know he smashed a Porsche in Connecticut and was arrested for driving 110 m.p.h. in a DeLorean on the Bronx River Parkway, and I have to believe he was pretty wasted during both of those incidents because he always seems to combine both events into one singular story. That patchwork narrative became the premise for the song "Rock Soldiers," the first cut on *Frehley's Comet*.

Ace's problem as a frontman was always abundantly obvious: His voice is terrible. But that's also his strength; like Jimi Hendrix and Courtney Love, his stunning inability to sing on key makes his music charming. KISS fans adored his contributions to *Love Gun* and *Dynasty*, as well as his exceptional 1978 effort, easily the best of the ill-fated KISS solo albums. And through most of the 1980s, *Frehley's Comet* sounded more like KISS than KISS did.

The value of *Frehley's Comet* is its quirkiness. I think it's cool that Anton Fig is the drummer. I like the tune that sounds like Journey ("Calling to You") and I love the song that sounds like a combination of Ted Nugent and the Jeff Twilley Band ("Love Me Right"). I find it intriguing that a male rock star would write a song that pays tribute to his doll collection ("Dolls"). And I am forever amused by Frehley's obsession with making sure all of his lyrics rhyme *exactly*. Dave Barry once pointed out that Steve Miller found a way to rhyme the word "Texas" with the phrase "What the facts is" (in that same song, Miller also managed to pair the word "justice" with the phrase "other people's taxes").

Poets refer to this literary device as "slant rhyme." Ace would never be so bold. His lines are always stiff, parallel rhymes—except for one awkward attempt to pair his own surname with the line "Don't be silly." Oh well. (**Jack Factor: $199**)

KISS, *Animalize* (1984, PolyGram): This was the best KISS effort from the sans makeup years, and it was pretty much Paul Stanley's baby (by this point, Gene Simmons was becoming infatuated with his film career and putting no effort whatsoever into songwriting). In fact, if you listed the twenty best KISS songs of all time, *Animalize* is the only post-Kabuki album that would have a tune to offer, the yowl-driven single "Heaven's On Fire." This was an extremely popular song in my junior high, and it prompted my neighbor to create a naughty little parody of the chorus: "Feel my meat / Watch my cock rise / Burn with me / My ass is on fire." Granted, this was only slightly more polished than "Weird" Al Yankovic, but I still think it was pretty clever for a sixth-grader who was burdened with the nickname "Ippy."

Animalize is the only KISS record that features Mark St. John on guitar; soon after making the record, he contracted an incredibly rare arthritic disorder that caused his left hand to swell to the side of a midsize rhinoceros. St. John would eventually recover and form White Tiger, a band most people mistakenly called "White Lion" or "Glass Tiger," which wouldn't have been a big deal if those hadn't been the names of other bands who were already more popular. But to be fair, St. John actually does a damn nice job on this LP, especially when you consider he was fundamentally a studio hack and was clearly instructed to play like one.

Beyond "Heaven's On Fire," the tune everyone seems to remember off *Animalize* is "Burn Bitch Burn," the closest Simmons ever came to writing a straightforward joke song (except of course for "Domino," which hopefully *is* a joke). The most memorable lyric was "When love rears its head, I want to get on your case / Ooh baby, I wanna put my log in your fireplace." We all thought this was hilarious . . . except for Ippy, who probably considered it to be a little lowbrow. (**Jack Factor: $200**)

*   *   *

Tesla, *The Great Radio Controversy* (1989, Geffen): This was glam metal to play inside the cab of a tractor—bluesy, denim, and downright *wholesome*: On "Be a Man," former cement truck driver Jeff Keith tells us to "do right by the ones you love, and always lend a helping hand." According to Tesla, this is what it takes to be a man. I guess nobody informed them that life ain't nothin' but bitches and money, and that's beautiful.

Traditionalists usually prefer their harder-rocking debut (1986's *Mechanical Resonance*) and kids who played hackey sack enjoyed 1990's deadheaded *Five Man Acoustical Jam*, but *The Great Radio Controversy* is still the best record Tesla ever made. It melds nonelectric instruments with unglossy riffing, and even a little Neil Young-ish pregrunge on "Heaven's Trail (No Way Out)." Unlike their peers, Tesla ignored the temptation to make formulaic power ballads and wrote normal AM radio relationship tunes, the best example being the bittersweet "Love Song." Of course, I still can't understand why the fuck this band cared who "really" invented the radio, and I still occasionally catch myself mispronouncing their name "Telsa," just like every other kid at my school. Come to think of it, we always seemed to erroneously call their first album *Mechanical Renaissance* too. Maybe Tesla turns kids into mindless deadheads (which I suppose is a pretty blatant oxymoron). **(Jack Factor: $217)**

Mötley Crüe, *Girls Girls Girls* (1987, Elektra): This is the Crüe's "dark" album, mostly because it's about drugs instead of the devil. Written by Nikki Sixx during the depths of his smack addiction, it's supposed to be about fucking strippers, but it's really about being fucked in the head. On "Wild Side," Vince Neil tells us that "A baby cries / A cop dies / A day's pay on the wild side." It seems that Sixx forgot to mention if this is supposed to be good or bad; judging from the context, he could really go either way. *Girls Girls Girls* ends up being a very nihilistic project, probably by accident; when Nikki tried to write a nihilistic album *on purpose* in 1994, it was slightly less successful than the introduction of New Coke.

The music on *Girls* . . . is more consciously bluesy than the other Crüe albums, hence the horrific live cover of "Jailhouse Rock." I tend to like the first three songs on side two (especially "Five Years Dead," mostly because it sounds like they're saying "*Bach* is dead," which actually makes more sense), and I've always enjoyed the sentimental throwaway "Nona," a tribute to Sixx's dead grandma (which is especially touching when followed by "Sumthin' for Nuthin'," a song about having sex with grandmas who are still alive). Of course, I'm not exactly sure how any of this was supposed to fit the image they were fostering at the time: Mötley had evolved from '81's "glam metal" to '83's "shock rock" to '85's "glitter pop," finally settling on this incarnation—some kind of leather-clad biker persona that mostly seemed like an homage to Al Pacino's *Cruisin'*. But you know, whatever. **(Jack Factor: $229)**

Warrant, *Dirty Rotten Filthy Stinking Rich* (1989, Columbia): The first release by the very first band I ever saw play live (May '89, West Fargo Fairgrounds, opening for Great White and Ratt), this magnum opus was dedicated to a girl who "lost her cherry but that's no sin / she's still got the box the cherry came in." That's pretty vapid and so are most of these lyrics, but it's the yummy kind of vapid. The album opens with a song about living on thirty-two pennies in a Ragú jar, but by the start of side two they want to light cigarettes with hundred-dollar bills and wear ocelot pelts to the farmer's market in rural Ohio, which is evidently what you do when you're a Down Boy.

If you experienced your first episode of finger-banging between August of 1989 and March of 1990, it probably happened while you were listening to "Heaven." However, the true value of this record is the Poison-esque rockers like "Big Talk" and "Ridin' High." You did not bang your head to Warrant; this was actually music you *danced* to (or at least shimmied). The bass sludge is almost non-existent, and the words are delivered with a pop earnesty typically reserved for people like Todd Rundgren. *Dirty Rotten* . . . was followed by the even more successful

Cherry Pie, but this remains a better project overall, mostly because it's smarter (in that vapid, yummy kind of way). It also has one of the greatest liner notes of all time: "All concepts by WARRANT." That's right—all *concepts* (by WARRANT). Hmm. Maybe this was actually supposed to sound like *Aqualung*. **(Jack Factor: $258)**

David Lee Roth, *Eat 'Em and Smile* (1986, Warner Bros.): Opening with Mr. Roth lying in a gutter and talking to a guitar about his "Yankee Rose," *Eat 'Em and Smile* bumps and grinds like the whore Dave is, all the way down to a closing stab at being glam metal's Frank Sinatra. The lineup is pretty solid (Stevie Vai on the six-string, Billy Sheehan on the four), and it absolutely blows the doors off Van Hagar's *5150*. Though Dave never made a decent record after this one, he gets major props for expertly building a record around a specific personality type: the horny white gigolo who's easy and crazy and wants to shoot you with his elephant gun. No artist has ever *needed* to make a solo album more than Diamond Dave.

At every wedding dance, there is always one uncle who drinks too much, dances too much, and tells the most ridiculous stories over and over and over again. He's the hero or the goat of every story he tells, and you can never quite tell if he's the most boorish jackass in your family or the most charming fellow you've ever met. David Lee Roth is that uncle, and *Eat 'Em and Smile* is his master work. **(Jack Factor: $275)**

Bon Jovi, *Cross Roads* (1994, Mercury): Purists always deride greatest hits records, usually claiming that the songs "lose something" when the order is changed. That's stupid, especially since nobody ever listens to a compact disc in its proper sequence anyway. I'll take the *Best of Blondie* over *Parallel Lines* eight days a week, and it certainly seems like everyone at the party has more drinks whenever we play *The Best of Van Morrison* instead of *Astral Weeks*. The same goes for this collection of Jonny B. Jovi's best stuff, and maybe even more so: It seems like the only good

Bon Jovi songs were the popular ones. This band has no forgotten gems whatsoever (except maybe "Love Is a Social Disease," but even that's a major stretch).

What they do offer is happy, sunshine metal that made all the girls shriek and all the guys wear styling gel. I doubt if Jon ever figured out what day it was from what he was drinking (or if he ever even got drunk), but "Wanted Dead or Alive" is a classic road song, copied poorly by about four hundred other bands. "Lay Your Hands on Me" and "Bad Medicine," the melodramatic opening tracks off *New Jersey*, still sound captivating. And in retrospect, "You Give Love a Bad Name" really isn't as horrible as I'd like to remember (if nothing else, it undoubtedly inspired Firehouse's "Don't Treat Me Bad," which I sometimes think might be among the forty finest songs ever released in the U.S.).

Jon Bon Jovi is kind of the Robert Frost of heavy metal. The great thing about Frost was that his poems weren't always about metaphorical bullshit; sometimes a poem about chopping wood was actually about *chopping wood*. Bon Jovi was the same way; he wrote literal lyrics and dulcet melodies, and they didn't worry about credibility or attitude or the legacy of Tony Iommi. We may remember Bon Jovi as the safest of all these metal bands and certainly the most stereotypically commercial, but they were real songwriters who simply tugged at heartstrings instead of brainstrings. That fluffy aesthetic is all over the cowboy-saturated *Cross Roads*. In fact, I even like the inclusion of "Someday I'll Be Saturday Night," despite the fact that Jon sounds a little like a bad Bruce Springsteen or a good Bryan Adams. (**Jack Factor: $288**)

Metallica, . . . *And Justice for All* (1988, Elektra): This inclusion is something of a contradiction, because every Metallica record prior to this one contains better songs. But . . . *And Justice for All* is far and away the most interesting work the group ever produced; never before had speed metal been so freaky. Seven of the nine tracks are longer than six minutes (two are longer than nine), and Kirk Hammett often seemed to be playing riffs backward (and sometimes sideways), but it never seems flashy or forced. Sometimes I think Hammett is the most underrated guitarist of his generation, even though he bores the piss out of me 80 percent of the time.

As is always the case with Metallica, the majority of the lyrics are apocalyptic hogwash, but this is still an incredibly smart LP that's legitimately experimental. Part of the sonic weirdness comes from a bizarre production decision: You can't hear Jason Newsted's bass lines at all on . . . *And Justice for All*, and that's intentional. Apparently, his musical exclusion was part of Newsted's "hazing" for having the gall to replace Cliff Burton, the original Metallica bassist who died when a bus fell on him in Europe.

To be honest, it's too bad that bass moratorium was eventually lifted. Ever since this LP came out in '88, Metallica has evolved into a remarkably average band who just happen to play really loud. Everything they've released in the past decade has been boring and weak, with the exception of one cool song about werewolves and a nice cover of Thin Lizzy's "Whiskey in the Jar." But maybe that's what people like me said about Zeppelin in '78. **(Jack Factor: $294)**

Van Halen, *Diver Down* (1982, Warner Bros.): Generally poohpoohed by most devout Halenheads, I find this their most endearing effort. Though it doesn't have a singular killer tune (like, say, "Unchained" off *Fair Warning*) and even though it's not frenetic or bottomless (like *Women and Children First*), it's the only VH album that never gets boring, even when it tries to be (i.e., the six minutes and twenty-four seconds of "Cathedral," "Secrets," and "Intruder"). The Marvin Gaye–penned "Dancing in the Street" has been covered by about two hundred artists, but Roth's is the best; I also prefer Dave's take on Roy Orbison's "(Oh) Pretty Woman" and the Kinks' "Where Have All the Good Times Gone!" (though I've never understood why the title of that particular tune is punctuated with an explanation point instead of a question mark; is this not a question, or is it just an enthusiastic cliché?).

Though I can understand why some fans take umbrage with the amount of unoriginal material on this project, I think that's an asinine complaint. Van Halen used to be the greatest cover band in the world, and that means a lot. At its core, the beauty of Van Halen is not Eddie's virtuosity or the strength of its incredible rhythm section; the beauty of Van Halen is that they were *fun*. Along with side two of *Van Halen II*, this was as fun as it ever got. **(Jack Factor: $333)**

Living Colour, *Vivid* (1988, CBS): Mick Jagger produced these rasta rockers, and he even loaned his bulbous lips to the backing vocals on "Glamour Boys," still one of the funniest songs I've ever heard, especially when one tries to imagine little nancy boy Mick claiming he's fierce. But Jagger's influence doesn't go much beyond that chorus (although he did score them the opening slot on the '89 Stones tour).

Vivid is not swaggering, jukebox metal; it's a well-lubricated record with lots of sheen and purpose. "Cult of Personality" is pretty much a thrash-o-rama that was whittled into a radio tune, but it always hits like a tsunami (I've actually seen it start mosh pits at wedding dances). I think Corey Glover's comparison of Gandhi with Stalin is supposed to make us think about the media (or something), but it really just reminds us that the guys in Living Colour aren't a bunch of morons, which should have been the least of their worries. The simple fact is that *Vivid* is fabulous when it rocks out, but it's pretty goddamn janky when it tries anything else. It's the same story with 1993's anachronistic *Stain*, a good album that always seems ashamed of itself. Living Colour is one of those hard rock groups who suffer from self-loathing; since all the members seem to think metal bands are stupid, they will ignore what they do best in order to be classified in a different category, even if that means singing a song titled "Open Letter (to a landlord)." When you consider how unintentionally rockin' *Vivid* turned out to be, it's frightening to think how awesome this band could have been had they actually tried. **(Jack Factor: $379)**

Skid Row, *Skid Row* (1989, Atlantic): Like a grizzly that stumbled across a bunch of honey-covered hippies, this is straight-forward carnage: hair-wagging, Bud-guzzling, boot-kicking, no bullshit rock 'n' roll (or *all* bullshit rock 'n' roll, if you follow my meaning). When I went back and found this cassette in my closet, I was surprised to discover this album came out as late as it did; I tend to remember the Skids being a bigger part of the '80s than they actually were.

If nothing else, Skid Row deserves credit for being honest; lots of bands claimed their next album was going to be "a lot heavier," and Skid Row is the only band who wasn't lying (1991's *Slave to the Grind* could swing with Megadeth). Still, this debut is the one that matters. The first four songs never relax; Sebastian Bach screams about mammary glands, somebody's sweet little sister (I'm guessing not his), and girls who smoke cigarettes when they cry. "18 and Life" was the pulp that made them famous, and it's one of the rare metal tunes that told a story (Rupert Holmes could probably cover it). "Youth Gone Wild" was their war anthem; it was actually the title of my high school yearbook when I was a senior (and I wasn't even on yearbook staff!). "I Remember You" might have been a bit too stereotypical as the obligatory power ballad, but Baz's range was better than most, and he was too damn anorexic (and too pretty) to ignore. To paraphrase the coolest fifth-grader I never interviewed, Skid Row rules ass. **(Jack Factor: $400)**

Cinderella, *Long Cold Winter* (1988, PolyGram): Nobody in the world sounds like Cinderella vocalist Tom Keifer. In the eyes of many, that's probably good. But in the realm of glam, Keifer might have been the most compelling throat around. If there was ever a dude who really *did* sound like the proverbial "cat caught in the gears of a combine," it was Tommy—and that's a compliment (at least when applied to *Long Cold Winter*).

Keifer actually had two voices: a baritone drawl (which he used in the introductions of ballads), and a maddening, nasal-injected screech (which he used for everything else). I realize I'm probably making this music sound horrific, and part of me suspects it probably was, but MAN, was that screech perfect for the first three tracks on this icy rock opera. "Bad Seamstress Blues" is legitimately clever, "Fallin' Apart at the Seams" is simultaneously poofy and menacing, and "Gypsy Road" is just a good, good, good, good, good song.

The hidden gems on *Winter* are on the flip side, namely "Take Me Back," which is a lot like the KISS hidden gem "Comin' Home" off *Hotter Than Hell*. What's weird is that Cinderella *also* has a song titled "Coming Home" (note the addition of the *g*), but it's a different vibe altogether. On "Coming Home," Keifer asks his prospective princess if she's "tough enough" for his love, which is probably a legitimate question: It would be tough to love any guy who was born with Tom's voice. But like I said, it was killer for bluesy poodle rock.

1988 was Cindy's peak; this record went triple platinum, just like their debut (*Night Songs*). I honestly believe Cinderella was one of the bands who were underrated by almost everyone, except possibly fourteen-year-old girls. Maybe I don't give mall chicks enough credit; maybe it's time to admit that fourteen-year-old girls are the only people in America who truly understand what coolness is supposed to look like. **(Jack Factor: $455)**

The Cult, *Electric* (1987, Sire): Ian Astbury and Billy Duffy have made a lot of records in their career (too many, frankly), but this was their best effort and certainly their most metal. The weird thing about the Cult is that they were a hard rock band that people who hated metal always seemed to dig; I'm constantly running into alt rockers who claim their favorite bands in high school were New Order, Erasure, and the Cult. Generally, these types sing the praises of 1985's *Love* (and for some reason, most old-school metal kids tend to align themselves with 1989's *Sonic Temple*), but *Electric* is the band's tastiest cream.

There is a surprisingly pleasant sameness to all eleven of these tunes, which spikes during "Lil' Devil" and "King Contrary Man" and dips into painful valleys during the hippy-dippy "Peace

Dog" and a godawful cover of "Born to Be Wild." The most memorable track is "Love Removal Machine," which is legitimately surreal; I've always wondered what a love removal machine would look like—probably something like an electric chair attached to a bottle of bourbon. Either way, Duffy's guitar licks sound more like Jimmy Page than Page's himself sounded on *Outrider*, and Astbury's coonskin cap is exactly like the one I wore for Halloween in 1979 and 1980, except I was probably a little cooler (but since I didn't know any fourteen-year-old girls at the time, I guess we'll never know). **(Jack Factor: $512)**

Poison, *Open Up and Say . . . Ahh!* (1988, Capitol): Ten seconds into this album, some girl is giving head to Bret Michaels, and "she goes down smooth, like a shot of gin." How smooth is that? Well, to be honest, not very. But that's what was great about Poison: Things like the relative smoothness of gin paled in comparison to the "greater concept," which didn't make any sense but always resulted in driving and looking for girls who were already drunk.✹

When *Open Up . . .* was released, I remember reading a bunch of reviews where writers claimed it lacked the "rollicking fun" of Poison's first album, *Look What the Cat Dragged In*. This con-

---

✹Driving around aimlessly and going nowhere is an aspect of small-town culture few people from urban communities truly understand, but it's pretty much the backbone of teen life in places like Wyndmere. We drove our parents' cars around the same path endlessly for several hours every weekend evening: The route ran from the Cenex station, north to Main Street (where you made a U-turn in front of the bankrupt lumberyard), down the residential stretch of Highway 18 for about a mile, east past the Tastee Freez (and through the town's only stop light), and then back to Cenex. The total distance of one rotation is 2.8 miles. Whenever you wanted to talk to someone in another car, you hit your brake lights twice when they passed you, which indicated that they were supposed to meet you in the parking lot of the high school bus barn. The fundamental goal was to make the local police officer follow your particular vehicle, which is why I'll always begrudgingly adore that Gin Blossoms song where the dude sings, "We can drive around this town / And let the cops chase us around."

fused me, because those same writers had all hated that first record, too. Bret and C. C. didn't get breaks from anyone; I remember hearing *fourth-graders* bitch about them. And that's probably why this album still seems so refreshing. If Poison cared what people thought of them, they certainly didn't act like it. They had debuted with an album that made kids want to steal Citron from their parents and cum in their jeans—*and then they made another!* C. C. DeVille played lead riffs that even I could figure out (and I can't play guitar), but he was better at sucking than almost everyone else in the world.

When the guys in Black Sabbath were growing up in Birmingham, they were all poor kids from an industrial neighborhood. When they got famous in the '70s, that social despair poured through their black-hearted music. The guys in Poison grew up in industrial Pennsylvania, and their youth was similarly grim. However, Poison got famous during the 1980s, and they fucking loved it. *Open Up and Say . . . Ahh!* is an Epicurean affirmation of all that is great about cheesy, plastic rock 'n' roll. It wasn't merely that Poison wanted nothing but a good time—they asked the world why they were supposed to want anything else. And in 1988, that was a good question. (**Jack Factor: $555**)

Faster Pussycat, *Faster Pussycat* (1987, Elektra): As a sophomore in high school, I didn't know who the fuck Russ Meyer was, so I thought this was a really wussie name for a rock group. Truth is, they *were* pretty much wussies, but they were some of the most streetwise wussies in L.A. (and if you don't believe me, go rent *The Decline of Western Civilization, Part II*). Almost of all of this LP is terrific, particularly the black-and-bluesy sleaze on "Don't Change That Song" and "Cathouse." Most of the initial attention surrounding this album was granted to "Babylon," a rap song that seemed like an attempt to rip off Anthrax's attempt at ripping off *Licensed to Ill*, but it sure seemed funny at the time.

However, it was the second side of *Faster Pussycat* that paid the rent. "Smash Alley" examined the downside of high heels and switchblades and also reminded me that I should probably listen to my Smashed Gladys cassette more often. "Ship Rolls In" was pretty much an Aerosmith song, but it wonderfully captured the identity of glam metal in three lines from vocalist/fellatio advocate Taime Downe: "You gotta roll with the punches, spin like a top / I ain't got much, but I got a lot of PER-SO-NAL-I-TEEEE / And that's all that counts." Taime, you're pretty smart for a wussy. **(Jack Factor: $580)**

Vinnie Vincent, *Invasion* (1986, Chrysalis): Like a Tasmanian devil whirling toward vaginas and self-destruction, the guitar-mageddon unleashed by ex-KISS wackmobile Vincent on this solo debut is so schlockily stunning that I still have to play this album at least six times every year.

Never was metal as brilliantly self-indulgent as it was on *Invasion* (which would soon become part of the group's actual name, hence the better known moniker "Vinnie Vincent Invasion"). After this first record, the group hired Mark Slaughter's throat and Vinnie went to hell, both as a rocker and as a human being (for all I know, Vinnie now lives on the moon and wears his Egyptian ankh makeup whenever he surfs the Internet for *alt.talk.creaturesofthenight*). But for select moments on *Invasion*, V. V. is the fastest, craziest, and downright *best* six-string shredder to ever wear pinkish lavender in public.

Right from track number one, you know what you're getting: "Boys Are Gonna Rock" has *two and a half* guitar solos. Singer Robert Fleischman screams about sadomasochism and ejaculations, but—for all practical purposes—this may as well be an instrumental album. At the conclusion of "Animal," Vincent plays faster and harder and faster and harder and faster and stupider and he's going nowhere but he's getting there fast and now your neighbors are banging on the wall and your bookcase speakers are starting to melt and your beagle is in obvious pain and suddenly you suspect that everything in your house is going to IMPLODE. And then Vinnie collapses, and then you hear six seconds of reverb. And then the next song begins (with a guitar solo). It should be also noted that *Invasion* ultimately ends with 151 seconds of Vincent replicating a car alarm (or perhaps a grain elevator). This is rock 'n' roll. This is rock 'n' roll? This is rock 'n' roll! **(Jack Factor: $675)**

Def Leppard, *Pyromania* (1983, PolyGram): First of all, let me say—purely as a fan—I probably prefer Lep's 1981 release *High 'n' Dry*. The title track on that record smokes everything here, and "Let It Go" is dandy rock candy. But I also realize that *Pyromania* is the better record. For a bunch of twenty-one-year-old alcoholics in need of personalities, the level of musical sophistication on *Pyromania* is amazing. I suppose the majority of that credit should go to Robert "Mutt" Lange, who earned the right to sleep with Shania Twain for producing an album this immaculate.

The knock against Def Leppard has always been that they're "overproduced," which is precisely what artists want when they ask Lange to engineer their records. Most producers—like Bob Rock, for example—took metal bands and tried to capture the "liveness" of the sound (when Rock did Mötley Crüe's *Dr. Feelgood*, he played up the guitar tones and Tommy Lee's orangutan drumming). Lange does the opposite; he works more like a smart copyeditor. Everything is polished until it's ultraclean and hyperefficient, so you only notice the main riff and the soaring vocals (this was even more obvious when he produced *Back in Black*).

Granted, this kind of recording philosophy doesn't work with a lot of artists. But it's a perfect recipe for a legitimately talented metal outfit, and that's exactly what Def Leppard was. "Rock! Rock! (Till You Drop)" is the ideal opening, and "Photograph" is the best Journey song ever made. Pyromania is infected with a bunch of pre-irony studio gimmicks (like the intro to "Rock of Ages" and the supposedly "space age" crap after track ten), but it doesn't have any bad songs, either.

Critics of '80s hard rock sometimes point to *Pyromania* as an example of what was wrong with the whole industry: The stock argument is that this record is sanitized arena pop that doesn't deliver *anything* that could affect a listener—the lyrics are about nothing, the music is perfectly calculated, there's no emotional investment by the artist, and there's not even a *constructed* sense of humanity. However, the only person who would come up with that kind of analysis is somebody who simply hates heavy metal and wants to make up a bunch of reasons to explain why. Fifteen years later, I can experience the same concepts I heard in my bedroom when I first got *Pyromania* from the RCA Music Service: Controlled aggression that cloaked an Orwellian fear (witness "Stagefright," "Die Hard the Hunter," "Foolin'," and "Billy's Got a Gun"). It's stupid to blame Def Leppard for being flawless. *Pyromania* was metal's *Pretzel Logic*—a studio master-piece that validated the genre. **(Jack Factor: $877)**

Guns N' Roses, *GNR Lies* (1988, Geffen): When we first heard this eight-song EP, we all thought the live material on side one was tits and the acoustic stuff on side two was girlie crap. Over time, the conventional wisdom revolved into the opinion that the "R" side was brilliant and the "G" side wasn't worth listening to. Ten years later, I have rediscovered the value of the former without losing respect for the latter (or maybe it's the other way around).

Lies opens with "Reckless Life," an accelerated rocker that would seem to be the résumé for the whole GNR experiment. That blows into a cover of "Nice Boys," which works because Axl Rose really does seem like a *boy*. Of course, that makes every-thing a bit awkward on "Move to the City," because suddenly Axl becomes a girl who stole her daddy's credit card—but by the time they're halfway through a rote version of "Mama Kin," nobody cares anyway.

Logic would dictate that the lyrics on the flip side should seem less shocking as time passes, but I find them more spooky today than I did in high school. As I grow older, I'm still intrigued by what Axl was so angry about. His inability to repli-cate this kind of ferocious emotion on future releases makes me suspect it must have been genuine; if it had all just been a show, you'd think he could do it anytime he stepped into a studio.

There seems to be something obviously wrong with Axl Rose's brain, and it's the kind of three-act neurosis that ruins a man's life, makes a man famous, and then ruins his life again (and usually in that order). Side two of *GNR Lies* is the peak of Act II. (**Jack Factor: $920**)

Ozzy Osbourne, *Blizzard of Ozz/Diary of a Madman* (both 1981, Jet): Obviously, this is kind of cheating, because I'm counting two albums as one. But it's almost impossible to separate these first two releases from Osbourne's solo career. If there is truly such a thing as "companion albums," these two would be the defining example (um . . . okay—I mean if you *don't* count *Rubber Soul* and *Revolver*).

Blizzard and *Diary* are, of course, the only two albums Ozzy made with Randy Rhoads, and Oz has apparently never recovered; Ozzy insists the twenty-eight months he worked with Randy seem longer than the rest of his life combined. He talks about Rhoads the way most people would discuss a deceased wife (on the liner notes to 1987's *Tribute*, he says Rhoads was what he had "dreamed about" in a guitar player and credits him with ending his depression). Part of that loss might be purely practical: Rhoads's ability as a player is—at times—stunning. The conventional wisdom is that *Blizzard of Ozz* is a masterpiece and *Diary of a Madman* sounds rushed and uneven, but I think they're equally excellent. In fact, I probably prefer the sophomore release.

Blizzard of Ozz was the perfect vehicle for Osbourne's solo ascension, because it's basically Sabbath music played wicked fast. There was a vaguely classical quality to Tony Iommi's playing, and Rhoads took that one step further (and got there quicker). Over his thirty-year career, "Crazy Train" stands as the best song Ozzy ever yowled. In his book *Running with the Devil*, Robert Walser points out how the guitar riff on "Suicide Solution" jibes with the lyrics: a cycling, disturbing drone that virtually mirrors clinical depression. Top to bottom, this is simply a good record—it's remarkably well-conceived and wisely structured.

Those two statements probably can't be made about *Diary of a Madman*, but it doesn't matter, because Rhoads's effort is even better. I generally find guitar solos pretty boring (doesn't everybody?), but I can listen to these; "Over the Mountain" might be more clever than ingenious, but it always blows me away. "Flying High Again" is intended to be this album's "Crazy Train" (it's even in the same place—track two), and I think it sort of succeeds in that attempt (it's also the last song Ozzy made that was indisputably pro-drug). There are a couple of nice slower tracks on *Diary*—I especially like "Tonight," which could have been a huge single had it been released five years later—but the real kicker is the intro to the title track. For no particular reason, Rhoads plays twenty-five seconds of the Doors' "Spanish Caravan." It's not central to the album (or even to the song), but it's *neat*. It's the kind of decision that all the guitar hacks who followed him never seemed to make.

I realize that Rhoads tends to get lionized because he died, and it's very possible that these records seem so remarkable simply because we are left with nothing else (except for a few early Quiet Riot demos). But this is very good rock music, and that has nothing to do with any plane crashes. (**Jack Factor: $1,000**)

Mötley Crüe, *Too Fast for Love* (1982, Elektra): Perhaps you're wondering why I'm including this album instead of *Shout at the Devil*, the Crüe record I so aggressively pimped in the opening pages of this book. Well, two reasons: for one thing, I'm sick of talking about *Shout*, and—quite frankly—this is a better LP.

I've never been too crazy about the popular opener "Live Wire," a song Mötley still plays in every concert. However, I adore "Come On and Dance" (even though it's almost impossible to dance to) and "Public Enemy #1" (even though the lyrics never mention what atrocity our antagonist supposedly committed). *Too Fast for Love* was originally released by the band independently on Lethur Records (they tossed them into club audiences while Nikki Sixx's boots burned), and the Elektra re-release still seems a little cheap; Vince Neil's vocals sound shallow, and at least in this instance it's not his fault. The guitars all sound like they're made of tin, but that gives everything an aluminum sheen. Light metal (or metal lite), I suppose.

The strength of *Too Fast* is the stylized trashiness; it's the Crüe at their glammiest and (one hopes) most sincere. Still, the crafty marketing of Nikki Sixx is already obvious: The cover art is such a rote *Sticky Fingers* rip-off that it qualifies as an homage—but almost none of its intended audience had ever seen the original! As a selling tool, Vince Neil's crotch worked *exactly* the same way Warhol groupie Jed Johnson's did. Just like the music, it was old material that seemed completely fresh to thirteen-year-old kids with no sense of history (like me, for example).

The title cut is probably the album's best rocker, while the closing ballad "On with the Show" is the finest slow song the band would ever make (it's twice as gut-wrenching as "Home Sweet Home," which basically means it's half as gut-wrenching as Big Star's "Holocaust" and one-tenth as effective as *Snoopy, Come Home*). The only misstep was the baffling exclusion of "Toast of the Town," the very first single Mötley ever released (and in case you're curious, the B-side was "Stick to Your Guns"). Fortunately, that track was reincluded on the '99 re-release.

It will be interesting to see how Mötley Crüe is eventually categorized by rock historians; I sometimes wonder if they'll end up being the '80s version of Nazareth or Foghat. They honestly deserve better. When you place heavy metal in a cultural context, *Too Fast for Love* is the kind of album that kind-of-sort-of matters. Whenever you forget what made glam metal so ridiculously popular, listen to this record. This is what happened when four Hollywood hobos got it right. (**Jack Factor: $1,333**)

Guns N' Roses, *Appetite for Destruction* (1987, Geffen): Well, this is pretty much it.

Appetite for Destruction is the singular answer to the question, "Why did hair metal need to exist?" After all the coke and the car wrecks and the screaming and the creaming and the musical masturbation and the pentagrams and the dead hookers, this is what we are left with—the best record of the 1980s, regardless of genre. If asked to list the ten best rock albums of all time, this is the only pop metal release that might make the list; it's certainly the only Reagan-era material that can compete with the White Album and *Rumours* and *Electric Warrior*. *Appetite for Destruction* is an *Exile on Main Street* for all the kids born in '72, except *Appetite* rocks harder and doesn't get boring in the middle. It bastardizes every early Aerosmith record, but all the lyrics are smarter and Axl is a better dancer.

Part of the credit for the success of this five-headed juggernaut has to go to Nigel Dick, the faceless fellow who directed all the videos for GNR's early singles. One needs to remember that *Appetite* was out for almost a year before it cracked the *Billboard* Top 10 in 1988. Most people assume that this was because of the single "Sweet Child O' Mine," but the real reason was the video for "Welcome to the Jungle." The first fifteen seconds of that vid explain everything we need to know: Axl gets off a bus in downtown L.A. with a piece of friggin' *hay* in his mouth (and evidently, he didn't do much chewing during the twenty-six-hour bus ride from Indiana, because it still looks pretty fresh). The first time I heard this song, I was riding the Octopus at the North Dakota State Fair in Minot, and I had no idea what the fuck it was supposed to be about—but I still kinda liked it. When I saw this video two months later, I realized that Axl wasn't welcoming *me* to the jungle, people were welcoming *him*. Suddenly, the whole album made a lot more sense: Axl Rose was screaming because he was scared.

From the brazen misogyny of "It's So Easy" to the pleading vulnerability of "Rocket Queen," the album is a relentless exercise in high-concept sleaze. "Nightrain" is my personal favorite; Axl insists he's "one bad mutha," and he proves it by waking up his whore and making her buy four-dollar wine with her Visa card. "Mr. Brownstone" is hard funk on hard drugs, and it cleverly tells us how rock stars are supposed to live—you wake up at seven, you get out of bed at nine, and you always take the stage two hours late. "Paradise City" is probably the musical high point; it has GNR's signature soft-heavy-soft vocal sequence and the best chorus in metal history. "Paradise City" still seems like a disco classic waiting to happen.

The flip side is a little dirtier, starting with the unsettling "My Michele" and the semisweet "Think About You." The material is dark and purposefully hidden (kind of like Slash's eyes, I suppose), and the drums are ferocious; it sounds like Steven Adler is setting off cherry bombs in his drum kit. And through it all, the guitar playing is stellar. On *Appetite for Destruction*, Slash invented a new style of playing that's best described as "blues punk." He simultaneously sounds raw and polished—the master craftsman who came to work loaded. It was a style that sold 15 million records, but almost nobody managed to copy it (including Slash, who never really got it right again—even when he consciously tried on 1993's *The Spaghetti Incident?*).

There are those who will argue that the best thing that could have happened to Guns N' Roses would have been death, probably in about 1991. They were certainly on the right path (in fact, the rumor persists that David Geffen wanted *Use Your Illusion* to be a double album because he suspected someone in the band would be dead before they could cut anything else). From a romantic (read: selfish) perspective, there's some truth to this argument; it would be nice if *Appetite for Destruction* was all we really knew about this band of gypsies; Axl would have never lost his hair and the Gunners would have never become such bloated disasters.

Since Rose legally obtained the rights to the name Guns N' Roses in 1991, GNR is Axl Rose for all practical (and impractical) purposes. Put Axl onstage with the starting five of the Quad City Thunder, and that qualifies as "the new Guns N' Roses." The group still exists, but it's almost like comparing Jefferson Airplane to Starship: As I write this, the ever-evolving lineup consists of Axl, Dizzy Reed, former Replacements' bassist Tommy Stinson, Buckethead (a robot-obsessed guitar freak who wears a Kentucky Fried Chicken bucket on his dome), Robin Finck of Nine Inch Nails, Brian "Brain" Mantia (the drummer from

Primus who replaced Josh Freese, the guy from the Vandals who played on the new Guns record but has also quit the band since the album's completion), and what amounts to Axl's buddies from high school. The next album's working title is *Chinese Democracy* and it's rumored to be aggressive industrial metal in the spirit of Led Zeppelin, filtered through the sensibilities of Stevie Wonder; I can only imagine what this will be like, although it's safe to assume it will be twice as good as Izzy Stradlin and the Ju Ju Hounds, three times as good Slash's Snakepit, and five hundred times better than anything Duff McKagan ever released. But it will never be as good as this, and I suspect Axl⊛ knows it. (**Jack Factor: $5,001**)

⊛This analysis was somewhat complicated by the May 11, 2000, issue of *Rolling Stone* magazine, which essentially described Rose as a nocturnal New Age freak who spends much of his time in Sedona, a pseudo-spiritual Narnia in the Arizona desert. The article implied *Chinese Democracy* will probably never be released, but I'm confident it will eventually come out—however, I have no clue when that will be. When I started writing this manuscript in 1998, I jokingly said I wanted to have it published before the next GNR record, and (at this point) I think I still have a legitimate shot. Meanwhile, my aforementioned buddy Mr. Pancake now lives near Sedona and told me he'd keep an eye out for Axl's aura.

February 18, 1989

The staunchly uncompromising,
previously untouchable speed metal
of Metallica is on the radio with "One"
(No. 78 on the singles chart).

The death of '80s heavy metal is sometimes compared to the extinction of the dinosaurs, and that's a perfect analogy, even though most of the people who make this argument don't understand why.

Everyone seems to think that dinosaurs lived for 165 million years and then managed to die in the course of one really shitty afternoon. Hacks usually describe the process as if it was a devastating collision of coincidence: The world bumped into a comet, the global thermostat dropped like an Acme anvil, and a bunch of furry little ferrets suddenly decided to eat all the T-Rex eggs in Eurasia. By suppertime, every Thunder Lizard on earth was eating dirt and awaiting petrifaction.

Obviously, this theory is flawed.

The historical reality is that the dinosaurs died quickly *in terms of the planet*, which is a hard concept for modern man to relate to. Hair metal's demise happened in much the same way: It died quickly, but only in terms of how society consumes pop culture. Retrospectively, the decline of the glam rock empire seems to have happened so rapidly that it already feels like it's been unpopular for twenty-five years; in truth, metal was still the biggest genre in rock as late as 1991. When Guns N' Roses released *Use Your Illusion 1 & II* in September of that year, it momentarily seemed like the defining moment for an entire generation: At midnight, thousands of people lined up at record stores to buy GNR's much-awaited follow-up to *Appetite for Destruction* as soon as it went on sale that Tuesday. At the time, this was a legitimately unique deal; although the concept of opening stores at midnight soon became commonplace for marquee records (which would include everything from Pearl Jam's *Vs.* to seemingly workmanlike releases from Green Day and the Wu-Tang Clan), no one in their twenties could ever remember this happening before. At the time, I was a college sophomore, and Guns had become my favorite band (MTV deserves some of the credit for that; they had been hyping the GNR record since May, filling my summer evenings with rockumentaries that featured rambling diatribes from a drunken Duff McKagan and bootleg concert clips of Axl Rose starting a riot in St. Louis). My friends and I spent hours hanging out at the one record store in Grand Forks that had an advance copy of the two discs, and we browsed for hours just to hear bits of the new record on the in-store stereo system. On Monday night, we all had about seven beers each and then stood in line on that brisk North Dakota evening, joining the endless masses of people waiting to get in the door of locally owned stores like Disc & Tape and Budget Tapes & Records. And what I remember most is that the majority of these people were clearly not "metal kids." Judging from their appearance, these conservatively dressed frat boys and sorority girls could have been fans of anything, or—more likely—fans of nothing. It may have been the first time I ever consciously took part in a cultural *event*.

But that was just the state of music in 1991. Heavy metal was the predominant music of the era, and Guns N' Roses was the genre's best band. Tower Records in Los Angeles sold 23,000 copies of those *Illusion* albums in twenty-four hours, and that made perfect sense. What most of us did not know (especially those of us in Middle America) was that 46,251 copies of some wacky little record called *Nevermind* had been sent to stores across the country for a September 24 street date. A new world had already been recorded; we just didn't know it yet. By Thanksgiving, I had a copy of *Nevermind,* as did all the people I knew who followed rock with any seriousness. By Christmas, it was filtering down to anyone who bought music in general (although that phenomenon seemed more tied to the "Smells Like Teen Spirit" video than it did to any sort of philosophical revolution). Butch Vig was a faceless assassin, and we all unknowingly purchased the death of W. Axl Rose.

The sad irony is that most metal fans looked at Nirvana *as* a metal band. It seems crazy now, but—for a few fleeting moments on the cultural calendar of early '92—the band that many casual rock kids compared (and sometimes even confused) with Nirvana was Ugly Kid Joe. The distinction between grunge and metal was initially unclear: Soundgarden opened for GNR; Alice in Chains originally called themselves "Alice N Chainz." The first time we heard someone mention the idea of an emerging "Seattle Sound," I recall my roommate mentioning he was happy because he liked Queensryche.

The biggest myth about the whole "alternative revolution" was that it happened overnight, and that it swept the commercial insincerity of the 1980s off the map on the strength of a few catchy, grungy guitar riffs from Aberdeen, Washington. That's not true. We live in an accelerated culture, but its acceleration is increased retrospectively. It would be almost three years before the world heard its second most important Gen X anthem, Beck's "Loser." For a college student, three years is a long time.

What made it seem so sweeping is that for people born in the early 1970s, the transformation was all too clear. I was able to become a major rock fan at a time when cock rock was thriving and growing (the summer of 1984) and exit college on the heels of Kurt Cobain's death, the ultimate example of how absolutely everything about rock 'n' roll (and its audience) had changed.

Of course, every hard-rock guy who's still touring swears that metal is as popular as it ever was; "It's just gone underground."

That's the battle cry of everyone from Warrant to Megadeth, and in some ways it's true. And not every band was struck by the cultural plague; obviously, Metallica figured out a way to expand their popularity and they have continued to sell more records than they ever did. Of course, some of that success was directly tied to the widespread decline of most of their peers. Even though Metallica mildly alienated some of their most loyal fans by becoming more commercial, there really wasn't anyone to steal their market share.

Bands like Marilyn Manson and Korn would seem like obvious extensions of '80s metal (Manson loves to rave about Judas Priest), but those antiaesthetic sensibilities don't wash with people who associate their tastes with the prettier, cleaner groups of the former decade. Industrial goth neo-metal suggests a different attitude, and—more importantly—it seems to specifically *belong* to a defined social sector within a defined demographic. Groups like Van Halen and Def Leppard were kind of made for everybody—guys, girls, stoners, bikers, farm kids, the JV debate team, even people who liked country music (in our football team's locker room, AC/DC was the original "crossover" band). This is part of the explanation as to why pop metal bands were so damn successful.

It's also a big reason why musical pundits were so dismissive of their style: Party-obsessed headbangers lacked the hipness of exclusion. Metallica was one of the few '80s metal groups who developed that kind of (ahem) "credibility." They were painfully serious and seemed to be playing music for different reasons than somebody like Jon Bon Jovi, and—at least at first—Metallica offered a sound that was legitimately more intense than the rest of the pack. Idiots always say that Metallica "sold out" between . . . *And Justice For All* and their eponymous 1992 Black Album, but that's nothing compared to their evolution from 1983's *Kill 'Em All* to 1984's *Ride the Lightning*, an album best remembered for the suicide ballad "Fade to Black." On their debut record, they had openly expressed a desire to go out and kill people; by their sophomore follow-up, they merely wanted to kill themselves.

It's my suspicion that when today's new generation of rock writers matures into forty-five-year-old bastards and starts running the media industry, Metallica will suddenly become more and more "important," perhaps even on scale with Led Zeppelin and the Who. They've managed to sustain a career that has stretched nearly two decades, and they've cleverly excelled at both sides of the cultural equation: Metallica started as an uncompromising underground band who appealed to a fringe hardcore audience, but they've seamlessly evolved into a commercial juggernaut that seems to release a new video to MTV every seventy-two hours. They have been the Madonna and they have been the whore, and future historians will ultimately adore them for both.

But Metallica never meant shit to someone like me. In fact, they kind of pissed me off. When I was a glamour-starved sophomore in high school, James Hetfield was ugly and humorless; when I was an elitist sophomore in college, he made witless sorority bitches like speed metal. Even when his songs were good, I hated their social ramifications.

Metallica was influenced by the so-called new wave of British metal (NWOBM), a collection of Europeans who played raw, needlessly complicated songs and lacked mascara, lip liner, and irony. These are groups like the power-hungry Judas Priest, the Samuel Taylor Coleridge-obsessed Iron Maiden, a handful of groups that described "heads" (Diamond Head, Motorhead, et al.), and a band called Tygers of Pang Tang who I've never listened to (not even once).

Musically, these were decent groups that serious (read: unlikeable) metal fans worship, and they will claim that these particular outfits have "stood the test of time" better than the American pretty boys. A better description would be that they still seem about as fun as they did when they were fresh (read: not very). The best NWOBM music came from Priest and Motorhead, especially when they would lean toward a slightly commercial sound (*very* slightly in the case of Motorhead). The biggest thing they did was to provide the theoretical inspiration for our next generation of unhappy fellows: speed metal (and speed metal's bastard son, death metal).

In June of 1998, I covered a Slayer concert at the Odeon Club in downtown Cleveland. The show was a sell-out, which surprised me at the time. It kind of illustrates how much blue-collar midwestern cities continue to love hard rock, regardless of how often the media tells them they should hate it.

This was the most intense show I ever attended. It was actually kind of terrifying, and I'm the kind of person who generally enjoys watching other people's self-destructive intensity. About a thousand people packed themselves into this tiny club near Lake Erie and went absolutely ballistic for two hours. Slayer would be Spinal Tap if they possessed even an ounce of irony, but—as it is—they are most serious band who ever lived. The result is absolutely punishing. Slayer is kind of like a guy who walks up to you in a bar and says he's going to rape your wife, burn down your house, shoot all your friends, cover your kids with acid, and then slowly starve you to death while rats nibble away at your emaciated flesh. Now, if this hypothetical guy is merely a drunken goofball, that kind of complex depravity seems hilarious (almost endearing). But if he's the one guy on earth willing (and able) to do all those things, you'd suddenly realize you're talking to the craziest, most sinister motherfucker who ever lived. Slayer is that one guy.

As a general rule, I'm an absolute media apologist. I constantly find myself defending depraved, socially reprehensible material, mostly because I genuinely support all of it. And like most social critics, I inevitably overlook the obvious whenever it comes to the marriage of art and life. And something happened at this Slayer concert that I cannot ignore, and it sure seems like a prime example of "the obvious."

Late in Slayer's set, I was standing near the Odeon's door, probably the most sedate part of the club. Frontman Tom Araya was delivering some fairly moronic between-song banter, and I honestly wasn't listening. Suddenly, Araya screams, "It's raining . . . blood!," which (obviously) meant they were going to perform

"Raining Blood," the last track off 1986's *Reign in Blood*, widely considered the greatest death metal album ever recorded. I don't know what makes *Reign in Blood* a higher artistic achievement than any other death metal LP (or even what makes it better than any other Slayer LP), but I don't have any argument against it either. I'll take Ira Robbins's word for it.

ANYWAY, what happened next continues to baffle me. As soon as guitarist Kerry King played the first chord—and I mean the *first* chord—a guy about fifteen feet away from me inexplicably punched the person standing in front of him. By mere coincidence, I had been inadvertently watching these two guys for the last ten minutes (they were in my line of sight), and they obviously had no ill will toward each other; in fact, I'm almost certain they had no relationship whatsoever. And it's not like they started moshing, either. The first guy made a closed fist and cold-cocked the other dude in the back of the head. And a little closer to the stage, something similar happened about five seconds later: A man hit a woman in the face for no apparent reason.

All these hooligans were dragged out of the bar by a few bad-ass bouncers and thrown face down on the sidewalk outside of the club (the Odeon staff does not fuck around). Like any good reporter (or—more accurately—like anyone trying to *act* like a good reporter), I scampered outside to see if these people were going to keep fighting. They didn't. In fact, they just stared at each other with blank faces, further accentuating the fact that these people *had never met before*. They had no tangible qualms with each other at all, and they couldn't even come up with a decent imaginary argument. Yet, for whatever the reason, they had started throwing punches at each other before the band could even bleat out the first words of one particular song (which are—in case you're wondering—"Trapped in purgatory / A lifeless object, alive").

Am I blaming this on Slayer? Well, no. These people were probably drunk, probably unstable, and almost certainly stupid. But there *is* something weird about how humans react to the sonic quality of speed metal. It has a funneling effect on one's mental

processes; everything becomes very linear. Somehow, that intellectual reconfiguration holds a strong appeal to a certain kind of
personality. If I were a scientist, I would conduct tests on people
who consider themselves loyal speed metal fans; I hypothesize they
would generally share similar cerebral patterns for problem-solv-
ing and argumentation (however, I'm only a journalist, so I'll simply talk about this as if it were already a fact).

What I can't understand (or—more accurately—pretend to
understand) is where this kind of hyperaggressive, no-love-till-
leather thinking comes from (musically, there's no equation to
explain it). The most interesting thing about speed metal is
that it really *was* groundbreaking (at least for a while); while the
new wave of UK metal is often cited as an influence, those bands
don't sound anything like contemporary speed metal. Metallica
and Megadeth usually claim they found their style by welding
British metal with a punk philosophy, and the conventional hipster wisdom is that punk was invented when some kid tried to
play "Communication Breakdown" in his basement and couldn't
figure out the chord changes. So I guess we are left to assume
that Led Zeppelin's eponymous debut was the first speed metal
album ever recorded (that is, if "we" are "a bunch of idiots").

My appreciation for bands like this—particularly the popular
ones, like Metallica—varies from moment to moment. It is difficult to listen to any full-length Metallica record, or even to sit
through an hour-long collection of the best Metallica songs
played in succession. If Led Zeppelin can be viewed as the Babe
Ruth of hard rock, Metallica is undoubtedly Hank Aaron: leaner,
more consistent over the long haul, destined to break all the
records—but somehow never *transcendent*. Still, their music
can be incredible for short stretches, and it makes you listen to all
other songs differently. It alters the boundaries of what popular
music can be. Metallica's first three records were stunningly
effective in creating a new kind of metal fan who perceived himself (or herself) differently from the other kids at school, and I
think a lot of that can be explained by the technical composition
of songs like "Seek & Destroy" and "Master of Puppets." One is

tempted to explain Metallica—and all speed metal—in an all too obvious way: *Heavy metal played faster.* But that's not really accurate.

When a series of notes reaches a certain speed, a David Banner-like metamorphosis occurs. This is especially true when these notes are played on an electric guitar. Listen to the final two minutes of "Animal" from Vinnie Vincent, a brilliant example of guitar masturbation that works. As Vincent plays faster and faster (and faster and faster), the instrument reaches a critical point where it suddenly becomes the equivalent of a police whistle; it's similar to how the sound of a passing train changes pitch because of the Doppler effect. The same sort of thing happens with the sequencing of guitar riffs. Let's say Slash started playing a familiar lick, like the lead riff from "Welcome to the Jungle." We all know exactly what Slash's style sounds like, so we'd recognize his musical signature even if he played it faster. This would continue as the riff would come quicker and quicker; it would still seem like Guns N' Roses, and it would still sound like a *rock* song. But at some juncture in the acceleration—and I can't specify when—it would suddenly become *speed metal,* and it would be impossible to connect with the original creation. Imagine watching a wagon wheel as the axle (or maybe in this case, the Axl) starts turning; at a specific speed, the spokes suddenly appear to be rolling in reverse. Granted, this is an illusion—but it's an illusion that's comparable to the very real way people consume speed metal differently from glam rock, even though the two animals are filed under the same section in any record store. There is a point of no return that changes the meaning of a sound.

What's always struck me about speed metal is that its fans are obsessed with lyrics, even though these lyrics are essentially indecipherable. Teenage speed metal fanatics inevitably write the words to entire songs in their school notebooks and place considerable significance on their themes. In the 1996 HBO documentary *Paradise Lost: The Child Murders at Robin Hood Hills,* convicted teenage sadist Damien Wayne Echols scribbled Metallica lyrics in his notebook alongside the work of antichrist super-star Aleister Crowley. While fans of party rock rarely cared about the words to their anthems, speed freaks demanded that their heroes write about *something* misanthropic, even if they didn't have any insight to offer.

That's probably how we got death metal. All of these speed metal bands were writing about dark, sinister issues, and eventually they made the logical leap to writing about the darkest, most sinister dude they could remember hearing about in Sunday school. Groups like Metallica and Megadeth (and Anthrax, sort of) were based around being unhappy, but somehow this evolved into upstart bands who wrote almost exclusively about killing themselves and/or their parents and/or the girlfriend they wish they had.

I've never seriously listened to groups like Deicide and Careass and King Diamond, and I don't feel much desire to place their work in a cultural context. It's not that I think these bands are dangerous; on the contrary, I think they ultimately play a positive role in the lives of kids who (for whatever reason) have dark fantasies and a desire to dwell on social emptiness. What I don't think they do is cross over into conventional culture; I don't think we've seen much of a mainstream societal pollination from death metal. It's an insular subculture that doesn't have legs. I suppose it's possible that these kinds of groups inherited some of their ideas from the goth scene, and it's just as possible that savvy death metal groups simply stole the sexy brand of satanism practiced by the Crüe, Maiden, and all three of Glenn Danzig's projects. However, I ultimately suspect that these artists simply thought dying was the only subject that was interesting to write about.

I don't know; perhaps there is a societal aspect to this world and I'm just not seeing it. There's still a thriving death metal scene in Florida, so maybe the presence of old people makes the concept of death more pertinent.

September 23, 1989

The Bulletboys debut record—
and its single "For the Love of Money"—
falls out of the *Billboard* 200
and disappears forever.

"Burn your bridges, take what you can get," crooned Gene Simmons on the unremarkable KISS song "While the City Sleeps," and that still seems like practical (if not necessarily amiable) advice. "Go for the throat, 'cause you paid your debt." According to scripture in the Book of Gene, there is no better revenge than living well.

The tune comes off the 1984 release *Animalize,* an album that also featured a track called "Get All You Can Take." This was the cassette I was listening to in my brother's Chevrolet pickup on the day that I made the worst decision of my life.

With the exception of gangsta rap, hair metal was probably the most unabashedly economic music ever made. And having money makes you do crazy shit: During Skid Row's peak, ectomorphic singer Sebastian Bach bought a pair of leather pants for a thousand dollars. The reason I know this is because I asked the six-foot-five Bach how much he weighed on his solo tour in January of 2000, and he said he still weighed 179 pounds, which was his touring weight in 1990. Bach's explanation for why he's remained the same size: "I still gotta get into those fucking pants, man. They cost me a thousand dollars."

When Vince Neil appeared on the cover of *SPIN* magazine in 1992, he was pictured lighting a cigar with a thousand-dollar bill (I guess he had enough pants). Logically, this should not have been the image rock bands wanted to foster (especially not "gritty" bands like Mötley Crüe, who sang about cats in the alley and rats in their snakeskin boots). But burning money certainly seemed acceptable at the time; Mötley Crüe had signed a six-record deal with Elektra for a reported $25 million. Of course, this was also the era when people thought movie characters like Gordon Gecko were fascinating. I can even recall my senior English teacher telling our entire class that Donald Trump was the sexiest man alive. It was a Golden Age of Glam Capitalism.

This story begins in the summer of 1989, when I was obsessed with being anywhere the stench of freshly laid asphalt was more prominent than the aroma of freshly cut grass. And this did not mean I wanted to run away to the big city; it just meant I wanted to be in a place that wasn't a farm. That place ended up being Wahpeton, North Dakota, which is about as dreadful a community as there is in North America. Wahpeton has fifteen thousand people and the worst of everything: There's nothing to do (except go to Hardee's), but it's not really a small town, either (you have to lock your car doors overnight, you don't recognize most of the people you pass on the street, and a lot of the middle school kids like to huff gas). Nonetheless, I aggressively pursued a summer job in Wahpeton where I was supposed to teach small children how to play basketball, and this gave me an excuse to escape from my house three times a week and drive the twenty-five miles to an outdoor recreational facility near the Wahpeton Zoo. And since I usually went to Hardee's after work, everything was pretty cool.

I can't remember any of the kids I coached and I don't recall teaching them anything of consequence, but I always enjoyed the drive. It meant an hour a day in my brother's shiny red pickup truck, and—as all metalheads know—pickup trucks have the finest acoustics in the world. Twenty minutes in the front seat of a Chevy Silverado is a better sonic experience than an entire afternoon at Abbey Road Studios, and the explanation for why is simple logistics: *The speakers are right behind your head!* That was a very loud summer. Lots of Ratt.

One day after "work" (i.e., watching eleven-year-olds miss left-hand layups), I stopped off at my bank to get some money from the instant cash machine. My family has always done their banking in Wahpeton, and since my hometown did not have an ATM, this was always kind of a neat luxury. I got my twenty dollar bill and I looked at my receipt, expecting to see about $80. Instead, I had a little over $3,200.

Something was afoot.

I walked in the bank and showed my receipt to the teller (which shows just how neat I thought that ATM machine was— I used it even when the bank was open). She told me that machines sometimes make mistakes and that I shouldn't worry about it. I followed her advice and went home.

A week later, I went to get cash again. This time, the receipt claimed I had $8,865. Again, I walked into the bank and informed the teller that I was not, in fact, a sixteen-year-old entrepreneur. This time she said it was probably a decimal point mistake, and I likely had $88.65 in my account. That sort of made sense (but not really). Still, I basically ignored the weirdness and went home. I mean, what else could I do?

At this point, you can probably see where this is leading.

I didn't get any more cash for almost a month. To be honest, my life really didn't have too many expenses (I could last a *long* time on $80, unless I was buying fireworks). However, one night my good friend Edd and my sort-of-friend Pud decided to see *The Dream Team* at the newly built Wahpeton four-plex, and I stopped at the bank to get a few frogskins. I got $20 . . . and found myself staring at a transaction slip that indicated I had $63,000.

This time, it was 6:45 P.M. and the bank was closed. There was no part-time teller to tell me it was all a misunderstanding, and I was in no mood to consider the consequences of my actions (or my life). Most of all, I remembered what I had learned from KISS. Burn your bridges, take what you can get, I thought. I should go for the throat, because I had paid my debt. I was going to live well, which would be my best revenge. I would give 'em hell.

I would rage against this machine.

I tried to withdraw $200. The electronic screen told me I couldn't take out more than $200 a day. For a second, this confused me. Then I did the math. I withdrew $180.

And then I was rich.

I had no intentions of making this into a recreational habit. However, I probably should have, because it ended up becoming a serious addiction. The size of the account varied wildly and inexplicably (sometimes it was as high as $75,000), and it was always more money than I could possibly comprehend.

And frankly, none of this seemed all that weird to me.

Sixteen is a dangerous age; you're just dumb enough to be really fucking cool. I suppose I thought about my future, but never beyond graduation. It seemed completely plausible that as long as I didn't get greedy, these withdrawals could just slip by detection until I went to college. All I needed to do was get out of high school and move somewhere else. As far as I could tell, that would be the equivalent of faking my own death.

Now that I had a bottomless wallet, I could seriously rock. I got my first CD player, and I replaced all five of my old Mötley Crüe cassettes with shiny new compact discs. I made all these purchases in one store, all within the span of fifteen minutes. My cousin was with me at the time, and I suspect he thought I was God. I bought a pair of $70 New Balance basketball shoes; when I blew out the sole during the first week of practice, I didn't waste my time returning them. I just picked up a pair of $85 Nikes. In Wyndmere, this was how rock stars lived.

Obviously, this scenario posed a lot of unanswered questions, and most of them were difficult to ignore (although I somehow always found a way). Whenever I got my monthly bank statement in the mail, the amount was always correct (and I was still writing a normal number of checks in my attempt to seem like an inconspicuous consumer). The big money was only available through ATMs, and there was no clear explanation as to why.

I tried to keep this fiscal phenomenon a secret and told only my closest friends, but high school kids are not exactly known for playing things close to the vest. As the school year progressed, there was a growing rumor that I had access to massive sums of money (fortunately, I think most of my peers simply assumed I was lying about this, which certainly would have been a more reasonable explanation than the truth).

There was also a fairly unavoidable ethical problem with all this thievery, and it was slowly starting to wear me down. In Penelope Spheeris's documentary *The Decline of Western Civilization Part II: The Metal Years*, the wise sage Paul Stanley explains the best part about having money is "not having to *worry* about money." However, that philosophy does not apply when the money you have is not actually yours. I worried about it constantly. Despite my best attempts at rationalization, I could not avoid the fact that this money was obviously coming from *someone*.

Of course, a little omnipresent guilt still didn't stop me from becoming an amateur (professional?) embezzler. I'd withdraw $20 just to see what level my balance was at (always half expecting—and maybe even hoping—to see "$80"), and inevitably see five figures of fantasy and request another transaction.

Months passed, and I kept banging my head. I got *Double Platinum* and the debut effort from Skid Row. I got *Surprise Attack* by Tora Tora (which I actually regarded as "underground" metal). I replaced my tapes of *Led Zeppelin IV* and *Van Halen II* with CD replicants, concreting my classic rock credibility. I even decided to buy all twenty-plus KISS releases, but only on cassette; even with free money, buying that many compact discs just seemed a little too decadent.

I still have all these purchases, and they continue to haunt me—or at least remind me—of my criminal past (in fact, whenever I'm looking through my CD racks and my eyes pass over that Tora Tora disc, it's the *only* thing I think about). My relationship to the music has been replaced by my relationship with its acquisition. I wonder if Cuban drug lords feel the same sensation when they look at their collection of speedboats.

Suddenly, it was April. I had been an independently wealthy seventeen-year-old for almost ten months. However, I had finally stopped using my ATM card. I could no longer handle lying in bed all night and thinking about all the things Catholic boys think about when they sin, particularly purgatory. Since the bank was partially at fault for all this, I assumed my offense could not legally constitute eternity in hell, but purgatory was totally plausible (and going to purgatory just seemed so damn *boring*—it would be like spending four thousand years in an airport). Sometimes I think if I had just kept up this abstinence, everything would have been okay; maybe I would have just gone to college and transferred my account to a different bank, and nobody would have gotten hurt. Maybe escaping from reality wouldn't have been as impossible as it should have been.

Unfortunately, I had to go to a track meet in Rosholt, South Dakota.

Rosholt is a small town just across the North Dakota/South Dakota border, and its high school hosts track and field meets twice every spring. These were always my favorite track meets of the season, because it provided the chance to mingle with girls from a whole different state (in the rural Midwest, track meets are the equivalent of Studio 54—I knew tons of guys who only went out for track in order to meet women).

The problem was that Rosholt's track was covered with black asphalt, so it got extraordinarily sticky whenever it was hot and extraordinarily hard whenever it was cold. If you were going to run in Rosholt, you needed to bring a wide assortment of spikes for your running shoes (the individual spikes are removable, so you'd screw in long spikes when the surface was warm and gummy and short spikes when it was cold and impenetrable).

I didn't know what the weather was going to be like in Rosholt, but I knew I wasn't prepared (at least in terms of spikes). I cut class and drove to Stan Kostka's Sporting Goods in downtown Wahpeton, where I could buy some one-eighth-inch spikes. But as I walked toward the store, I suddenly remembered I had spent the last of my available cash on Slaughter's *Stick It to Ya*. (This was because Slaughter—along with Faster Pussycat—was the open-ing act for the KISS *Hot in the Shade* tour coming to Fargo in late May, and I needed to familiarize myself with their work.)

I had my checkbook, but I decided to just pop into the bank and get $10 from the ATM. Spikes are cheap, so why write a check for $2.99?

I slid my card into the machine's metal mouth. I punched in my four-digit code, 1805 ("18" being my high school football num-ber, "05" being my jersey number for hoops). I hit the key that sig-nified "cash from checking."

My transaction was denied.

I repunched my numeric code. Again, denied.

And then—for reasons I shall never quite understand—I went into the bank to complain.

Perhaps this is precisely what Raskolnikov would have done had he been in my sneakers, but I seriously doubt it (and since I've never actually read *Crime and Punishment*, I guess I'll never know). Frankly, it was a pretty audacious move, perhaps influ-enced by the way David Lee Roth used to demand that concert promoters provided a huge bowl of M&Ms in his dressing room before every concert, but all the brown ones had to be picked out by hand.

The teller was a nice college girl with Scandinavian hair, librar-ian glasses, and a red sweater that seemed a little too warm for April (and yes, I really *can* remember all this). She listened to my polite complaint and directed me to an older women who was sitting at a desk. The woman called up my account on her com-puter and suddenly became very serious. She made an inner-office phone call and made sure I could not hear what she was saying, even though I was sitting three feet away. I was fucked. A third woman came over to the desk; she was wearing a sensible pantsuit, and I thought I was going to pee.✪ She asked me to come with her, and we silently entered the bank's inner sanctum. I had never known that banks had such places. Where were we

---

✪Or maybe vomit.

going? Was she going to lock me in the fucking vault? I wondered if she just didn't feel comfortable shooting me in the lobby.

We sat down in a relatively empty room and I listened to the air conditioner, even though it seemed way too early in the year for air-conditioning (it occurred to me that this might explain the teller's need for a sweater). The woman asked me if I was comfortable. I said, "I don't know." She pretended to smile, and I tried to make eye contact while holding an expression that tried to simulate bewilderment. We had a nice chat, and this woman explained how this "error" had occurred.

Now, I have been legally advised not to give any details about how—or why—this "error" happened (however, I will say that the explanation is much, much simpler than you'd possibly imagine). And as soon as my female jailer felt I was completely aware of the specifics of our little misunderstanding, this nameless woman in a sensible business suit made a simple, unemotional request.

"We need you to give us two thousand one hundred and sixty dollars."

I pretended to seem shocked. In truth, I had expected the amount to be even higher, although I had no idea how much. I contemplated freaking out and feigning hysterics, but I was afraid that would only change my problem without really improving it. I shuddered a bit and I took some exaggerated deep breaths to create the illusion of confusion.

But then I noticed something.

This woman looked nervous.

Some journalists will tell you that—over time—they have learned to read people's faces during interviews. This is one skill I never had to learn. I could tell this woman knew she was almost as fucked as I was. The process of explaining the situation had unconsciously validated what she already knew: Her bank had made the kind of mistake that banks are not supposed to make. Moreover, I was a minor. I was seventeen, and I looked even younger; I couldn't be charged with a crime. I couldn't be charged with anything. And I was a good actor. I could tell everyone I had no idea what I was doing, and it would seem credible. I could claim that I was too irresponsible to balance my checkbook and that I never even glanced at my ATM receipts. I could insist I was just a feeble-witted headbanger who didn't understand the value of money. Besides, I had even told the bank about it—twice!

If I fought this, I could get off.

I could get off.

I could get off.

Unfortunately, "getting off" would create another problem, and that one was even worse. Even though I had spent ten months buying a whole shitload of nothing, my parents had no idea about any of this. White-collar crime is not something you discuss over a roast beef supper. And even though I could trick the rest of the world into thinking I was just an ignorant teenage simpleton, I could not trick my parents. My mom would know. I would have to tell my mom I had accidentally withdrawn $2,160 over a ten-month period, and I would have to look into her disappointed face while she pretended to believe me.

I thought about the way so many of my friends bitched about their parents; they all seemed to think they were destroying their lives. I never felt like that. My parents were undoubtedly crazy, but they never did anything except make my life better. I was their seventh and final child, and they did not need this. To this day, I never want them to know anything about my life that makes me seem like the horrible person I truly am. In fact, the thought of them reading this book keeps me awake at night. It makes me want to get drunk.

In seconds, I decided that the news of my great rock 'n' roll swindle must never reach my parents. The pantsuited woman behind the desk may have been nervous, but her silence was the kind of inadvertent negotiation that could have made fictional Gordon Gecko filthy fucking rich. I played the only card in my deck: I pulled out my checkbook and wrote a check for $2,160.

Did I have that much money in my account? Of course not. I had to be creative, and this required even more deception. When I was eleven years old, my dad had suffered a stroke. He recovered, but somehow this event resulted in my underage sister and me earning money we couldn't spend. My father had been technically disabled by the stroke, and we somehow got money to supplement the lost income (which we certainly needed, because my mom was a housewife). The money was deposited into an account in my mother's name, which I would gain full access to when I turned eighteen. This money was intended for college. But when I explained this to the anonymous, nervous banker lady, she agreed to transfer that money straight into my checking account (a wildly inappropriate move that further solidifies my suspicion that I could have beaten the rap).

To this day, I am paying off the financial aid loans I took for my freshman year of college.

I did not feel like David Lee Roth when I walked out of the bank that day. I didn't buy any track spikes either. Instead of returning to school that afternoon, I drove around the countryside and cried, listening to the KISS cassette *Hotter Than Hell*. It dawned on me that if I had never purchased *Hotter Than Hell*, I would have only had to repay $2,150. The meaninglessness of that realization buried me like an avalanche of gravel. Fuck, what difference would *that* make? There was no singular purchase that had sealed my fate; there was no eight-hundred-pound gorilla sitting in the corner of my bedroom. I had somehow pissed away two grand of my future, one blistering power chord at a time.

In 1996, the KISS reunion earned $43.6 million in revenue, by far the year's most successful tour. Obviously, the decision for Paul and Gene to reunite with Peter and Ace was a good one. Meanwhile, nobody really knows how much money KISS lost to bad decisions like 1981's *Music from the Elder* and the doomed 1979 "Super KISS" tour; according to former KISS business manager C. K. Lendt, those losses were far greater than what they made in the '90s (particularly when you factor in inflation). But what continues to make KISS so appealing is that all of these decisions—the brilliant ones, the bad ones, and especially the downright idiotic ones—were all made for the same reason: *Because this was rock 'n' roll.* When Paul was about to record his 1978 solo album in Beverly Hills, he showed up at his rented studio on the first day and decided he didn't like the acoustics. He demanded that they change studios, which would waste $60,000. Predictably, his management advised against the move. Paul supposedly said, "Well, it's cheaper than not making an album." This is a terrible argument, but it's a damn good point. I only shelled out $2,160, but I completely understand where Paul was coming from: It was cheaper than looking like the idiot and the liar that I was.

"Burn your bridges, take what you can get."

Well, okay.

"Go for the throat, 'cause you paid your debt."

True.

"Livin' well is the best revenge."

Sort of.

"So give 'em hell."

I tried, Gene. Really. I tried.

September 10, 1990

Warrant releases *Cherry Pie*. In a CD review for my college newspaper, I call this record "stellar." It is three years before I am allowed to review another album.

The film *Velvet Goldmine* opened in most major markets on November 6, 1998. In the cinematic community, this was news, but only mildly so. Simply put, *Velvet Goldmine* was a good—but by no means great—movie. Chronicling the British glam rock era of the early '70s, Goldmine was visually interesting and generally fun (assuming you love glam rock and gayness), but the story was questionably conceived and poorly executed. It may actually seem better twenty years from now, when the connections between fact and fiction won't seem so impossible to separate.

However, the release of *Goldmine* was major news for people who were considered "pop cultural journalists," and I was one of those people. The hot topic that autumn was the "glam revival." Due to a weird collision of coincidences, every social pundit in America seemed to be claiming that glitter rock—and particularly glitter fashion—was poised to sweep the world. To be honest, it was basically just because of this one movie and Marilyn Manson, who had recently re-invented himself as David Bowie for his latest release, *Mechanical Animals*.

But in this day and age, two of anything makes a trend. That forced me (and everybody like me) to write stories with headlines like "Glam Rock Is Back On the Attack!" It just so happened that Manson was playing in nearby Cleveland the week after *Velvet Goldmine* opened, so our timing was especially fortuitous. Here's the article I wrote for *The Beacon Journal* in Akron on November 13 of that year (and remember, this story was written for a pretty broad audience, so please excuse the pedantic nature of the introduction . . .):

CLEVELAND—When Marilyn Manson struts onstage at the 3,000-seat Music Hall tomorrow night, it's very possible—in fact, probable—that he will be sporting prosthetic breasts.

He will be covered in pasty white makeup, and he'll wear highly impractical platform shoes. And instead of donning all black, he will likely be dressed in angelic white (or possibly hot pink).

This alien, androgynous look is Manson's new attempt at shocking people. Of course, there's really nothing *new* about it: Manson is simply trying to lead the so-called "rebirth" of glam rock, a bygone genre that's having a cultural (if not necessarily musical) effect on the state of rock 'n' roll.

Glam rock was born in Britain during the early 1970s. Categorized by outlandish costuming, bisexual attitudes and synthetic pop songs, it was defined by U.K. icons like David Bowie and groups like T. Rex, Sweet and Mott the Hoople. American bands combined the theatrical elements of glam with a harder style of rock, starting with Iggy and the Stooges and evolving into Alice Cooper and KISS.

The original life span of glitter rock was brief—it started in 1970 and was dead by '74. But interest in the high-heeled era is peaking. Manson's latest album, *Mechanical Animals*, is an unabashed throwback to Bowie's 1973 *Aladdin Sane* LP. The cover of the October issue of W magazine declares "Glam Rock Is Back," and the accompanying story suggests glam fashion will be influencing runway models this winter. Even Tuesday's *Live! With Regis and Kathie Lee* had a segment on glam chic.

Perhaps most telling is the buzz surrounding *Velvet Gold-mine*, a film that chronicles the glitter era in semifictional terms. Currently showing at Cleveland Heights' Cedar Lee Theatre, *Goldmine* has received mixed reviews. But flaws in the movie's plot seem secondary to its spacey soundtrack and provocative, sexually ambiguous cinematography. In fact, *Goldmine* costume designer Sandy Powell insists the picture is "really a fashion movie."

Amazingly, there's even a renewed interest in the *second* era of glam: the much-maligned hair metal years of the 1980s. Sony is rumored to have signed Cinderella, Ratt and Great White to new recording contracts for a yet-to-be-named subsidiary label.

"I don't know if Sony is chasing a specific look, but I do know those bands are doing very well on club tours," says Cinderella publicist Byron Huntas. "There's definitely interest in '80s glam. When we played at the Key Club in L.A. on Oct. 2, Marilyn Manson was in the audience. Billy Corgan [of Smashing Pumpkins] was recently spotted at a Ratt show. People love this stuff."

Meanwhile, a handful of neo-glam rockers—Spacehog, Blur and Nancy Boy—have used glitz and posturing to achieve mild notoriety. But all that glitters is not gold; though Manson gets bushels of media attention, his much-publicized album has already fallen out of the *Billboard* Top 20. People may be talking about glam, but they don't seem to be buying it.

"At this point, the glam revival is more about theory than it is about music," says Barney Hoskyns, the U.S. editor of the British magazine *MOJO* and the author of *Glam! Bowie, Bolan and the Glitter Rock Revolution*. "A movie like *Velvet Goldmine* is a very structured attempt to comment on what glam meant, along with a story line that has heavy homoerotic overtones. But it's not going to get average kids on the street to parade around in silver boots with six-inch heels."

Hoskyns thinks the hype surrounding glam is primarily coming from the fashion industry. Musically, he's not surprised record buyers have been less enthusiastic.

"The term 'retro' has become such a buzz word," Hoskyns

said. "Everything is described as retro these days. I think people are starting to pull away from brazen replications of the past."

Dennis Dennehy at Geffen Records says the illusion of a glam revival is probably a collision of coincidences: Manson's new look, the release of *Velvet Goldmine* and the return of pop metal just happen to have occurred at the same time.

Still, Dennehy suspects the spirit of glam rock is making a valid resurgence, even if it's being manifested in a different way. At least he hopes it is: In February, Geffen will push a debut album by the band Buck Cherry, a group on the DreamWorks label that Dennehy favorably compares to the New York Dolls.

"Glam was always about sexual freedom and drug experimentation. People are interested in those themes again," Dennehy says. "AIDS and the heroin epidemic don't cast the cultural shadow they did five years ago. I'm not trying to say those situations are any less important, but people have grown accustomed to living with them. It's just become part of life. Artists feel like they can be rock stars again, and that's what glam is all about."

I include this article for a couple of reasons. Obviously, it's notable; it seems crazy to talk about glam metal without mentioning the reemergence (or at least the *supposed* reemergence) of the incarnation's original animal a decade after the fact. I also think the potential (albeit unlikely) signing of Cinderella and Ratt to Sony is a little more than a minor anomaly; in fact, I'm kind of afraid that glam metal·will completely come back in vogue before I can finish this damn book. At the very least, I'm absolutely certain it will eventually have the kitschy, contrarian appeal of dance pop and new wave. The '98 glam revolt might be a harbinger of another full-on retro explosion that's just around the corner.

However, my main motivation is to introduce Hoskyns into this equation.

As the article states, Hoskyns is an editor for *MOJO*, one of the few British rock magazines that is (a) readable, and (b) remotely accurate. He's written books on the Doors, Prince, and the Band (and he also coauthored a book titled *The Mullet: Hairstyle of the Gods*, so he certainly must understand *something* about hard rock). The fact that I had the chance to interview him at all was kind of a fluke; our newspaper received a promo copy of his book *Glam!* on Monday the ninth, and I was supposed to have my story finished by Tuesday afternoon. At about 11:00 A.M. on Monday, I called Simon & Schuster and asked if I could somehow get a hold of Hoskyns as soon as possible. They told me to fax a request, which is publicist slang for "get fucked."

At 3:00 P.M. the next day, my story was basically done. But seconds before I sent it to my editor—and to my absolute and utter surprise—Hoskyns suddenly called me from his home in Woodstock, New York. He sounded feminine, but that's just because he's very, very British. However, Hoskyns describes himself as an "Americaphile" (which seems like a completely alien term to anyone from the States, but—truth be told—the world probably has a helluva lot more "Americaphiles" than it has "Anglophiles"). And after he fed me some excellent material for my story, we had a friendly, unprofessional conversation about '80s glam metal. This had kind of become my habit; while in the process of working on this book, I basically asked everyone I ever met about their thoughts on heavy metal. It really didn't matter who the fuck they were. Even if I was interviewing H. Ross Perot, I was gonna slip in a question about Trixter.

But I will always remember Barney Hoskyns. Why? Because he basically shredded the entire premise of my project in less than 120 seconds. And this was *before* I told him what I was doing. I hadn't even mentioned I was writing a book. Without provocation (and while discussing the "beauty" of Marc Bolan), he touched on the return of hair bands in the early 1980s. Suddenly, I saw my window of opportunity. "That's an interesting point," I said. "And now that you've brought it up, I'm curious: Was there any value to '80s glam metal?"

And this is what he said:

"Only if you want to seem extremely ironic, or if you just want to be one of those rock critics that doesn't want to toe the party line. If you're trying to ask me if I saw any credibility in Poison, I'm certainly not going to say 'yes.' They were awful. It was all so overdone; it was so calculating. There was no invention. A band like Mötley Crüe just wanted to be a stupid rock 'n' roll band with a bunch of tattoos. And ultimately, all those groups looked the same, anyway."

At this point, I had a lot of mixed emotions. On one hand, this man had eloquently crystallized every fear I had about trying to create a book about heavy metal, and I suddenly felt like I was the stupidest blockhead in America. Yet—on the other hand—I was pretty damn impressed by how quotable this dude was. And he just kept going!

"Now, I wouldn't lump all those bands into one group," he continued. "Van Halen was funny; I always thought David Lee Roth was a witty, clever guy. But when you got down to the really horrific bands like Quiet Riot and London . . . oh, my God. You were just seeing this putrid, commercially cynical, idiotic image of what somebody thought a Sunset Strip glam band was supposed to look like."

I started to suggest that he was being a little too flippant with his cultural criticism. Certainly, he was exaggerating his argument for effect, right? I mean, even critics agreed that Guns N' Roses was a good band, right?

"I thought Guns N' Roses was really tired," he continued. "They were exactly like everybody else, except they were a little more obsessed with getting into detox. I have no idea what anyone ever saw in Axl Rose. It seemed like so many people wanted him to be some kind of subversive voice from a small town, kind of like Kurt Cobain. But he was never a Cobain. He never meant anything important."

At this point, it seemed as if Hoskyns was literally reading from my text and mocking me. Of course, the simple reality is that his feelings on '80s metal are a more prototypical reflection of the rock community (and the global community) than mine. And that's unfortunate. Hoskyns is a smart guy, but he hates heavy metal for all the wrong reasons.

"Hating metal" actually has a lot to do with liking it. Actually, that's true for popular music in general. People who take rock music seriously in a literal sense always seem to be missing the point. I enjoy hating musicians far more than I enjoy appreciating them. As far as I'm concerned, when someone becomes a rock star, he quits being a person. I'm not being sarcastic, either. That's how it's *supposed* to be.

Whenever the subject of Kurt Cobain comes up, I always catch a lot of flak for implying that there was something truly wonderful about his suicide. I can totally understand why that suggestion would make someone want to punch me; as a member of the human race, it doesn't seem like there is anything positive about a genius who kills himself at the age of twenty-seven and leaves an infant without a father. But from a cultural perspective, Cobain's suicide was the only "great" thing that happened to music in the 1990s. He is the only artist of my generation who was indisputably sincere.

Most people have a very fucked-up relationship with musicians: They want to pretend that famous artists think about them as singular individuals. Joe Q. Fan has a personal relationship with Sting, so he likes to believe Sting feels the same way about him. I notice this every single time I've been backstage after a concert for a "meet and greet" session with a touring musician. A "meet and greet" is a situation where a band sits at a table after a show, and a few fans and industry types get to shake their hands and have something autographed (usually a black-and-white photo of the group supplied by the road publicist). Most of the time, the entire entourage is composed of the people who promoted the gig, a handful of random superfans who won backstage passes through radio contests, and three potential rock sluts.

The road manager runs these folks through like an assembly line, and the band is always sweaty and bored. Most groups are almost never rude (in fact, some are amazingly cordial), but it's really just part of the job. The young, wild-eyed rockers would usually prefer to be out getting drunk and getting laid, and the older established stars would obviously prefer to be having dinner with their spouses. But they sit at these tables (typically set up in the locker rooms of sports arenas) and methodically sign pictures with black felt pens, and they listen to a few dozen people insist they are their "biggest fans," a lot like the chick from *Misery*.

After the "meet and greet" is over (which is almost always *exactly* thirty minutes), the band stands up and leaves town, and they will do the same thing in another city tomorrow night. But the people who momentarily shook hands with Ozzy or Slash (or whoever) will talk about this for the next five years. They will tell people how they "met" Gene Simmons, and they will inevitably says something like, "He was a really nice guy." Which basically means the artist in question did not purposely spit on them.

I hate to classify rock fans as idiots, but they usually are. They don't understand that they are consuming an art form in a macro format. They are not getting anything *special* from these performers. If the Replacements' "Sixteen Blue" touches their life in a wonderful and specific way, that has very little to do with Paul Westerberg. What Westerberg did was write a great song that is (a) catchy, and (b) populist. He's brilliant, but not because his music can speak to an individual; he's brilliant because he can speak to millions of individuals and make each one of them feel like he's specifically talking to them. In an emotive sense, Westerberg helps people affect themselves, and he can do it on a mammoth scale. But diehard Replacements fans refuse to think of his songs in this way. If they did, it would make the whole experience of listening to "Sixteen Blue" on a lonely Friday night a lot less meaningful.

I suppose that explains why people so desperately want to take pop music seriously; it makes meaning out of four simple chords and elementary poetry. But that's always what was so great about Nirvana—and Cobain's death. For once, *it was all real*. People were always obsessed with calling Cobain "ironic," but nobody (myself included) ever noticed that he was the one guy in the whole scene who was *never* being ironic. He sang about hating life and wanting to die, and the cacophonic crash and beautiful wail of Nirvana's music was precisely how sadness sounds. And he validated everything he ever said by carrying through with the ultimate act: a high-profile suicide that was delivered to the world by the media, just as they had delivered "Smells Like Teen Spirit" in 1991. The scale of Kurt's death was a reflection of his public life, which was really the only part of his life any of us knew. He was—and is—the only pop genius of my generation. He gave people exactly what they really wanted, and he did so with absolute sincerity. I don't see how anything could ever be more effective than an album as good as *Nevermind* and a shotgun blast to the face.

But does that mean that Cobain is beyond reproach? As a person—yes. But as a rock star? No. He was a rock guy who talked a lot of shit most of the time. When he was pogoing and screaming on MTV, he was doing it for our entertainment. When something is put out in the public, it loses its human qualities (for example, if you hate this book, I certainly wouldn't expect you to pretend you like it in order to spare my feelings, particularly since this book is almost certainly the only reference you have to me as a person). Hating (and sometimes mocking) music is just as important as loving (and embracing) music. They are basically the same emotive function, separated only by the tone of one's voice.

That's why I say Hoskyns hates '80 pop metal for the wrong reasons. When you get right down to it, the main problem had nothing to do with its social philosophy or the lack of artistic creativity. The biggest problem was that the vast majority of metal songs were simply *boring*. And the paradox is that the music was especially boring whenever the artists made conscious attempts to be intellectual or creative .

Metal (and all of rock music, really) has always grappled with the stupid logic of "virtuosity" and the relatively groundless argument that complex construction equates with greatness. Sometimes it does, sometimes it doesn't. It is easy to illustrate this with extreme examples; I don't think any normal pop fan would suggest that Joe Satriani is a better guitarist than Keith Richards, even though there's no doubt that Satch is countless times more proficient. To argue otherwise would be like saying George Will is a better writer than Ernest Hemingway because George uses bigger words, longer sentences, and more complicated arguments.

Hard rock's obsession with virtuosity was partially an attempt to legitimize the genre and make it seem valid, which (on rare occasions) it did. If nothing else, it made it seem relatively inaccessible. The beauty (and stupidity) of punk was that anyone could do it; if you had a guitar and a garage and two friends, you were probably two weeks away from playing a gig. That was not the case with heavy metal. The idea of learning the chops for "Surfing with the Alien" or the intro to "Mean Streets" was basically impossible, unless you were pretty damn musical. As a metal kid, there was always the idea that our music was secretly *smarter* than what was on Top 40 radio. The fans of quick-fingered guitar rock saw their music the same way teen movies usually portrayed burn-out kids: They looked like shit and nobody gave them any credit, but—underneath that tough, lazy exterior—they were really the brightest kids in the class (kind of like Judd Nelson in *The Breakfast Club*).

Sometimes this assumption was right. Obviously, you had Eddie Van Halen and Randy Rhoads. Both of those players were raised with classical backgrounds, and one assumes they would have been wonderful talents in whatever sonic medium they pursued. There seems to be a universal belief that someone like Rhoads could have been a world-class oboe player, if that had been the cool thing to do. Of course, Rhoads gets a little extra credit for having died in a plane crash. Nonbreathing people get all the breaks. Clearly, the easiest way to become "great" is to get "good" and then get "dead." Rhoads is now an axe legend and will be forever (relatively speaking), and his work on those early Osbourne albums *is*—at the very least—very good. But was he as great as everyone seems to remember? Maybe, but probably not.

"I've never seen anyone become a better fucking guitar player by dying than Randy Rhoads," Lemmy Kilmister told me in

1998. "Nobody ever talked about him when he was alive, but suddenly everyone started saying he's some kind of fucking genius. He was a nice guy and a very good guitarist, but he wasn't a Hendrix or a Clapton or anything like that."

Whether or not Rhoads was really that great really isn't the issue, though. The issue is that his style—and particularly his "goal," for lack of a better term—has been copied exhaustively. So has Eddie Van Halen's (to an even larger degree), as well as that of guys like Ritchie Blackmore and Jeff Beck. These ardent followers were the patron saints of the whole "guitar school" chic movement that spawned some of the dullest music of the late twentieth century.

The music of Yngwie Malmsteen was shit. It was virtually unlistenable. Like an intricately designed maze that went nowhere, it epitomized pretension—which was exactly what so much of the era's good metal never had. Malmsteen was cursed by three things: a tremendous amount of technical musical prowess, the complete absence of any musical soul, and a horrific unwillingness to pick a stage name. No rock guitarist ever fused classical influences to metal with such unabashed abandon; he even preferred song titles like "Icarus' Dream Suite." At the time of his greatest glory (which was never really ever, but for the sake of argument we'll say 1985), all the guitar mags loved raving about the genius that was Yngwie: a speed demon who could jam a million shrieking notes into half a breath, and did so under the premise of art. He called his debut album (and his backing band) *Rising Force*, and that was how the hard rock community initially perceived him. There was a moment in time when metal insiders suspected that the future of metal was held in the rapid-fire paws of Malmsteen; even though he hadn't sold that many records, there was a strong belief that—in time—*every* metal band would sound like Yngwie Malmsteen.

But Malmsteen never sold records. He did not reinvent metal. In fact, he never even became famous; today, he's remembered only by obsessive guitar freaks (and by people who like to make fun of '80s metal, I suppose).

Ultimately, Yngwie had four problems. One was the ridiculous name, which wasn't really his fault since he was Swedish, the Holy Land of ridiculous names. Another was his attitude, and that was his own fault. Malmsteen openly referred to himself as a genius and constantly attacked the metal genre, even though that was his only audience. He was flatly unlikeable. A third was his musical direction. Regardless of its sonic merits, Malmsteen's style made the mistake of moving metal away from its roots. He never seemed to understand that he was really playing for an updated version of the kids who loved Sab and Zep, two groups who were really just heavy blues bands. When you listened to a record like *Odyssey*, you never really knew what it was—it sounded like rock, but it didn't *seem* like it. There was nothing visceral or angry about it, the songs were sterile, almost robotic. Malmsteen took the blues out of rock 'n' roll, and the sex and drugs disappeared with it.

But the real problem (number four) with Malmsteen's music is what I stated before: It was boring. In fact, it seemed to create a whole new way for music to suck. It was boring in that way that made you feel vaguely ashamed, kind of like reading *Moby-Dick* or A1 newspaper stories about Kosovo. It made your eyes glaze over; the instrumentals would play on and on, the pyrotechnic scales would climb higher and higher, and it gave you nothing but tinnitus.

Now, that criticism is not the same as suggesting Malmsteen's material *said* nothing, because most metal said nothing (and sometimes even less). Music that doesn't have a point is totally acceptable. But this kind of rock—this so-called impressive metal—wasn't even fun. It was laborious. Critics like to accuse '80s metal of being pompous, and I usually disagree with that assessment; I don't think the majority of hard rock bands displayed as much pretension as the alternative bands who replaced them. But the handful of metalheads who were the exception to that rule took pomposity to an entirely different level.

For the most part, these were all guitar guys. I remember reading an article where Steve Vai actually referred to himself as a "guitar god." It was a really lousy article, so my hope is that Vai was being sardonic and the journalist somehow didn't pick up on it. But part of me thinks Vai was probably being serious. After all, he did make an instrumental album called *The Passion and the Warfare*, and the whole thing sounded like one song. I guess that was the point: that passion *is* warfare. Which I assume most people agreed with anyway, even before they heard fourteen consecutive guitar solos.

Dokken was a really boring band, mostly because George Lynch is a supposedly "incredible" guitarist. I can barely remember how any Dokken songs go, because the melodies had no hook. Living Colour was sometimes very good, but sometimes extraordinarily dull; once again, the blame falls on the talent of the guitarist, in this case Vernon Reid. Reid can be very cool on occasion. He rips shit up on the Public Enemy song "Sophisticated Bitch" but he works so hard at the "less is more" guitar philosophy that he somehow manages to jam excess simplicity into every song, ultimately turning all that "nothing" into "too much something." Joe Satriani surfed with an alien, but mostly it was stupid. Every Whitesnake song that wasn't a smash single is for narcoleptics only, especially when the aforementioned "guitar god" joined the group (Vai was much better when he was with David Lee Roth, mostly because Dave told him to scrap the Guitar Institute bullshit and just get out and push). I also recall a lot of people insisting that Europe and Enuff Z'Nuff were a bunch of long-haired geniuses—*Rolling Stone* even compared Enuff to the Beatles, and I guess both bands did sing about girls named Michelle—but everyone who liked to rock out thought they were crap. For those of you keeping score at home, Europe is remembered for the single "The Final Countdown." Enuff Z'Nuff is remembered for nothing, except maybe for that *Rolling Stone* thing (and that might be an urban legend).

Another good reason to hate heavy metal is Ted Nugent, or—more accurately—people who are *like* Ted Nugent. Every time I go to a big rock show, I see herds of these kind of men, and they always make me wish I had the power to give people polio.

As a singular entity, Nugent is not wholly terrible. He didn't make much good music during the glam '80s, but his musical legacy was always within earshot. The vast majority of his best songs are about (or at least make reference to) vaginas, but his guitar playing has always been pretty bad-ass. All the hair bands who consistently ripped off the riff from "Cat Scratch Fever" usually hit pay dirt (L.A. Guns, for example). I tend to enjoy both of Nugent's songs that prominently feature the word "wang," and the seemingly endless "Stranglehold" was a mainstay in Dr. Johnny Fever's playlist on *WKRP In Cincinnati*. So it's not like we didn't know who Terrible Ted was.

Even as a human, Ted is palatable. His "political" take on all that liberal, leftist bullshit is refreshing, and there's something weirdly charming about his maniacal desire to kill every deer in North America. I certainly have no qualms with the idea of killing animals. After years of research, I have come to the conclusion that animals enjoy being eaten; they think it's fun. If Ted wants to ice a few thousand ungulates before he takes his own dirt nap, I won't hold it against him.

My problem with Ted Nugent is that guys who aspire to be like him—or just *are* like him by default—make me feel ashamed for liking hard rock. They have no sense of humor, and they beat people up and they kill cats for no reason. They get totally fucked up on Budweiser anytime they're in public; if they smoke pot, they only do so when they're already drunk, so they never get mellow (it just makes them a little less predictable, which isn't necessarily good). Once you become friends with these people (and if you're from a small town, you will), you can never relax. If you get drunk with these guys and pass out, they will write on your face with a black Magic Marker. They will literally piss all over you. They will steal your car and intentionally drive it into a ditch. Ex-cons always talk about how the rules of society don't apply inside the walls of a prison; I have to assume the penitentiary experience is akin to partying with a bunch of Nugent disciples. If you're not consciously being an asshole to someone else, you will become a victim. And what can you do? Nothing. And why not? *Because these are your goddamn friends.*

Over the past decade, the main band that is ridiculed for being a bunch of white trash imbeciles is Lynyrd Skynyrd. I honestly think a lot of that baggage came from an early clip of *Beavis & Butt-head*: In the very early *B & B* vignette (way back when it was only a four-minute segment on MTV's *Liquid Television*), a drunken, aging redneck declares that somebody should "Play some Skynyrd, man." In a matter of months, this became a familiar taunt to toss toward idiots (I can't prove that this otherwise forgettable MTV moment was the absolute origin of the anti-Skynyrd movement, but it certainly seems more than coincidental). I can understand why Skynyrd is an easy target for ridicule; their overt appreciation of the Confederate flag made them seem a wee bit racist, and their overplayed, bourbon-soaked swamp rock seemed outdated the moment is was released. But the ignored reality is that Lynyrd Skynyrd was a brilliant collection of songwriters: Their records have a regional quality that's usually only heard in hip-hop or old country, and the lyrical content is remarkably gutsy (when you consider the demographic of their core audience, releasing an antigun anthem like "Saturday Night Special" could have been career suicide). The assertion that Skynyrd is the music of the dumb is unfortunate, even though it sometimes might be a little true. But if anyone should be shackled with that label, it should be Ted and his crossbow of doom.

Obviously, this is all pointing to a clear contradiction. The logical reader is asking, How can you attack Yngwie Malmsteen for being pretentious and "smart," and then proceed to rip Ted Nugent for fostering low-grade humanity and being boorish and "dumb"? It would seem that the Motor City Madman presents a product that is perfectly opposed to the Swedish fretmonger, so it's hypocritical to despise them both.

But it's not.

It's not because they are not really opposites. They both suck, but for totally unrelated reasons. Malmsteen was *pretentious* in the literal sense of the word—people often say "pretentious" when they mean artsy or conceited, but it really means pretending to be something you're not. Yngwie pretended he was a hard-rock Mozart because normal people didn't like his music. He used classical training to hide from his own mediocre songwriting. And by the same token, Nugent was *boorish* in the literal sense: He was clownish and rude, but in a rustic way. There was no theater or irony to his caveman persona, and it established the wrong kind of credibility. Sexist, jingoistic, anti-art rhetoric can be clever—but only if the motive behind it is to *entertain*, not to *persuade*.

Right now, the most popular example of American low culture is professional wrestling. The World Wrestling Federation's *Raw Is War* is the most highly rated program on cable television, and Ted Turner's World Championship Wrestling is not far behind. Not surprisingly, the wrestling industry has a close relationship with heavy metal, particularly '80s metal. The most popular personality in the "sport," Steve Austin, has his own compilation of rock anthems titled *Steve Austin's Stone Cold Metal*—it includes two KISS tracks, the Scorpions' "Rock You Like a Hurricane," an old Def Leppard tune, and Austin's theme song "Stone Cold" by Rainbow. The WWF and the WCW both have multiple records that promote wrasslin' through metal (in fact, the WCW has a tag team sanctioned by KISS). Even the low-grade ECW (the industry's "extreme" third tier) has a pretty decent collection of metal acts covering other metal acts (Motorhead performs "Enter Sandman," Bruce Dickinson does a Scorps song, etc.).

The connection between wrestling and metal is pretty obvious: They're both redneck obsessions dripping with wry humor. Pro wrestling particularly appeals to wife-beating trailer park residents, drunk college sophomores, and acerbic cultural pundits; that's pretty much the same audience for Mötley Crüe in 1999. Wrestling is not stupid—it only tries to look that way. And the same can probably be said for Ted Nugent. The danger is that the people who love wrestling (and metal) the most don't want to see the joke. And it's not that they're fools who don't "get it": They get it completely. They just prefer to consume the satire as reality. Self-righteous TV critics used to criticize *All in the Family* because they feared the audience would be confused by Archie Bunker's prejudices. What these critics were too stupid to realize is that people who related to Carroll O'Connor's character knew he was a bigot and they knew he was supposed to be a negative image. *That's why they liked him.*

In the same way, there are people who watch wrestling because it's considered trashy and idiotic. Elitists go to operas they don't understand because it makes them feel separate from the rest of society; blue-collar drunks watch pro wrestling for the exact same reason. Artists like Nugent foster that kind of anti-intellectual perspective. What probably started as a gimmick (at least from the perspective of the record companies) has evolved into a very real, somewhat scary philosophy. People rail against the posturing of metal, but the real problems begin when the posturing ends. That's when an artistic image becomes an actual personality type. That's when people start to see aggressive music as a call to actual aggression, and the enemy becomes anyone who doesn't openly embrace stupidity. And (to paraphrase sports radio host Jim Rome), that's when you hear the six most dangerous words in North America: "You think you're better than me?" Whenever that phrase is uttered in a small-town bar, somebody is going to lose teeth.

Some things are funny because they're true. Ted Nugent would be funnier if I ever got the sense he was lying.

June 27, 1992

The world premiere of Guns N' Roses' "November Rain" video.

By the time MTV turned ten years old in 1991, pretty much every rock video made by a major label artist was pretty sophisticated. Every metal artist was churning out videos (Mötley Crüe made five for *Dr. Feelgood*), and Saturday night's *Headbanger's Ball* was an essential part of MTV's weekly programming. Though a lot of the vids still looked the same, they were higher-grade knockoffs; technology made everything look more expensive and professional. In 1992, Skid Row made a simple black-and-white clip for "Monkey Business" that was just the band rocking in a desolate field (with a monkey), but it was doctored and tweaked enough to get substantial airplay all summer.

However, one band took the potential of video and pushed it to its ultimate extreme—so far, in fact, that it's unlikely any rock group will ever again try anything as ambitious or insane. The band, of course, was Guns N' Roses. The project was the ultra-expensive, ultimately unsuccessful *Use Your Illusion* "video trilogy," and it may have been the decision that turned GNR from the biggest band in the world into . . . well, into what they are now.

What Guns N' Roses tried to do (or, more accurately—what Axl Rose tried to do) was take the three ballads off *Use Your Illusion I* and *II* and become George Lucas. Without fear of hyperbole, it can be said that this was the most ostentatious video concept ever attempted by a major rock artist. The goal was to make three videos that could stand alone (and therefore enter MTV's heavy rotation), but they would also be interconnected in a way that they could be watched in sequence, much like a twenty-two-minute art film. Though I recognize the mild absurdity of this self-indulgence, I also think Guns N' Roses has never been given proper credit for attempting something that was legitimately formidable. In many ways, making three intertwined videos is a much more difficult assignment than making a conventional rock film (like *The Wall* or *Stop Making Sense*). The audience for videos is consciously expecting—almost *demanding*—a collection of eye-catching images not connected by a narrative. People who went into a movie theater to see something like *The Song Remains the Same* knew what they were getting into, and they watched the event as a feature. GNR expected people to follow a crazy, non sequitur story line that was (a) usually incomplete, and (b) dependent on their ability to recall videos they *weren't* watching. In retrospect, it was an almost impossible task.

In theory, here's what the *Use Your Illusion* trilogy was supposed to mean —or at least what I can deduce from watching it a few dozen times (I realize Rose has periodically commented on what all this was *supposed* to teach us, but that doesn't necessarily relate to how it came across on the TV). Regardless of the artistic intent, the plot seemed to work like this: "Don't Cry" was the first video, but is actually the second act of a three-act play (thus, "Don't Cry" contains the story's conflict). "November Rain" was the second video, but it's actually the story's first act (even though it opens with the beginning of the third act and ends with the conclusion of Act II). "Estranged" is the third act and supposedly the conclusion, but it has clips from both Act I and II and really doesn't explain anything at all.

On paper, this obviously makes no sense. On screen, it's only slightly more clear. But this is how a concept video works when you take it to its most logical (illogical?) extreme. This *is* "art," although history has not treated these videos very well.

Released to TV soon after the *Use Your Illusion* records hit stores on September 17, "Don't Cry" opens with a baby who has extremely (in fact, unrealistically) blue eyes, immediately followed by the image of a crow. The next shot is Axl walking through a blizzard, holding a bottle of booze and a gun. The significance of these clips is alluded to later in the production, but never explained. However, we soon get to the important stuff: Axl, looking very pissed off about *something*, gets into a fight with housemate Stephanie Seymour, the Victoria's Secret supermodel who was Rose's real-life lover. Seymour has a gun and Rose violently pushes her against a wall, which is a little disturbing in retrospect, particularly since Seymour would later accuse Rose of abuse (they eventually settled out of court; a 1995 issue of *Parade* magazine indicated that Rose's insurance company agreed to give Seymour a settlement of $400,000, but Rose's lawyers denied any payout).

This is a great example of what was so uncomfortably compelling about Guns N' Roses. Unlike other metal artists, Rose was completely willing to combine his personal life with his public persona: Not only does he use his real girlfriend, he openly addresses his two greatest demons—violence and misogyny. Later in "Don't Cry," we learn the apparent reason for the domestic dispute: Rose has been unfaithful (or at least very friendly) with a blond girl at a piano, causing Stephanie to slap the woman and start a cat fight. Once again, the action is a glimpse into Rose's psyche; he has projected another of his weaknesses (jealousy) onto Seymour, and he's also exposed his personal sexual fantasies in a somewhat negative way (Rose has often admitted that he loves to watch lesbian sex, and the girl-on-girl fight in this video is far more sexy than scary).

Since "Don't Cry" was the first of the three videos (and arguably not even part of a larger trilogy, depending on who you believe), it's a little more autonomous than the other two clips; when it first moved into MTV's rotation, even diehard fans had no idea this was part of a larger project, so "Don't Cry" needed the ability to stand alone. During the chorus, the band is shown performing on the top of a building with a helicopter in the foreground. Axl wears flannel and a Jane's Addiction T-shirt, while Slash wears a sign that asks "Where's Izzy?" For most GNR followers, Slash's sign was the most intriguing part of the clip, because—at the time—Izzy Stradlin was rumored to be quietly quitting the band (Izzy, who cowrote "Don't Cry" but does not appear in the video or any leg of the trilogy, officially quit the group in November of 1991). Shannon Hoon, the lead singer of the band Blind Melon and a key contributor to the *Use Your Illusion* albums, also appears on the rooftop. Hoon would die of an overdose while touring in 1995, thereby destroying the theory that all pop stars become legends if they die early.

At the time of its origin, most people thought "Don't Cry" was an attempt at video surrealism that had no clear purpose. However, there were some overt references to the other videos (even though none of the viewing audiences knew they were supposed to be looking for them). Rose is shown thrashing in water, which connects with the conclusion of "Estranged." One scene has three Axls in the same room simultaneously, obviously suggesting a multiple personality disorder (we also see Rose talking to a female psychiatrist). Another shows a grave marker that indicates W. Axl Rose was born in 1962 and died in 1990. Later videos would never explain the syllogism for the second date.

My favorite part of "Don't Cry" is when Slash consciously drives a car off a cliff, and the car immediately explodes. In the next sequence, Slash plays his solo at the cliff's summit, and then he throws his guitar over the edge. Without getting too obvious, the symbiotic relationship between the car and the instrument tied Slash back to his own *Appetite for Destruction*. However, these scenes have no bearing on the overall work, and they seem to have been included simply because it seemed like a cool idea that someone might misconstrue as symbiotic. The same can be said for the closing shot, where we see the original infant from the video's opening, only now it has incredibly green eyes. It links the beginning of the piece with the conclusion, but it has no significance on anything (unless we are to assume that Axl is implying that he had a twin brother who was separated from him at birth, a concept that is just stupid enough to be possible).

The understanding that this was going to be a trilogy emerged with the next video, the epic "November Rain." When it premiered on *Headbanger's Ball* in the summer of 1992, it was hyped by MTV as the greatest video ever made. Immediately after its virgin broadcast, VJ Riki Rachtman looked directly into the camera and earnestly said, "That [*pause*] . . . was amazing." This was funny for three reasons. It was funny because Rachtman was acting like *he* had just seen the video for the very first time. It was also funny because Rachtman actually had a cameo *in* the video, which seemed like a conflict of interest but was mostly just weird. However, the main reason it was funny was because "November Rain" was a ludicrously overblown mini-movie that absolutely did not work as a music video.

As time has passed, my take on "November Rain" has softened. When I watch it now, it seems like a big, better-than-average attempt at doing something "historical," and in that respect it was successful. Like Michael Jackson's "Thriller," it's the kind of video that's only played during MTV countdowns (the sequence changes slightly every Memorial Day weekend, but "November Rain" typically places fourth or fifth on MTV's list of all-time videos, behind "Smells Like Teen Spirit," "Thriller," Madonna's "Vogue," and Peter Gabriel's "Sledgehammer"). The obvious problem is its length, and videos are hard to edit down (Metallica's "One" faced the same quagmire, and fans were always upset by the edited, less-powerful version of that video).

The director for the three videos was Andy Morahan, an established videographer who earned a living by directing videos for rock superstars (including George Michael's "Father Figure"), commercials for Guess jeans, and that horrible third installment of the *Highlander* film series. While most of Morahan's work with GNR is structured around Dadaistic imagery, "November Rain" is not. "November Rain" follows a traditional (almost cliché) dramatic narrative: It opens with Rose taking pills to cure his insomnia, only to dream about the joy of his wedding and the death of his wife (once again portrayed by Seymour).

The early moments (minutes?) of "November Rain" are in a

concert hall, but the sequence is obviously not from an actual Guns N' Roses tour. They are performing with a symphony, and Rose is at the piano doing his best Elton John impersonation. This setting is supposed to make concrete the Homeric nature of this endeavor, but it was a bad decision; critics who had already begun criticizing GNR for being a bloated '80s dinosaur ripped this video to shreds. There is one especially silly silhouette of Duff McKagan holding his arms in the air in a Jesus Christ pose. "November Rain" is probably the most unpunk video ever made.

Things improve when we are transported to a country church, just in time for the Wedding of the Roses. Stephanie is the hottest bride in rock history, and Slash is the shaggy best man. To be honest, very little happens in this video, especially when you consider it lasts for over nine minutes. One scene seems to suggest a bachelor party, but Seymour is in attendance. Several shots are so common that they could almost be real footage from an actual celebrity wedding (and since Rose and Seymour broke up before they got hitched, this video effectively acts as their faux wedding album). For casual fans, the most memorable scene is probably the extended guitar solo, when Slash stomps outside after the exchange of the rings.

The turning point in "November Rain" is when the wedding reception is interrupted by the kind of downpour that only happens in movies. Everyone runs for cover, and some idiot inexplicably dives into the wedding cake. The music become somber, and suddenly Seymour is dead. The wedding has become a funeral, and it closes with Axl crying at the foot of her grave.

Thus, we are left with the central question of the *Use Your Illusion* video trilogy: "How did Stephanie die?" The intensity of speculation wasn't quite on par with "Who shot J. R.?," but people like me *were* interested. The conventional wisdom was that Axl would be this story's version of Kristin Shepard. There is a brief shot in "November Rain" were Axl is walking the streets alone, and he passes a sign that reads GUNS. The double entendre is rather obvious, but the narrative hint is more important: Perhaps Rose shot his wife (and got away with it). Back in "Don't Cry," Seymour has a scene with a gun in her hand, so maybe she killed herself accidentally during a struggle with Axl. Or did she simply commit suicide? These were the questions that we expected to be explained by the video for "Estranged." All the weirdness in "Don't Cry" and all the melodrama of "November Rain" would suddenly make sense, like the nifty deus ex machina conclusion to *The Purloined Letter.*

This, of course, never happened. We ended up feeling more like Joseph K in Franz Kafka's *The Trial* (or maybe it was more like Keanu Reeves in *The Matrix*). The only thing we learned was that you should never cast your girlfriend in a long-term video project.

Back when this little concept was cooked up, Rose clearly assumed he and Stephanie Seymour were going to be together forever. When their relationship spontaneously combusted soon after "November Rain," the concept was essentially trashed beyond recognition, even though the band would never admit it. This was not like a soap opera, where they could just find a new girl and have a narrator say, "The role of Axl's rock bitch is now being portrayed by Nastasha Henstridge." The charm to this story was that everyone knew Rose and Seymour were a real couple, and she wasn't so much a *character* as she was a *metaphor*, although I don't know what for (maybe that's what the original plan for "Estranged" would have pointed out).

Instead, we were delivered a consciously weird, horrifically expensive video that tries to write around the fact that Seymour was out of the picture. Her absence became the proverbial "elephant in the corner," particularly when Rose (and director Morahan) needed to make unavoidable references back to the first two vids.

"Estranged" begins with the dictionary definition of the track's title, which is too small (and too long) to read on a TV screen. The song itself is pretty good, but the opening seconds are very overwrought; Axl's battered pleas are placed against a police raid of Rose's palatial estate while the singer sleeps in a cubbyhole. At first, we all thought this was going to lead to the arrest of Rose for his wife's murder (and maybe it was, in the original script). Instead, we cut to performance footage from a massive L.A. concert venue. Rose wears a Charles Manson T-shirt, which nicely coincided with his most recent controversy (in the fall of 1993, GNR released the covers album *The Spaghetti Incident?*, which included Rose's unlisted version of the Manson-penned folk song "Look At Your Game, Girl").

There are a few clever notions in "Estranged" (Slash wears a T. Rex shirt, publicly crediting the original top-hat top cat), but it's mostly forced and uneven. Rose again plays the multiple personality card, and water permeates everything (even some of the camera shots have the wavy, distorted look of liquid). Sunset Strip becomes a river filled with computerized dolphins. Slash floats down the Strip like a phantom, performing his guitar solo in front of the Rainbow and the Roxy. No one even notices him; he is now a stranger in his homeland. Guns N' Roses has become so internationally famous that they're no longer welcome in their jungle.

In perhaps the most blatant abuse of stardom ever attempted in a rock video, the turning point of "Estranged" takes place on a rented ocean liner. Axl leaps off the mammoth ship and thrashes in the rough sea. Gilby Clarke tries to rescue him in a rowboat (apparently, Clarke was only added to the GNR lineup to rescue Rose from sea-faring disasters). Clarke fails. Axl is going to die . . . until he is saved by dolphins.

I find it necessary to admit that long before this video was ever conceived I had a substantial prejudice against dolphins. They are my least favorite member of the animal kingdom. Everyone seems to think dolphins are cute and "intelligent," but they're best described as ugly and impractical. I don't want to come across as insensitive, but show me a person whose intelligence equates to that of a dolphin and I will show you a fucking retard. In my opinion, they are the most overrated mammals on the planet. Thus, I hated the conclusion of this video with a passion that I usually reserve for highway patrolmen, inner-city panhandlers, and the WNBA. It was both senseless and annoying, and—quite frankly—pretty unoriginal. The only part that was interesting is the fact that Slash makes his guitar sound a little like the squeaks of a dolphin, a connection no one noticed when we first played *Use Your Illusion II*. Apparently, Rose had the vision for this video years before it was ever made.

"Estranged" concludes with Axl's Converse shoe coming to rest on the ocean floor and Rose sitting *with* a dolphin, grinning into the camera like Norman Bates at the end of *Psycho*. I never understood how this was supposed to be insightful (or cool, or funny, or even interesting). It basically reminded me that Axl Rose only seemed brilliant as long as none of us knew what he was trying to do. As soon as we got the idea, it was just another stupid video.

November 15, 1992

**I get drunk
and go to a hockey game.**

As I write this, I am taking shots of some really horrific Durango tequila. It comes in a plastic bottle, and it costs $7.59 a liter. I am cutting it with Mountain Dew, and I am drinking each shot over my kitchen sink, just in case I vomit. And I realize that I will have to write the rest of this chapter tomorrow, when I'm not fucked up.

I hate the fact that heavy metal is a big part of the reason why I behave like this. And I especially hate the fact that when I'm not drunk, I'll never be able to explain why this is so bad.

Am I blaming Trixter for my stupidity? Am I pointing an accusing finger at Mark Slaughter? Nay (or—more accurately— no). But I am totally wasted, and I'm alone in my apartment, and I'm stupid. And I love it. And hard rock is part of the reason why I love it. And even though I feel great right now, I know I should hate it. And when I try to expand on these thoughts tomorrow, I will not remember why. At best, I will be slightly impressed by how accurately I type when I'm drunk.

(the next day)

Well, it turns out I'm actually a horrible typist when I'm drunk (I just went back and fixed my mistakes in the previous three paragraphs; my main problem seems to be the word "and," which I kept spelling "nad," which I suppose isn't that big of a problem in the scope of the universe). However, I *am* a bit impressed by my drunken logic, if not necessarily by my drunken work ethic.

There's no doubt in my mind that I have a serious drinking problem. And while I would never blame heavy metal for this, it certainly makes it more fun.

Even though I almost never think about it, I should probably hate glam rock for what it does to my body. It's clearly helping me drink myself to death. When I'm all alone, and I've had my eighth or ninth drink, and there are no old buddies or estranged girlfriends to call on the telephone, I inevitably find myself going into my closet and digging through my high school cassettes. This is when I get into the vintage shit: Bon Jovi's *New Jersey*, '90s Tesla, *Animalize*, Drivin' N' Cryin' (who really weren't a metal band at all, but "Fly Me Courageous" fits my personal parameters), live Ozzy, a dubbed copy of Faster Pussycat's *Whipped*, and a bunch of metal-based rap like 2 Live Crew and Tone Loc and Anthrax's "I'm the Man."

This stuff sounds great when I'm getting drunk. I rock out in my apartment. I play air guitar and work on my Paul Stanley shuffle, and I chug bottles of Rolling Rock during guitar solos. Some nights, this is all that I do. I get home from work after a bad day, skip supper (so I can get drunk faster), and start throwing heavy metal tapes into my stereo. I get so fucked up that I can't even masturbate. When I wake up the next morning, there will be empty bottles all over my living room and a bunch of W.A.S.P. tapes piled on my couch. I will have horrific digestive problems, and I will not be able to eat anything except Cocoa Puffs.

Judging from the two hundred words I wrote last night, it appears that I despise this kind of behavior when I'm drunk (or at least I try to make myself think that I do). The strange thing is that I'm totally fine with it now. Isn't this the opposite of how drunks are supposed to act? I always thought alcoholics were people who constantly bemoaned and lamented their binge drinking whenever they were sober, only to break down and deny they have a problem when they start to maniacally pound shots. I've always been the opposite. When I'm straight, it always seems like being drunk would be a logical alternative to anything else I'm doing, even though I'm certain that it's certainly going to destroy me (or at least destroy my life).

In fact, I think I'm going to make myself a drink right now.

(forty-five seconds later)

The synergy between booze and hair metal is as exquisite as that of the brandy and ginger ale currently glimmering in front of me. Heavy metal is a drinker's medium and a drunkard's realm. Bruce Kulick's whining guitar sounds more palatable when your skull has been dulled by booze, kind of like the way Novocain helps distance the sound of a dentist's drill. Hard rock also speeds up the inebriation process—those dopey singalong choruses are the musical equivalent of a dozen frat boys standing on the bar and chanting "Go! Go! Go! Go!"

"When you were in Mötley Crüe, you were expected to be drunk all the time," says Crüe drummer Tommy Lee. "People would come backstage after a show, and if there wasn't a beer in your hand, they'd be disappointed." Public metalheads face a similar scenario. When you start associating yourself with the rock 'n' roll lifestyle, there is a social obligation to start drinking at 4:20 P.M.

When I was a sophomore at the University of North Dakota, I wrote a sports column for the college newspaper, but it really wasn't about sports, even though I constantly referred to Mookie Blaylock (and I mean the man, not the band). My column was really about everything else—particularly what I espoused to be the best way to live. In a general sense, this meant being drunk all the time. In a specific sense, it meant *me* being drunk all the time, especially if I was in public. When I started this gimmick (and that's exactly what it was to begin with), I didn't drink that much more than most male college students. But then I stumbled (figuratively and literally) into an incredibly effective persona.

It was a Friday, which was the same day my little sports column was always published. In this particular column, I discussed (and mildly criticized) a member of UND's basketball team for getting a DUI. If I recall, the hook to the column was that I was a fucked-up alcoholic and that it would be hypocritical of me to pass judgment on an athlete for practicing the same behavior, which was precisely what I was doing anyway, and that was somehow the joke. Or something.

ANYWAY, early that same afternoon, my friend Chad Hansen called and told me to meander over to his place so we could have a beer before he went to visit his girlfriend. This girlfriend lived five hours away in western North Dakota, and since Chad had no car he had to catch a ride from some other dude driving in the same general direction (who, if I recall correctly, was a guy named Chad Love, who I still think had a remarkably cool name for a white guy). Sadly, Chad Hansen lived in a fraternity house. Fraternities were no place for a hard-rockin', nonconformist, edgy young journalist like myself; frats were filled with rich kids who wore sweaters around their hips and listened to Steve Miller and chanted "Go! Go! Go! Go!" But I liked Chad and I liked free beer, so I went over. I always went over.

The subsequent plot of this anecdote is obviously not unique to anyone who's lived a slacker past: Chad #2 is supposed to pick up Chad #1 at 3:00 P.M., but Chad #2 doesn't arrive until 6:30 P.M., thereby forcing me and Chad #1 to drink an entire case of Busch Light. So now it's dark and cold and I'm walking back to my dormitory and I haven't eaten supper and I'm a fucking disaster, and I still somehow convince my friends to carry me to that night's UND hockey game. But as they haul me into the packed Englestad Sports Arena, a strange metamorphosis occurs: I instantly become legitimate. Everyone in the building sees "that guy from the newspaper" who *claims* to be a drunk, and it turns out he really *is* a drunk, and he's dancing like Axl to the national anthem. I realize that intoxicated people always make the mistake of thinking they're the coolest person in the house, but this time I was actually right. And this would set a very dangerous precedent.

For the next two and a half years, I felt as though I had to be drunk (or at least drinking) whenever I was out in public. I came to the conclusion that this was what people wanted from me, and—quite honestly—I'm pretty sure my perception was accurate. I became my own personal publicist and I created my own little public identity, and it quickly became reality. It's the same thing that happened to Tommy Lee (only he took it a million steps further). Being a predictable public booze hound is really just another example of constructed glamour: A band like Mötley Crüe told me what being a superstar drunk exemplified, and then I persuaded myself to embody it. Drinking became a job.

Speaking of my beloved Crüe (and about getting drunk), I recently watched VH1's *Behind the Music: Mötley Crüe* for about the eighth time. As a historical document, it's not all that insightful; the only thing I really learned was the reason they put umlauts over the *o* and *u* in their logo was because they were drinking Löwenbräu when they came up with the name. I also learned that Razzle Dingley, the drummer of Hanoi Rocks who died in Vince Neil's '84 car wreck, may have been from Finland (previous sources had always indicated Hanoi Rocks was a Norwegian metal band). Most importantly, I was reminded that hard-rock guys always refer to cocaine as "Krell" (according to David Lee Roth, "Krell" was the name of an extinct race of aliens from a 1956 movie called *Forbidden Planet*; Dave never explained the logic behind this slang, but he swears he fought some killer "Krell Wars" with Ozzy Osbourne when Van Halen opened Black Sabbath's '78 tour).

Behind the Music is an especially delicious train wreck for old metal fans. It completely plays into the unhealthy voyeurism that former rock kids like me can't deny. All the episodes are structured exactly the same: An artist (1) starts with nothing but a dream, (2) rises to multiplatinum success, (3) succumbs to the drugs and booze and sex that come with that success, (4) crashes into bankruptcy, and (5) rises from the ashes. In Mötley Crüe's case, this happened three separate times.

Part of this comes off as pathetic. Rob Zombie told me he

despises *Behind the Music* and thinks it should be called VH1's *Stupid Idiots Who Lost All Their Money.* Zombie feels the reason people like these stories is because of social perversity: We enjoy watching heroes fail. "I can't understand why people think that's cool," Zombie said. "Sometimes I think people want musicians to be stupid so they can laugh at them when they hit rock bottom. They want to be able to tell their friends they saw some loser from Guns N' Roses explain how he went broke."

I don't doubt that there's some truth in that. *Behind the Music* certainly promotes the idea that musicians are stupid people who can't handle prosperity. However, these melodramatic rise-and-fall stories have a special meaning for people who used to have a very real "relationship" with these spandex-clad angels.

For example, take the aforementioned Vince Neil auto wreck. The year 1984 probably marked the height of my Mötley Crüe obsession. It was winter, and I was listening to *Shout at the Devil* every day (and I mean every day). My metal friends and I often discussed the upcoming Crüe record that was scheduled to hit stores later the following summer. We knew the word "pain" was part of the record's title, and—at least according to Nikki Sixx's interviews—it was going to be exactly what we wanted, regardless of what that might be (it was going to be "heavier," "bluesier," "harder," and it was going to have a bunch of hit singles while still being "less commercial").

Since we didn't have MTV and nobody listened to the radio, the North Dakota metal community found out about Vince's car wreck through the local newspaper. Mötley Crüe was just big enough to warrant an AP story whenever one of its members killed somebody, and I remember being mildly excited when I saw a nine-inch article about an accident involving Vince Neil Wharton, the lead singer from the "rock 'n'roll band Mötley Crüe." To me, that line was the most offensive part of the entire article— Mötley Crüe was *not* a "rock 'n' roll band." Bruce fucking Springsteen was in a "rock 'n' roll band." Mötley was a *heavy metal* band. I immediately questioned the reporter's credibility.

At the time, this event did not seem like a tragedy. Before the death of Razzle, I had never even heard of Hanoi Rocks. Hardly anyone had; I'm sure the untimely death of their drummer was the greatest thing that ever happened to their commercial viability. My main concern was that Vince was okay—that is to say, okay enough to finish the new record.

Not only had Neil killed his co-pilot, he had also rammed into another car, badly injuring its two passengers (one of them was a woman who suffered permanent brain damage). As an adult, I now realize that normal people go to prison for this sort of thing. But that never crossed my mind as a twelve-year-old. I was somehow naive and jaded at the same time: Part of me didn't think *anyone* could go to jail for an *accident* (that was the naive part), and part of me already knew that famous people never go to jail for *anything* (that was the jaded part).

There was another kid in my high school named Eric; he was three years older than me and the vortex of the burgeoning Wyndmere metal scene. Eric had long hair and took guitar lessons (he could play "Smoke on the Water"!), and even though he was an honor student and a fundamentally good person, all the local parents hated him (especially mine). Today, Eric is a doctor, but in 1984 he aspired to be as sinister as most adults assumed he was: On a fateful autumn night in 1985, he and two other ruffians vandalized an abandoned schoolhouse with an axe (a crime that remains "unsolved"). This was about the same time Eric took to calling himself "Nikki."

ANYWAY, I stayed over at Eric's (Nikki's?) house one night, and I remember that he had the Neil newspaper article taped to his wall. It would be easy to look back and suggest that he did this to "glorify" the act, but that was not the case. It was because this story validated the existence of Mötley Crüe. One of "our" people was making news in "their" world. This is a very common paradigm held in small towns. If somebody who grew up in your community wins a Nobel Prize, you cut out the newspaper story and put it on the bulletin board; if someone from your town grows up and becomes America's most depraved serial rapist, you cut out the newspaper story and put it on the bulletin board. It's just nice to see someone doing *anything*.

I can completely remember discussing Vince's accident that night; we were listening to Twisted Sister's *Stay Hungry* and had finished playing with Eric's Intellivision. The reason I remember it so vividly is because Eric was drinking a beer. This was a new experience for me. I wasn't even drinking—I was just *hanging out* with somebody who was. We were in the basement (Eric essentially lived in the basement), and he nonchalantly took an Old Milwaukee from the fridge and replaced it with a warm can from the storage closet. He asked me if I wanted one, and I said "no." I'm not sure if Eric was showing off or trying to coerce me into drinking, but I really doubt it was either. He was not prone to such behavior (especially since we were the only people in the room).

In retrospect, this does not seem dangerous (or even very rebellious). But I'm stunned by the unknowing hypocrisy of my adolescent mind. I was unwilling to drink a beer, and I was mildly disturbed by the fact that my friend was, but I saw nothing wrong whatsoever about Vince Neil getting wasted and destroying a total stranger's brain. Here again, the separation between my reality and the world of my idols is staggering. I obviously felt no human kinship to Vince Neil at all. His lifestyle and his music were equally unreal. I did not see his drinking as good or bad; I simply saw his drinking as *his*.

But that would not always be the case.

As I look back at my career as an alcoholic, I can usually break it down in one of two ways: by booze, or by the band that came with it. For the purposes of this discussion, I will do both. I began drinking earnestly during the second semester of my freshman year at college (roughly one year before the aforementioned hockey fiasco). This is what I normally classify as my "early whiskey period," but it can also be referred to as the "Crüe months." At the time, Mötley Crüe was still my favorite band, and since this was an introductory period to alcoholism, I used Nikki Sixx as a reference point. Nikki (along with Van Halen bassist Michael Anthony) was an adamant supporter of Jack Daniel's whiskey, so that's what I liked to drink. And when I say "drinking," I basically mean sitting in my dorm room with three other guys, watching movies, and getting loaded. Like most new drinkers, I was still struggling with beer consumption. Beer is like coffee; you have to force yourself to drink it for months before you actually think it tastes good, and then you want to drink it all the time. At this juncture, whiskey made more sense, because we'd mix it with Coke, and then it would taste like really bad Coke. One bottle of Southern Comfort could get four of us drunk (the reason we replaced Jack with SoCo was because we were always broke, and—when you get right down to it—what the fuck did we know about whiskey? In fact, I still don't understand people who know a lot about alcohol. I'm sure I'll never remember the difference between "whiskey" and "bourbon," even though I'm more than willing to pour both down my gullet).

The summer after my freshman year (this is 1991), I lived with my goofball sidekick Mike Schauer. At the time, Mike was obsessed with Warrant, so I pretended to hate them. My main argument was that they had too many guys in the band; I was a big supporter of four-member groups, while Mike favored five-man ensembles (our other major argument was over whose Nintendo baseball team was more "popular" with the simulated Nintendo fans). Nonetheless, we still listened to a lot of *Cherry Pie* over those three months (as well as ample doses of Skid Row's *Slave to the Grind*), and that seemed to foster the consumption of Coors and Budweiser. Warrant was more of a populist party band, and their music was not founded on being wasted every moment of the day. In fact, Warrant even appealed to the three girls who lived next door to us, so we actually dabbled in "social drinking," a concept Mike and I had never before understood. We still weren't very good at it—one of us usually puked (usually Mike, who was always prone to puking)—but it was still a different kind of booze-soaked insanity. Beer was much more user-friendly. I'm sure if Warrant had kept putting out decent records, I'd own one of those home-brewing kits.

Fall of 1991 was when we all "discovered" Nirvana and Pearl

Jam, and that prompted the Vodka Age. Beer suddenly seemed antiquated; frat boys and football players drank Budweiser. Of course, *we* drank Budweiser too—but only when we listened to Guns N' Roses. All those L.A. metal bands loved Bud, even after they got rich. It was another example of six-string patriotism: Heavy metal was the most American of musical genres. After a hard night of bloated commercialism and meaningless sex, Budweiser helped you unwind like a man, even though it's made from rice.

That spring, my friends and I started aggressively going to keg parties; this became the driving force in all our lives. All week long, campus conversations focused on where the parties were going to be that weekend. Friday night, you drank in your dorm room until it got dark (7:20 in the winter, 9:05 in the summer), and then you hit as many parties as you could. If keg cups cost $3 at the door, you viewed it as a wonderful bargain; if they were $4, you had to drink as much as possible to break even; if they were $5, you went somewhere else. Of course, if you were a girl, cups were always free, but you were halfway expected to eventually put out.

Here's how the process works at a normal keg party: As you drink yourself into a zombie, you walk around and ask everyone where they are going to party tomorrow night. Saturday night, you see these same people and ask them if they had a good time the night before. These are your "keg party friends." You know nothing about them and you have never spoken to them sober, and that is perfectly fine. If you see these people during daylight hours, you will exchange a knowing glance that recognizes your relationship but does nothing to deepen the bond (and if you *do* talk, it will only be to figure out who is having a party). There are dozens of people I shared every weekend with for over a year, and I couldn't guess where 95 percent of them live today. However, I will never forget the street location of every good party house in Grand Forks (the top five were as follows: Sixteenth and Fifth, 123 Walnut, 2100 University Avenue, the kickass studio apartment across from the Ski & Bike Shop, and the loft above

Popolino's Pizza on Gateway Avenue). I can honestly say it was the happiest period of my entire life.

Unfortunately, this is also the hardest period to categorize musically. People who throw keg parties tend to play really shitty music. Sometimes they would just turn on MTV and jack the volume up, so I remember hearing Ace of Base constantly. I was also tight with a balding high school track legend named Shane who lived in a house commonly known as the Mule Barn, and his parties were dominated by solo Ozzy (*No More Tears, No Rest for the Wicked,* all that Zakk Wylde shit). Osbourne was a good role model for these gatherings, because the primary objective was to appear pathetically and psychotically drunk in front of as many people as possible. If you were going to throw back twenty-two glasses of warm beer and totally freak out and instigate a fight and start crying and punch through a TV screen, it was absolutely essential to do so with at least forty strangers in the house. Granted, this kind of behavior wasn't very "glam" (it's hard to look glamorous when three of your friends are trying to incapacitate you before the cops come), but it was very "metal." It was wildly popular to play the "Jekyll and Hyde" card: You acted affable and happy and quiet whenever you were straight, and then you became a depressed, suicidal wild man after a dozen drinks. Lots of folks in my social circle were obsessed with behaving this way on a weekly basis; I guess we all thought this course of action would make people think we were "dark" and "misunderstood," and somehow this would get us laid. Ozzy claims he did this every day for about fifteen years. Maybe it worked for him.

By the time I was a junior, I was more "media savvy," which basically meant I now consciously made lifestyle choices that were dictated by famous people. I really got into the whole Guns N' Roses mystique, particularly Slash, and particularly trying to act like Slash at parties. This sparked my "late whiskey period," only this time I really *was* drinking Jack Daniel's, because now I was getting Pell grants. I swore that Jack Daniel's was all I would drink for a year, and for a while that's exactly what I did. I usually drank two 750 milliliter bottles every week (when I cleaned out my dorm room at the end of that academic year, I found empty JD bottles hidden absolutely everywhere—including four *in my sock drawer*). By now, I was pretty well established as a local writer (I was my university's contrived version of the "wacky controversial columnist"), and I tried to foster the same reputation that Slash seemed to display: "He's talented and popular—but will he live to be thirty?" That's *exactly* what I wanted people to say about me. And I'm pretty sure some of them did (although not as many as I'd like to pretend). I would drink Jack Daniel's until I was dazed and incoherent, and then I'd sit in the corner and watch people at the party whisper about who I was. Even when I was too drunk to walk, I could always tell which people recognized me from the picture that ran with my newspaper column. I loved that pathetic admiration; I loved being wasted in public; I loved the strange credibility that comes with being the most self-cancerous superstar in any given social situation. I could not dance with Mr. Brownstone, but I would swallow anything you poured in front of me.

After a while, I got bored with this shtick (or maybe I ran out of money—I honestly can't remember). Me and my little posse spent the next few months hanging out in a dorm room occupied by Mr. Pancake (who was a biology major with no relationship to Mr. Brownstone), and we'd watch the Canadian teen drama *Fifteen* while drinking Busch Light pounders (which truth be told was always the most universal staple in all our drinking diets). Our musical leanings were becoming more "collegiate" (at least temporarily), so it didn't seem like it mattered what we were drinking. I'm sure the guys in Pavement drank beer, but they didn't exactly make a point of talking about it. We saw lots of pictures where Eddie Vedder looked drunk (there's one especially memorable MTV interview where he's holding his head and surrounded by empty bottles), but it wasn't part of his message. It did not seem like Pearl Jam drank to have fun; they drank because they were sexually abused (or they were worried about people who were, or something like that).

Of course, this didn't stop us from drinking, but it did erode our supposed motivations for doing so. Now we drank because that's what we did.

Now I'm twenty-eight, so I drink in actual bars. The only bars I like are neighborhood dives where no one else goes, and these types of places don't play hair metal. They usually play Dean Martin or the Carpenters, which is usually what I want to hear anyway. Today, I mostly drink brandy and ginger ale, a concoction that has come to be known as the Witty Chuck. The Witty Chuck (and you can actually order this by name at Duffy's Tavern in Fargo and the Double Olive in Akron) is a wonderful drink for three reasons, which is ironic, because it only has two ingredients. The reasons are as follows: (1) it tastes good, (2) it has some kick, and most importantly, (3) it makes you witty. I'm serious— *it makes you witty*. Most people become stupid and belligerent when they get drunk, but not people who drink the Witty Chuck. After three elixirs, they turn into Dorothy Parker. You'll find yourself winging zingers at everyone in the bar, and they will all have to admit that you are the wittiest person alive. People will love you, and some of them will insist on buying you waffles at Denny's. Trust me on this one.

Of course, as I already mentioned, I do occasionally get wasted in my living room to get "back to my roots," which is '80s metal and whatever alcohol I can find in my kitchen. "Drinking is my profession. Drums are just a hobby," Dokken percussionist Mick Brown said in 1985, and some nights I can see where he's coming from. "I have to admit that I'm a pretty bad influence on a lot of people. The girls who hang around me will take a couple of days off from their jobs, and then find out they've been fired when they return to work. And they get really torn up. I just go, 'Listen, if you can't handle it, then don't hang around me. I don't want to ruin your life just for having a good time.' I'm a party professional. I stay in on New Year's Eve because all the amateurs are out."

This kind of behavior was clearly not too responsible of Mick (and it probably cost him a few girlfriends), just as it's probably not too sensible for me to get loaded while I listen to *Tooth and Nail* all by myself. But I can't deny my heart: I like to drink, and I like to rock. You think I'm an idiot? Fine. You don't have to come over.

January 27, 1997

A reunited (and substantially grizzled)
Mötley Crüe perform "Shout at the Devil '97"
at the American Music Awards.

The release (and subsequent success) of Bush's *Sixteen Stone* in 1994 represented the first crack in Seattle's grunge empire, unquestionably the most important musical force since punk. Though the album itself was generally quite good—"Machine-head" was one of the most metal-esque tunes of that year—*Sixteen Stone* set a dangerous precedent: If a bunch of handsome art students from Britain could go hyper-platinum as a post-Cobain clone, the state of Sasquatch rock was at maximum saturation. The formula had been set in concrete; parody was soon on the horizon. Bush was a good band who just happened to signal the beginning of the end; ultimately, they would became the grunge Warrant.

Seemingly seconds after grunge began to falter, the possibility of a "metal revival" started to surface on the lips of all those rock pundits who exist solely to start musical revivals they'll eventually bemoan. At first, it was total kitsch; the only bands who talked about '80s hard rock in interviews were joke bands who realized that mentioning Winger made reporters giggle. It evolved into rediscovery; fifth-graders found their parents' Def Leppard and Metallica cassettes the same way I found my brother's CCR 8-tracks. Suddenly, *Appetite for Destruction* and *5150* were classic rock. By 1996, ironic pop stars were still mentioning glam rockers in interviews, but now it was harder to tell if they were joking. Dave Grohl would claim that Dio-era Sabbath was awesome (he has a particular appreciation for "The Mob Rules"), and everyone would smirk—but then the Foo Fighters would release a song that sounded like Ozzy solo material (if you don't believe me, listen to their contribution on that ridiculous X-*Files* soundtrack).

Pretty soon, you couldn't swing a dead cat without hitting somebody who was blathering on about the "new metal" movement. The most obvious example came with the advent of Ozzfest, an economic juggernaut that proved to be the most successful tour of 1997 (pound for pound and dollar for dollar, it squashed the media-exulted Lilith Fair festival). The first Ozzfest tour had a couple of major draws: It featured Marilyn Manson at the peak of his Q rating, and it delivered a reunion of the original Black Sabbath lineup (sort of . . . actually, drummer Bill Ward was too "exhausted" to perform, so they recruited that ponytail guy from Faith No More and they only played about four songs per night, but then again, how much can you really expect from three fifty-year-old Brits who spent half their life eating acid and pretending to worship the devil?).

Still, Ozzfest wasn't the same (at least not to me). To an '80s metal kid, Ozzfest didn't seem like heavy metal. Oh, these bands were certainly heavy, but they weren't any more fun than the morose alt rockers who sang about how they were creeps and losers who hailed from Olympia (where everyone evidently fucks the same). Bands like Coal Chamber, Powerman 5000, and Fear Factory aspire to be Gen X versions of Black Sab, but they fail miserably; they mostly seem like Soundgarden, but without the brains or the melody. Poison may have been a dumb, loud pop band, but that's light-years better than being a dumb, loud grunge band. On both the 1997 and '98 Ozzfest bills, there was a definite *type* of fledgling hard rock act—they all wanted to somehow combine the sonic sludge of late '80s metal with the dour disaffection of early '90s industrial AmRep rock. It consciously offered the worst of both worlds.

Slightly more promising—and the operative word here is *slightly*—are the hip-hop–obsessed metal groups that merge funk rock guitars with desperate rap vocals. Packs of these mongrel groups popped up everywhere in late '98, and the lead dingo was Korn. The lovable jackasses in Korn absolutely fascinate me: They are the first band that I can honestly say I don't "get." I understand why they're popular, and I've seen them live twice (and enjoyed them once). But Korn was the band that made me realize I was no longer a target market for hard-rock bands.

Most rock groups dream of being bigger than the Beatles. Korn does not share that dream. In fact, they don't even think about the Beatles. At all. Ever.

"I've never owned a Beatles record. I've never even listened to one," insists Fieldy, the mono-named Korn bassist. "The Rolling Stones, Led Zeppelin—those bands haven't influenced us in any way. Nobody in the band ever listened to that stuff. Our musical history starts with the Red Hot Chili Peppers and early Faith No More. As a band, that's where we begin."

For rock purists (or even for anyone who casually enjoys FM radio), that kind of inflammatory statement is enough to qualify Korn as a heretical joke. They have an unabashed disrespect for the history of rock, and the band appeals to an audience almost entirely composed of aggressive, confused males. Yet there is something that can be said about Korn that can't honestly be applied to almost every other rock group that has ever existed: Korn is legitimately new. The band leads a wholly original pop generation; for perhaps the first time, rock music has completely disconnected itself from its roots. As of late, Korn vocalist Jonathan Davis has taken to mentioning how buying *Shout at the Devil* changed his life (and for many of the same reasons it changed mine), but it's impossible to hear any of Vince Neil's influence on Davis's singing style. Korn is neither an extension of—nor a reaction to—classic rock; the band does not support or mock tradition. Quite frankly, Korn has no relationship whatsoever to the people who invented their art form.

It's almost as if Korn embodies everything old people hate

about kids. They fuse the three most obnoxious elements of modern music: the down-tuned throb of metal, the mind-numbing rhythm of rap, and the inaudible howl of hard-core thrash. The goofballs in Korn wear baggy pants and stupid retro sneakers, but they're obsessed with new technology and hold a perverse adoration for consumerism. In fact, when I talked to Fieldy in autumn of 1998, he actually conducted the interview on a cell phone from a shopping mall in Irvine, California.

"I think like a fourteen-year-old. Our whole band thinks like fourteen-year-olds," he said, without one milligram of irony. "You have to."

In 1987, Korn would have probably been classified as a straight-up rap band (probably as an unfunny version of the Beastie Boys). Davis doesn't really sing (in fact, half the time he seems to be whispering), and there are no guitar solos or signs of musicianship. Korn's main pupils, the Jacksonville-based band Limp Bizkit, are even more connected to hip-hop and have managed to become just as popular; Bizkit vocalist Fred Durst admits he'd actually prefer to be a straightforward hip-hop group, but it's impossible for white guys with metal overtones to get credibility in a predominantly black industry.⊗ The band 311 is kind of in the same boat, only with more Chili Pepper funkiness, more pot, less street cred, stupider lyrics, and a preppy "boy band" cuteness that rivals N' Sync.

It should be noted that all these acts are fiercely unwilling to adopt the label of "heavy metal." They are a hybrid of hard rock and rap, but they only choose to recognize the latter. When Korn created and headlined their highly successful "Family Values" tour, the second biggest act on the bill was Ice Cube. Consequently, a group like Korn truly does represent its audience; the current teen populace sees "glam metal" as an archaic load of shit

⊗Limp Bizkit also received much of the blame for the riots at the Woodstock '99 rock festival, prompting MTV's Chris Connelly to scoff at the "inexplicable anger" from the Bizkit's "white, upper-class audience." I guess this aggression was "inexplicable" because white rich people are always unspeakably happy about being white and rich.

that belongs to a wholly different generation of imbeciles, but they like the look and lexicon of hip-hop. The only obvious influence they take from the metal era is the emphasis on fashion—and that applies to both clothing and lifestyle. Korn is very conscious about how they appear, and their audience pays attention.

"I remember the first time we toured as headliners, and I looked out the window of the bus. Every kid was wearing Adidas," Fieldy said. "It was an entire crowd of kids who dressed the way we do. We called Adidas and told them they owed us money. I mean, we probably helped them sell an extra million pairs of shoes, because every real Korn fan wears Adidas. It's fucking unfair. They should have at least given us fifty thousand dollars."

Much to the surprise of absolutely no one, Adidas did not respond to Korn's financial request. Despite the free advertising, the familiar three-striped shoe company probably doesn't appreciate Korn, especially since the band likes to suggest that *Adidas* is an acronym for "All Day I Dream About Sex." But this is typical behavior for a group that loves the bad-boy albatross hanging from their necks. Korn members always project themselves as a potential train wreck; their nasty reputation was further solidified when a rash of schools banned students from wearing Korn T-shirts in class. Davis mentions his drinking problem in virtually every interview he gives (every song on their '99 album *Issues* was about his alcoholism, just as Alice in Chain's record *Dirt* had only been about Layne Staley's heroin problem), and all five Kornsters are constantly declaring their love for Coors beer.

"We're all alcoholics, but we don't care. I don't get too sensitive about it," Fieldy said. "I get drunk every day. It has nothing to do with being in this band either, because we were all alcoholics before we ever started Korn. It's not a big deal for any of us, except for maybe Jonathan, but that's just because he's really sensitive about everything. I always do my job. I always get up in the morning. If drinking ever becomes a problem, I'll just quit."

The crazy thing about Fieldy's quotes is that he's being serious. He probably does think Adidas owes him money, and he probably does think that you can drink every day until you suddenly feel like quitting. These wishes will become reality at about the same time Korn learns how to spell. But my favorite part of his insight was the cagey understanding of his fan base: "Every real Korn fan wears Adidas." That's the kind of brand loyalty that only metal and punk fosters. In the mid-1980s, girls dressed like Madonna, but Madonna never demanded them to do so. She never said, "Every real Madonna fan wears fishnets and wedding veils." But metal bands have done this kind of thing since the dawn of guitar rock. Korn is simply a little more open about it.

Rage Against the Machine shared several aesthetic elements with Korn, but they also offered some major differences. Rage was equally obsessed with rap stylings and unconventional song-writing (there are no real melodies to be found on their albums), but they *were* highly musical. Guitarist Tom Morello is an expert at making weird noises with his axe; in fact, he's so good at it, Rage always makes a big deal about stating that all the sounds on their records were "made by guitar, bass, drums, and vocals" (they even include a little warning on the jacket of their CD). In the 1980s, Vinnie Vincent used to do the same thing, and so did Queen in the 1970s. Regardless of all the espoused explanations for why this is important, the bottom line was the same for all three: Musicians are silly, vain people, and synthesizers make creating rock music seem too easy.

Nonetheless, Rage Against the Machine was one of the better bands to emerge over the past decade, even though it's kind of hard to discuss them without laughing. For almost a decade, they were the most stupidly serious band on the planet. Rage's first album was released in 1992, and the record's principal topic was the perceived innocence of Indian activist Leonard Peltier. Prior to getting this CD, I generally believed that Peltier was wrongly imprisoned, but now I'm not so sure; I always assume Rage vocalist Zack de la Rocha only supports guilty people. I'm skeptical of pretty much everything he advocates, even when he's right. It was a full four years before the Machine released a second album, probably because it took a while for de la Rocha to find new things to be pissed about. On 1996's *Evil Empire*, the subject matter shifted to the Zapatista Liberation Movement and Mumia Abu-Jamal's unjust death sentence for the murder of a cop. Actually, one would think that Rage would have supported Abu-Jamal even if he *were* guilty, since they seem to think most cops deserve to get shot.

If there was ever an illustration of how remarkably impressionable teenagers can be, it is the success of Rage Against the Machine. I cannot fathom fourteen-year-olds jumping around their bedroom and screaming about "profits for the bourgeois," but it obviously must happen. Without much radio support, Rage became a commercial heavyweight, and it's to Rocha's credit that he's made it cool to be informed about current events. Of course, I'm not sure how kids are necessarily supposed to apply these issues—when de la Rocha sings, "Fuck you, I won't do what ya tell me," I doubt if too many eighth-graders consider the plight of Mexican freedom fighters. They probably just refuse to do their geometry proofs for math class.

But here's the rub: A few of them probably *do* think about Zapata. They care, and they love it. And that's really who Rocha seems to be singing for. You can get loaded and mosh to "Guerrilla Radio," but that's like using cooking sherry to get smashed. Ultimately, I don't see even a glimmer of '80s metal in Rage Against the Machine. They're really a louder version of *War*-era U2, except Rage had the sense to quit while they were ahead.❀

I guess what I'm saying is that all the predictable suspects are innocent. Rage Against the Korn Chamber 5000 can't carry glam rock into the twenty-first century. But who can? It's a perplexing problem. There are only a handful of candidates who seem willing to try, and most are failing miserably. But there are a select few who seem to understand what Axl was yowling about.

The best of these bands is undoubtedly the Donnas, a band

❀We hope.

that's so awesome it makes me want to smoke angel dust and kill somebody. The Donnas are four teenage[*] California girls who sing songs like "Leather On Leather" and "Wanna Get Some Stuff." Their second album, *American Teenage Rock N Roll Machine*, was the only legitimately *great* record released in 1998. Since all the semifoxy mommas in the band have renamed themselves "Donna," a lot of people think they're the new all-girl Ramones (and they do have one song that's totally a Ramones rip-off called "Gimme My Radio," not to mention an entire first album that sounds like it was recorded in a bomb shelter). However, *American Teenage Rock N Roll Machine* is absolutely glam metal. "You Make Me Hot" shamelessly steals two guitar riffs from Mick Mars—the bridge replicates the riff from "Too Fast for Love" (which they eventually covered for real on 1998's *Get Skintight*), and the final seconds duplicate the conclusion of "Public Enemy # 1." Guitarist Donna R. is an avowed Ace Frehley disciple (she plays "Strutter" in the studio the way Ace played it on *Alive!*), but she mostly seems taken by the way Ace *looks* when he plays guitar—the whole swaying, drugged-out, "I cradle my axe like a newborn baby" routine. It should also be noted that vocalist Donna A. strongly resembles Sebastian Bach, except not quite as feminine.

From what I can tell, the only band who might rock harder than the Donnas is Nashville Pussy. Their debut album (*Let Them Eat Pussy*) is pretty horrible, but the accompanying stage show is super-awesome delicious. The singer is an ugly redneck who used to front an even crappier band called Nine Pound Hammer; the guitarist is his wife, a long-haired freak with breasts that are always trying to escape to freedom. The bassist used to be a sexy 'n' scary (mostly scary) six-foot-four model who's the sister of NBA journeyman Cherokee Parks. She liked to blow fire.

The Pussy's style is a synthesis of Lynyrd Skynyrd and Motorhead, but the posturing is *total* glam rock—it's beyond the point

---

[*]Of course, they'll all be twenty-one by the time this book comes out, which might mean they're already irrelevant.

of parody. When I saw them open for Marilyn Manson, they rocked my pants off in an almost literal sense; I suspect Manson likes them because the show is unabashed performance art, kind of like a poor man's (poor lesbian's?) version of White Zombie. White Zombie no longer exists, but mastermind Rob Zombie continues to churn out music in exactly the same vein (1998's *Hellbilly Deluxe* could have been released as the studio follow-up to 1995's excellent *Astro Creep: 2000* and no one would have raised an eyebrow). Particularly when witnessed live, Zombie seems exactly like an old metal act—sort of like W.A.S.P., except with slightly better music. The only problem is that Zombie is a little *too* smart; his theatrics are so consciously stupid that they're cartoons, and he does them with a self-referential understanding that not even KISS possessed (and this is both good and bad). I think the highest compliment you can give to Rob Zombie is that he leads the only industrial art rock band that doesn't suck. But to most people's ears, the result is a contemporary type of heavy metal that fully accepts its 1980s roots.

Philosophically, Kid Rock is another glam disciple. Hailing from Detroit Rock City (or at least a Detroit Rock Suburb), the Kid (who files his taxes under the name of Bob Richie) used to party with the Insane Clown Posse, a pair of (ahem) "wigger" joke rappers who refer to their fans as Juggalos and once claimed that KISS "stole our shit." ICP is totally hilarious, but they're hardly influenced by heavy metal; they mostly appeal to the preteens who are even too dumb for Limp Bizkit. ICP does not play anything that can be classified as "music." Kid Rock, on the other hand, bangs for real. On 1998's *Devil Without a Cause*, he sounds a little like the early Beastie Boys, except Kid is not being sardonic. His "message" is about the social importance of strippers, methadone addicts, alcoholics, and "all the questions without any answers" (perhaps he's referring to the sound of one hand clapping). In an earlier chapter, I compared Led Zep to Babe Ruth and Metallica to Hank Aaron; that being the case, I suppose Kid is Bill Veeck— his whole show is nothing but attitude, gimmicks, and midgets. My favorite Kid Rockism comes from "I Am the Bullgod," where

Kid admits he can't even mow the lawn without smoking dope behind the garage. Now *that*'s rock 'n' roll. Kid has all the standard metal obsessions (comparing himself to a cowboy, gawking at lesbians, wearing fur coats, using "fuck" as a verbalized pause, etc.). His video for "Only God Knows Why" is almost a shot-for-shot replica of Mötley's "Home Sweet Home." And it's more than his lyrics or imagery: *Devil* unleashes some heavy guitar action, and instead of merely stealing samples, there are a few semioriginal creations. Kid Rock's white trash sensibility makes him seem drug-addled and a little ridiculous, but I love the fact that he's so earnest about this shit.

Speaking of earnest: With his bald dome and propensity for wearing his heart on his sleeve, Billy Corgan could be perceived as the Charlie Brown of modern rock. However, the now-defunct Smashing Pumpkins were also a remarkably heavy rock act, and the only person who seems willing to accept that reality is Corgan himself (a Van Halen superfan who hangs out with Tony Iommi and is only half-joking when he compares his music to Judas Priest and Mountain).

The person I most often compare Corgan with is John Fogerty, another prolific songwriter with world-class pop sensibility and a desire to completely control everything he's involved with. The grim facial expressions he and his bandmates displayed during their rise to popularity downplayed their metal roots, as does Corgan's drought-strickened skull. But the actual *music* Billy writes often has a metal edge—or at least his better stuff does. The two Pumpkins records that are the least metal (1991's *Gish* and 1998's *Adore*) are multitudes weaker than the material that came between (*Siamese Dream* was rockin' like Dokken, and a few tracks on *Mellon Collie and the Infinite Sadness* dripped of the Rainbow and the Whisky). *Machina: The Machines of God* goes so far as to include the song "Heavy Metal Machine," which *Entertainment Weekly* called "KISS for eggheads." I realize *EW* was trying to be snarky, but that's just about the highest compliment a guitar-based alt rocker can get.

I would never seriously label the Pumpkins as a prototypical "metal band," but they often operated under the same structural parameters: swirling, heavy guitars augmented by a straightforward rhythm section. Since Corgan understands songwriting better than Nikki Sixx or Warren DeMartini, he disguises his banger tendencies more deftly (resulting in well-deserved critical acclaim from every possible direction). But those of us with the right kind of radios detect a conspiracy. We all know that Corgan is actually keeping glam rock alive, even though the rock press doesn't want to believe it. And that's why he can get away with it. Keep acting pretentious, Billy. We "understand."

As I write this paragraph, it appears that the original lineup of Veruca Salt will never record again. This is too bad, since I liked both of their albums (especially the second one that nobody bought). Veruca also made an EP with Steve Albini, a producer who makes such a big deal about hating metal that everyone halfway suspects he probably loves it, which he doesn't, but I guess that's the idea. Albini once told me that Led Zeppelin was a horrible rock band, mostly because they had "the worst vocalist in music history." His willingness to make that statement in public seems to be the only possible explanation as to why he got hired to mix the 1998 Page-Plant album *Walking Into Clarksdale*. I will never understand cool people.

I don't think I ever listened to the Veruca Salt EP that Albini worked on, mostly because it had a really stupid title. But I'm guessing it was probably pretty decent. Veruca was fronted by two righteous rock bitches: the sniveling prima donna Nina Gordon, and the sniveling bad-ass Louise Post. Gordon did most of the singing, but Post did all the work; she always claimed her main influence was Angus Young, but her fast machine had a cleaner motor than AC/DC ever did. Both *American Thighs* and *Eight Arms to Hold You* have way too much filler to be classified as genius, but the good stuff is stellar: "Seether," "Straight," and "Don't Make Me Prove It" have that sense of *hardness* that categorized early Skid Row and Judas Priest. This is the best modern example of a group that's hard, but not heavy. Veruca Salt reminds me of a Mexican middleweight in the mold of Julio Cesar

Chavez—they'll jab the piss out of you, cleverly setting up an overhand right that is a little louder than you'd expect. These women have great taste in power pop, and they also had some real visual flair (the video for "Volcano Girls" was the best use of bungee cords since "Panama"). I'm still not exactly sure why former best buddies Nina and Louise now hate each other; rumor has it that one of them (I think it was Louise) was sleeping with David Grohl, who eventually dumped her for Winona Ryder, thereby casting Veruca Salt into unexplained turmoil. I don't know; I guess I never read *Charlie and the Chocolate Factory*.

Even though their first album is kind of crappy, it's nice to see that a band like Buckcherry is trying to jump on (or possibly jump-start) the glam wagon. A full six months before their debut, Geffen (acting as an arm of DreamWorks) was hyping Buckcherry as a "Sunset Strip band," which is industry lingo for "hair metal slut rock." The first song I heard from Buckcherry was the cocaine-praising single "Lit Up," which nicely replicates the core riff from Ace Frehley's "Shock Me." This got me excited, because I suspected the Bucks might be as cool and shameless as the Donnas (a hope I had also held for the Prissteens). Unfortunately, the rest of the LP is an attempt to write their own "original" material, much of which sucks. Buckcherry makes a concerted effort to sound like an Uzi Suicide-era GNR, but they deliver a muddled jalopy that seems more like Jackyl jamming with Tracii Guns. Still, it *is* glam metal, and it probably deserves to be mentioned here.

I suppose I also need to give a shout out to Lenny Kravitz. Mr. Kravitz is many things. He's a musician, but he looks like a model. He's half-black, but he's also half-Jewish. He's the son of one TV star (the late Roxie Roker) and the ex-husband of another (Lisa Bonet). He's a Jesus freak, but he also likes to bang Australian songstress Natalie Imbruglia. He's kind of a metal guy, but he's also kind of a funk guy—and that somehow makes him an alternative balladeer. And he's the best dresser in rock 'n' roll (at least if you're a fan of hemp pants). "Are You Gonna Go My Way" sounds like Sly and the Family Stone jamming with Rush, which equates to a totally rocking version of Living Colour (except good).

At this point, I am tempted to go all Chuck Eddy on you and include a bunch of other bands I like that have no relationship to metal whatsoever. When Eddy updated his "pretentious and funny" *Stairway to Hell* in 1998, he included his list of the 100 Best Metal Records of the 1990s; the ranks included high-intensity acid rockers like Weezer and Cornershop. Eddy swears his criteria for inclusion on his list is that at least half the music on any given record sounds like metal *to him*, which makes me wonder just how loud he plays his stereo. I suspect Chuck's whole reason for doing the updated list was to reiterate how much he loves Rancid, who he evidently sees as the Gen X equivalent of Kix.

As I scan over the rest of my CDs from the '90s, the only band that seems legitimately misplaced and—by virtue of all cultural barometers—*should* have been an '80s group is Stone Temple Pilots, a group constantly attacked by the press as the worst band of its generation. Much of that has to do with one song, the Pearl Jam rip-off "Plush." Though the song itself does seem strikingly similar to some of the material on *Ten*, the real problem was its presentation: In the accompanying video, vocalist Scott Weiland tried to look like Eddie Vedder, even mimicking his physical affectations. This singular decision put STP in a hole they never emerged from, which eventually prompted Weiland to become a heroin addict and even become friends with Courtney Love.⊗

The sad irony is that almost everything Stone Temple Pilots released after their 1992 debut (*Core*) was damn good. *Purple*

⊗Love's ability to fool intelligent people continues to baffle me. In 1991, she made *Pretty on the Inside*, and it was about as remarkable as a bucket of vomit warming in the afternoon sun. By 1994, she had married Kurt Cobain and— *surprise!*—proceeded to "write" a record that's pretty amazing (and seemingly unconnected to her debut in almost every possible way). Tragically, Kurt died the week before it was released. Courtney subsequently stopped making music . . . until she renewed her friendship with Billy Corgan and—*surprise!*— released *Celebrity Skin*, another exceptional record with virtually no sonic relationship to *Live Through This*. Funny how this keeps happening. I hope Courtney starts sleeping with Trey Anastasio of Phish, because I'd love to see Hole become a jam band.

(1994) was critically ripped to shreds (particularly by *SPIN* magazine), but it stands up as one of that year's best efforts. Though "Smells Like Teen Spirit" is unquestionably the decade's most important rock song, "Interstate Love Song" is probably the best one to listen to. I have heard it hundreds of times, but when it comes on my car radio I never touch the dial. At least for cruising purposes, it's an almost flawless tune. *Tiny Music . . . Songs from the Vatican Gift Shop* was another vastly underrated album that suffered more from the band's janky reputation than from any ill-advised songwriting.

Every little nuance of STP makes them seem like they should be an '80s metal band, from their charismatic, drug-addled frontman to their Zeplified riffing and earnest respect for melody. They possess the beautiful combination of virtuosity and imbecility that makes metal my favorite kind of music. But on a guttural level, I never feel like STP can be called a *metal band* (even though they would have made a great one). They seem to fit in a new class of pop music that is almost undefinable. Along with everyone from the Black Crowes to Helmet, Stone Temple Pilots are just a "modern hard-rock group." I'm sure all of those outfits would prefer that designation to being called "metal bands," but the amorphous category of *modern hard rock* is actually a mild criticism. Musicians are always insisting that they want their own identity and they don't want to be pigeonholed into a "type," but once they achieve that aspiration, it somehow makes them seem less consequential. Unless you leave a massive body of world-class work (like Prince or R.E.M.), being autonomous is usually more admirable than effective. The quest for musical immortality is not a simple one, and being able to do many things well is usually not as effective as doing just one thing perfectly.

In 1997, Queensryche released an album called *Hear In the Now Frontier*. I did not buy it, but I ended up winning it at a bar while I was watching a *Monday Night Football* game between the Pittsburgh Steelers and the Jacksonville Jaguars. Some radio station was broadcasting from the establishment, and they were asking trivia questions (actually, the questions weren't really "trivia," per se—I won by knowing what Tulane University's nickname is, which seemed more like a current events question, but who am I to bicker with authority?). My prize was the soundtrack to the movie *Elizabeth*, which I traded for the Queensryche disc. Ironically, the guy who had won the Queensryche CD got it for *not* knowing the answer to the question, "What was the name of the most recent Queensryche album?"

ANYWAY, I did not make this trade because I had a particular affinity for Queensryche. I never even owned any of their albums, but my old college roommate loved them. Mike (that was his name) was an especially big fan of *Operation: Mindcrime*, a conspiracy-driven rock opera about a nun who gets pregnant and tries to brainwash society (or something like that). Most people remember Queensryche for the song "Silent Lucidity," which came off the 1990 *Empire* album. That single caused casual fans to believe that Queensryche was a lot like Pink Floyd, which (at the time) seemed like an insult to us metalheads. Looking back, the comparison was certainly understandable.

Upon my acquisition of *Hear In the Now Frontier* (which had to be the worst album title since PE's *Muse Sick-N-Hour Mess Age*), I decided to mail it to Mike, certainly the nicest Queensyche fan I ever lived with. But before I did, I thought I'd give *Hear In the Now Frontier* a spin in my CD player (and come to think of it, Alanis Morissette's *Supposed Former Infatuation Junkie* was a pretty awful album title too).

As I listened to Geoff Tate's earnest voice, I was dumbstruck by something I would have never expected in a thousand years: This record sounded *good*—certainly as good as those old Queensryche records that hard rock critics always described as "vastly underrated."

The inexplicable sonic success of *Hear In the Now Frontier* got me thinking about why most of the '80s metal bands fail when they try to make contemporary albums. What did Queensryche do that everyone else seems to miss? My gut reaction was that maybe Queensryche had *always* been different, and that their technical virtuosity superseded the limitations of the genre. It wouldn't be a bad argument, because Queensryche did take cues from less predictable sources. While the connection to Floyd was a little overstated, there was a lot of Queen in Queensryche (or at least a lot of Brian May). There was also a lot of Rush and Yes, two bands that never sounded contemporary (even when they were).

But this thinking does not hold up to scrutiny. Lots of bands could argue that they were different from the rest, and that didn't stop them from flopping over time. Iron Maiden took more ideas from classical music than they stole from Aerosmith. A band like Dream Theater never sustained any musical relevance, and they were (and are) *exactly* like Queensryche. I actually saw Dream Theater when they opened for ELP and Yes in the autumn of 1998, and it reminded me of Spinal Tap's "jazz odyssey" period.

I was nearly ready to give up thinking about Queensryche altogether, mostly because I thought the value of *Hear In the Now Frontier* was a musical anomaly that was probably due to my admittedly low expectations. But then David Giffels explained everything. David Giffels is one of those guys who seems to have lived a charmed life: He was a Cleveland Cavaliers ball boy, and then he fronted a cool rock band, and then he married a beautiful woman who's half-Italian and half-Cherokee, and then he became a script writer for *Beavis & Butt-head*, and then he cowrote a book documenting the 125-year history of the Akron rubber industry, and he renovated a nineteenth-century home, and then he explained to me why Queensryche doesn't suck.

David seems to think a band's longevity isn't necessarily dependent on what they produce; it's more dependent on "what they're about." At first, that almost sounds like ridiculous hippie talk, but it's actually pretty astute. His example was the Rolling Stones: As a bunch of sixty-year-old men strutting onstage in front of 35,000 baby boomers, the Stones look pretty stupid. However, no one cares how pathetic they look, and that's due to two reasons.

The first reason can be explained with my own theory: I think the Stones are now loved by people who don't actually like them and never really did. I know bushels of people in their thirties and forties who paid $125 to see the Rolling Stones in concert, and very few of them know anything about the band. I wrote a feature story about the '99 Stones concert in Cleveland, and the majority of the ticketholders I interviewed outside Gund Arena knew nearly nothing about the group's history. Many of them never even owned any of the Stones records; they were all listening to the Carpenters and KISS and the Cars and *The Blues Brothers* soundtrack and all the other omnipresent 8-tracks of the era. *Sticky Fingers* is a wonderful and important record, but I rarely find it when I look through most folks' old record collections. However, I stumble across copies of Head East's *Flat as a Pancake* constantly. According to the Recording Industry Association of America, *Flat as a Pancake* only went gold, which proves just how useless record figures were before the advent of Soundscan. There is no way that album only sold 500,000 copies. There are four people *in my family* who own that fucking record.

The Rolling Stones no longer represent Rolling Stones fans. They now represent "baby boomer rock 'n' roll," and every aging boomer wants to believe he or she still rocks. That being the case, they really have no choice but to love Mick Jagger—no one else is left. You can't really go around acting excited about Uriah Heep. If you want to participate in the music of "Your Generation," the Stones are just about the only option. That's why people who never listened to *Beggar's Banquet* are suddenly buying *Hot Rocks* on CD and insisting that Ron Wood has always been their personal Christ. The same thing happened when the Eagles reunited in the early '90s: My brother paid over $100 bucks to see the Eagles, and I *know* he never listened to them in the 1970s. Back in 1977, he would probably have preferred to see Ted Nugent pick up a crossbow and shoot Don Henley in the face.

But there is also a second reason for the Stones' eternal youth, and that brings us to Mr. Giffels's theory. Any pop musicologist will tell you that the Rolling Stones earned their spot in rock history by tapping into the blues—even if every Stone had all died in 1973, they'd still be important in a sonic sense. They are the epitome of the white British blues band; Cream, Zeppelin, and early Fleetwood Mac took the concept further, but the Stones were the true source. They connected Howlin' Wolf to Bill Haley, and Jagger rubbed that combination against the crotch of the Western world. It may have been a great *show*, but it was always about *the blues*. If you strip away everything else, the Rolling Stones are simply a blues band (it's similar to how Nirvana was simply a great punk band—once you carved away the nonsense and the hype).

In other words, the Stones are "about" playing the blues. Consequently, they are able to get old and still matter. No one would ever call B. B. King an "old fart." No one would ever accuse R. L. Burnside of being a dinosaur. These terms only seem to apply to white rock musicians who rely on modern gimmicks. If the Stones suddenly faded into social mediocrity and could no longer sell out the Pontiac Silverdome in twenty-eight minutes, Keith Richards could still get critics' attention by picking up an acoustic guitar and meandering down to the crossroads. As a bluesman, he's probably just now entering his prime.

A similar comparison can be made with a band like Queensryche. Queensryche was never "about" heavy metal, even though they were a metal band. Mostly, Queensryche was about trying to be ambitious and interesting; you never threw on *Operation: Mindcrime* when you were drinking Busch Light and hoping to get laid (in fact, my buddy Mike usually played *Operation Mindcrime* when he was reading his accounting textbooks). They were obsessed with integrity and—at least among metalists—highly political. Much of their political content leaned in the direction of naive libertarian gobbledygook (as is so often the case with civics rockers), but at least they thought about *something*. If Poison can be seen as metal's hippies, Queenryche would have been metal's yippies (and I suppose that would make Slayer the Weathermen). It wasn't fun music, and it wasn't supposed to be. It was supposed to be a labor of love.

That's why Queensryche doesn't sound idiotic a full decade after they mattered. They don't have to convince anyone that they still fuck strippers or sacrifice children onstage, nor do they have to reinvent themselves as intellectuals. Instead, *Hear In the Now Frontier* is the same kind of record they would have made in 1987, and it has the same kind of impact (granted, that impact is marginal, but it's still better than seeming like a bloated caricature). Queensryche is like an Elvis who was never particularly good-looking, but who also never got fat.

Still, crediting Queensryche is probably counterintuitive, since it doesn't really make sense to attack rock bands for lacking longevity. That's not part of the job description. Nobody ever considers the importance of longevity when a band is young; when people buy a CD from a new artist and like what they hear, they might hope that the band's tour goes through their town, and if they really like the album they might even express interest in buying a couple more of the artists' previous releases. However, no teenager ever buys an album and then says, "Gee, I hope these guys make seventeen more albums over the next twenty-five years." Why should I care what Axl Rose will be doing when *I'm* forty?

Let's be honest: It's more or less taken for granted that rock bands don't have staying power. The moment we're born, we start dying; the moment a musician gets famous, he starts to fade into oblivion. Every pop act that earns major commercial success with one album (or especially with one single) always faces the same criticism from anyone outside of their audience: "In five years, no one will know who these guys are." And most of the time, that's true. This, of course, is good. If everyone who became famous *stayed* famous, we'd all go bankrupt buying forty new records every Tuesday.

Starting the late '90s, there has even been a cultural movement celebrating musicians who fell off the face of the earth. Predictably, the main culprit behind the retro-kitsch revival is VH1. They occasionally broadcast a show called *Where Are They Now?*, and the premise is to reacquaint us with people like the

Captain and Tennille and Men Without Hats. It's kind of a brilliant coup; even though the producers at VH1 showcase these one-hit wonders with hardcore sarcasm, the artists always love to participate: It puts them back in the spotlight they so dearly miss, and (more importantly) it almost always spikes sales of their back catalog. The wonderfully shameless E! network uses a similar approach with its *True Hollywood Stories,* although E! tends to focus on canceled sitcoms and child stars who go nuts, rob video stores, make porn flicks, and kill themselves. As a whole, our culture has become fascinated with public failure.

Metal acts rarely benefit from that fascination, though. The feeling seems to be that glam rockers took themselves too seriously to warrant playful memories. Here again, we see the emergence of a peculiar contradiction: People describe glam metal music as fun and crazy, yet they also remember glam metal artists as pretentious. The conventional opinion seems to be along the lines of, "Fuck Kip Winger. He's probably working in a gas station, and that's what he deserves." (Actually, Kip released a solo album called *This Conversation Seems Like a Dream,* a title that's only better than *Hear In the Now Frontier* because it seems like it's mocking the Smiths. But I think you get the general idea.) Nobody really wonders where old metalheads are today, and it's because we can't imagine them as adults. They might as well have melted.

More than any other musical style, heavy metal is tied to youth. Living the teenage dream is a gorilla on every glam singer's shoulders. That ideal can usually be expressed for about two (maybe three) records. After about the fourth album, the concept of expressing the ideals of America's youth comes off as flatly ridiculous. And after that, it's just pathetic.

David Lee Roth is a frequent guest on *The Howard Stern Show,* and he's an ideal subject for Stern's brand of entertainment. Dave tells lots of rambling stories about whores and cocaine, and it's reminiscent of a retired NFL quarterback who honestly believes he could still go out and throw for three hundred yards against the Packers whenever he gets a few shots of scotch in his gulliver. This is the perfect medium for a man in

Roth's position: He's a marvelous storyteller, and it's improving his legacy. Even though Van Halen ended up selling more records with Sammy Hagar than they did with Dave, there's never an argument over who was the only true frontman of that band.

Yet Roth would look like a fool if the original Van Halen ever reunited.✪ The thought of a balding man trying to howl and do backflips is not appealing, and that's basically all Roth can do. He doesn't deny it, either. "Of course I'd rather be bouncing around and touring the country," he said when I asked if he still hoped that Eddie would call and make an offer. "I'm a one-trick pony. That's the only thing I really do well. Anything else I've ever done is merely a way to finance my one trick—arena rock."

The problem is that "arena rock" is not like fly fishing for walleye or throwing horseshoes: The window for being able to do it with any social relevance is very small, especially when you play heavy glam. Metal frontmen are supposed to be vocally aggressive and recklessly edgy, and they're supposed to represent the kind of animalistic sexuality that is only found in seventeen-year-old males. Consequently, the only hard rockers who can survive are the ones who consciously ignore the beautiful stupidity of this archetype. And almost none of them are willing to do that.

As I look at my own personal CD collection, my eyes gloss over the hair metal bands who still make records today. Almost all of them are insipid, and it kind of makes me sad. For all its bally-hooed hype, *Psycho Circus* was probably among the worst three or four KISS albums the group ever released (placing it in a class with *Crazy Nights* and *Hot In the Shade*). KISS still puts on the best live show in the universe (I've seen 'em nine times), but it's basically parody and they basically admit it. Stephen Pearcy's post-Ratt project Arcade was as bad as you'd probably expect it to be, and Ratt's '99 record tanked. Taime Downe of Faster Pussycat now heads an electronica group called the Newlydeads ("Things just ran their course," Downe explained. "I just wanted to do differ-

---

✪ And I'm really afraid they will.

ent shit."). Extreme released an album in 1995 titled *Waiting for the Punchline*; since singer Gary Cherone jumped ship for a brief tenure in Van Halen, I suppose they're still waiting. Def Leppard still makes new music, and maybe British people care. I know I don't, even though *Euphoria* debuted at No. 11 on the charts. The biggest glam metal release from 1999 was a live Guns N' Roses record, but all of its songs were recorded between 1987 and 1993.

Almost no one has surrendered, but the war is long over. Twisted Sister's "We're Not Gonna Take It" is used in a Comtrex commercial, and Ozzy's "Crazy Train" hawks Japanese cars. You find a lot of "greatest hits" packages, and you see aging bands playing state fairs and rib festivals, usually hoping to sell 50,000 copies of a new record on CMC, a North Carolina–based label that is now home to a dozen old metal acts. A notable exception to all this is Mötley Crüe; the Crüe are once again trying to become Aerosmith, but this time in a different way.

Aerosmith was the craziest, wildest American band of the 1970s, and then they hit rock bottom. Joe Perry left the band to start the Joe Perry Project, which flopped like a beached whale. Meanwhile, the Perryless Aerosmith was ever crappier. They all eventually got clean and uncool, leading to a reunion. With the help of Run-DMC, they even became an MTV staple. At the dawn of a new millennium, it can honestly be said that Aerosmith is "more popular than ever." That's a cliché that publicists love to tag on dinosaur rock bands, but in this case it's true. They have made only one good song in ten years ("F.I.N.E."), but they are still a supergroup.

"You want to survive and you want to have long-term viability," Tom Hamilton told me in 1998. "We have recorded some songs that have gone on to be very popular, and that has given us more time to rock. For example, I realize *Get a Grip* was a commercially successful album, even though I thought it was off-balance and had too many ballads. But we'll do whatever we have to do to keep making records and to keep touring. Aerosmith doesn't mind being a pop band sometimes."

Aerosmith beat the system by outliving it. And just as Mötley used Aerosmith's musical template in 1982, they are using their marketing template at the dawn of the millennium. When they kicked Vince Neil out of the group in the early '90s, they picked up a new singer (John Corabi) and made one of the worst Soundgarden rip-off albums of all time. Neil's two solo attempts were actually okay, but he still had no future. Nobody was the least bit surprised when the two parties got back together and decided to make one more run for the money. They've even purchased (and re-released) their entire Elektra catalog. These guys have bills to pay.

I keep trying to make myself like the result, 1997's *Generation Swine*. It's not easy. Oh, there are occasional glimpses of the band I discovered in fifth grade—they even do a revamped industrial version of "Shout at the Devil." But it's mostly a bunch of shit. The day *Generation Swine* was released, I remember walking into a record store and talking with the two guys who were working behind the counter. They loved the new Crüe material—but only as a comedy album. Over the next twenty minutes, they played the album's opening track four times, always laughing like hipster hyenas at the same set of lyrics: "I'm a sick motherfucker / I'm a sweet sucka mutha." Even goofier was the tune written and sung by Tommy Lee about his child, "Brandon." Every time Lee sang the chorus, "Brandon, I love you, you are the one," he tagged on the line "Brandon, my son." It almost seemed as though Tommy was making a conscious effort to remind everyone he was not gay. You'd think having 15 million people watch you get a blow job from Pamela Anderson would be more than enough to validate your heterosexuality. *(Reader's note: It now seems the always unpredictable Lee has quit the Crüe to become a rapper with the group Methods of Mayhem. It's horrible, but not nearly as bad as I expected. He's been replaced—at least temporarily—with ex-Ozzy drummer Randy Castillo and Samantha Maloney from Hole.)*

Still, I legitimately enjoyed the *Swine* song "Afraid," a dulcet number that reminded me why I liked Nikki Sixx's songwriting in the first place. I felt same way when I heard "Bitter Pill," one of two new songs on the Crüe's second greatest-hits compilation that came out in the fall of '98. "Bitter Pill" replicates the main lick from Foreigner's "Hot Blooded," and it lets Vince sound the way I want to remember him.

Fuck it, I have to be honest: I'm a metal fan, okay? I like listening to Mötley Crüe. I still watch my 1986 VHS copy of *Mötley Crüe Uncensored*, and I still love the part where Vince walks down the stairs of his fake house and says, "Duuuude." I know I make it sound like analyzing this music was all some sort of intellectual exercise, but it's part of my life. And for a few uncomfortable moments of my past, it was pretty much the only thing in my life.

Every year, *Entertainment Weekly* has an issue it calls "Guilty Pleasures" where all their writers sing the praises of Patrick Swayze and *Charmed*. It's obviously an effective idea, because all my friends and I read the issue and spend the next seventy-two hours coming up with our own lists over e-mail. Part of the annual process is trying to define exactly what a "guilty pleasure" is, and my friend Pat probably came up with the perfect explanation: "A guilty pleasure is something I pretend to like ironically, but in truth is something I really just like." If I was straight with myself, that would be my take on glam metal. Very often, I inexplicably embrace the same ideas that I just finished railing against: Part of me wants to insist that heavy metal really *is* stupid. I make fun of people who love the same bands I loved (and still do). Social pressure has made me cannibalize my own adolescent experience.

We all want to be cool, and it's hard for some of us to admit we're not. When I tell people I came from a town that didn't have a single stoplight, I make myself smile, even though I don't know why this is funny (or why it should be embarrassing). When I admit that I spent many nights assuming I would die a virgin, I act like I'm being self-deprecating, even though I'm mostly being honest. When I remember how confused I was while I drove up and down the empty streets of my snow-packed hometown, I try to be wistful, even though I fucking hated having no one to talk to. And when I read my high school journal and realize what a homophobic, racist, sexist, and genuinely *unlikeable* person I was at the age of seventeen, I force myself to laugh. But I'm being a hypocrite, and I know it. In so many ways, that *was* my life. With the exception of some legitimately good parents and a better-than-average jump shot, I had nothing else . . . except for the cassettes on my dresser and the pentagram over my bed.

Hair metal was a wormhole for every midwestern kid who was too naive to understand why he wasn't happy. I may have been a loser, but Vince and Axl and Ace and Ozzy were cool *for me*. They allowed me to live a life I never would see, and I never had to leave my bedroom.

I absolutely could not relate to Mötley Crüe. And that's why I will always love them.

Epilogue

When I started writing *Fargo Rock City* in 1998, it was never my intention to change anyone's mind about the value of heavy metal music. There has never been a moment in my life when I wanted to convince the world about the relative awesomeness of White Lion, nor was there ever a day when I aspired to create the definitive, annotated history of Dokken. I just tried to write the book I had always wanted to find in a bookstore. And I think I did that, sort of. Yet as I look back at how my life has changed —and particularly the way I *perceive* my life—since the release of *Fargo Rock City* in May of 2001, I suddenly feel like I understand how Nikki Sixx must have felt in 1988, minus the money and the heroin and the marathon sex with Vanity. To quote Guns N' Roses (or *Cool Hand Luke*, depending on how you look at it), "Some men you just can't reach."

Superficially, I feel as though the core premise of *Fargo Rock City* has been totally vindicated; there has certainly been a resurgence of interest in '80s metal over the past few years. Actually, *resurgence* isn't really the right word; what mostly happened is that all the people who secretly loved metal during the 1980s are now too old too worry about being cool. Meanwhile, 17-year-old kids are buying *Appetite for Destruction* because they're too young to know it's unfashionable. When I watched Sum 41 play "Shout at the Devil" and "You Got Another Thing Coming" on MTV's 20th anniversary special, it was oddly reassuring to see a new generation of kids digging the same music I had loved for all the same reasons. Sum 41's affinity for pop metal isn't the least bit surprising, either: There's just no logic for not liking a Mötley Crüe song if you're the kind of person who aspires to rock.

However, what I've come to realize is that logic has nothing to do with how people look at anything, including this stupid book. That's why I suddenly relate to all the bands I wrote about. It's always been my theory that criticism is really just veiled autobiography; whenever someone writes about a piece of art, they're really just writing about themselves. Upon watching the reaction to *Fargo Rock City*, I'm now certain that theory is empirical truth.

Now, there's obviously a glaring hypocrisy to what I'm about to write, because (a) many of the reviews of this book have been remarkably complimentary, and (b) I work as a newspaper critic *for a living*. So it's not like I have no idea how criticism works; I'm completely aware of how arbitrary it inevitably is. True story: When I was still working in North Dakota, I used to eat lunch with my girlfriend next to a swimming pool (we always enjoyed getting roast beef sandwiches from the Hardees' drive-thru and eating them on the concrete steps next to the public pool in downtown Fargo; for some reason, it always reminded us of eating at Alcatraz). During one such meal, we had a massive fight about the status of our relationship, a status that seemed to change every 18 minutes we were together. I responded to this argument by going back into my office at the newspaper and writing a review of *Balance* by Van Halen, which I referred to as the single worst album ever recorded. Now, granted—*Balance* generally sucks. But it's probably not the worst album ever recorded, or even the worst album of the '90s (that would undoubtedly be something by Dave Matthews). The real reason I hated *Balance* so much is because I thought I was never going to kiss my girlfriend again, which—in truth— didn't have all that much to do with Sammy Hagar's larynx. But this is exactly how newspaper criticism works, and anyone who tells you different is either (a) lying, (b) stupid, or (c) actively employed as a newspaper critic. I'm not suggesting that the subject being reviewed is ignored completely, but other intangible factors are involved. And unless the media becomes operated by robots, that will always be the case. I am completely aware of this.

Which is why I feel like an idiot.

I feel like an idiot because I was still ridiculously bothered by the criticism of *Fargo Rock City*, even though I knew it was meaningless. Every time I read someone complaining that the title of the book was "deceptive," I got depressed; this is because I probably hate the title of this book more than any-one else on the planet, and I felt that way from the very beginning. (I wanted to call it *Appetite for Deconstruction*, but everyone talked me out of it.) I was always confused when a writer would accuse me of being too ironic, especially since a few other writers claimed that I wasn't being ironic enough. It was continually frustrating to have people express disappoint-ment over the fact that *Fargo Rock City* wasn't the book they *assumed* it was going to be (i.e. more of a conventional mem-oir, more of a straightforward rock critique, more of an objec-tive history of hard rock, more of a homage to Twisted Sister's *Stay Hungry* LP, and so on). And it's still hard for me to under-stand why so many people fixated on the drinking chapter, beyond the fact that that it gave writers something obvious to psychologically analyze.

However, these are all personal issues. These are just exam-ples of me being oversensitive, and it's probably sort of pathetic for me to write an epilogue just to strike back at my faceless crit-ics. But I have at least one issue of complaint that I think is valid, and it has nothing to do with me: Generally, people reacted to *Fargo Rock City* not as a book, but as a philosophical extension of the music I wrote about. There is a certain class of people who refuse to accept that heavy metal was important, or even mildly interesting. In fact, the mere suggestion appears to make them mad.

The same summer *Fargo Rock City* was released in hardcover, two other books about loud '80s music arrived in bookstores. The first was *The Dirt: Confessions of the World's Most Notori-*

ous Rock Band by Neil Strauss, and the second was *Our Band Could Be Your Life* by Michael Azerrad. Both of these books are way, way better than mine. However, they both make for interesting comparisons to *Fargo Rock City*, and I think these comparisons prove my point. *The Dirt* was about the escapades of Mötley Crüe, the first and last band mentioned in *Fargo Rock City*. To the surprise of no one, the group's stories are relentlessly entertaining: *The Dirt* is like *Hammer of the Gods*, amplified by 11, minus the music. And the key is that "minus the music" part. I don't think the oral history of any band has ever been so exhaustively documented without really talking about the group's music *at all*. On the rare occasions when the Crüe's songs are mentioned, they're immediately dismissed; even Nikki Sixx and Vince Neil admit that two of the Crüe's biggest albums (*Theater of Pain* and *Girls, Girls, Girls*) were more or less shit. It's sort of sad, really; even the guys in the band have convinced themselves that their music was appalling.

So . . . are Nikki and Vince right? I don't know. Maybe. I like both of those albums, but I'm certainly not going to try and convince anyone that *Theatre of Pain* is Carole King's *Tapestry*. I'm not a Mötley Crüe apologist.[✲] But how can music that was the soundtrack to the lives of so many teenagers not be culturally important, even if it was overproduced and derivative? The one thing I wanted to show with *Fargo Rock City* is that pop music doesn't matter for what it is; it matters for what it does. The greatest thing about rock 'n' roll is that it's an art form where the audience is more important than the art itself. Whether or not "Home Sweet Home" was terrific is almost irrelevant; the fact that a million future adults *believed* it was terrific is what counts.

That brings me to the subject of *Our Band Could Be Your Life*, a brilliantly written book that serves as the perfect antithesis for *Fargo Rock City*. Michael Azerrad wrote about 13 indie bands from the 1980s that comprised the musical under-

---

[✲] Well, okay . . . I'm *sort of* a Mötley Crüe apologist.

ground: The Minutemen, Mission of Burma, Sonic Youth, Big Black, et al. Essentially, Azerrad writes about the artists whose art was a direct response to Def Leppard and Tesla and Bon Jovi, and the insights are fascinating. But even as I found myself loving the book, I found myself hating most of the artists he wrote about. In fact, they reminded me of why I loved Poison in the first place. Bret Michaels was important because he never tried to be; he just wanted to be cool, which was once the single biggest goal in my life. Too many of those indie bands were consumed with the misguided belief that their destiny was to recalibrate the American mind; they tried too hard to seem significant. Despite all their espoused organic passion, everything they did was calculated: They knew precisely how unwilling revolutionaries were supposed to act. There will always be this bizarre consensus that sporadically interesting, consciously under-produced music is inherently transcendent, mainly because almost no one appreciates it. And that defines the concept of elitism.

Obviously, Azerrad disagrees with me on this issue, and his argument is that a band like Fugazi never overtly said "we're important," nor did they ever technically demand anyone to live in the manner they embraced. *But that sentiment was there.* It's almost always riding shotgun with the music rock critics tend to adore. I eventually interviewed Azerrad about his book, and I asked him to speculate on the differences between a kid who went to a Black Flag show at a Moose Lodge in 1981 and a kid who went to a Van Halen show at The Forum on the very same night. This is what he said:

"Obviously, the kid at the Black Flag show is a bit of an independent, investigative thinker. He or she probably had to read about Black Flag in a fanzine, and he or she can look past glossy production to see the gist of a band. That takes a certain independence of thought and a leap of imagination. Someone who makes their way to a Black Flag concert in 1981 is obviously different then the kind of kid who's at Van Halen, because the Van Halen kid only reads mainstream publication and listens to the radio, so that's all he knows. For the person who goes to the Black Flag show, music is probably more important to them. But that's not a value judgment about them as a human being."

Wrong. That *is* a value judgment. What it says is that the kid who likes Black Flag is a *better* music fan than the kid who likes Van Halen. And that's ridiculous. It's possible these two hypothetical kids like Black Flag and Van Halen for diametrically different reasons, but its just as possible they like them for the exact same reason ("Man, these guys fucking *rock*!"). The true difference is that—20 years later—loving Black Flag meant you understood the unbridled intensity of the raging underclass. Loving Van Halen meant you liked to party. Consequently, loving Van Halen meant your adolescence meant almost nothing.

Azerrad thinks my feelings about the exclusionary aspects of Black Flag and Sonic Youth is a product of my own insecurity; I don't know, perhaps there's a grain of truth to that assertion. There is a paradox to the fact that—though I honestly love '80s metal—I almost never listen to it anymore, beyond Guns N' Roses❂ and Vinnie Vincent Invasion. But maybe that's why I can suddenly understand what it must have been like to be Nikki Sixx, back when he was writing music that normal people loved and intellectuals loathed, even though neither faction was really paying attention to the songs; they merely loved or loathed what they wanted those songs to represent. I'm sure Nikki spent more than one night in the studio thinking, "Man, this record is crap . . . *but this crap is who I am.*"

In the introduction to *Fargo Rock City*, I stated that I was

---

❂ Funny (or maybe not so funny) side note: While I wrote *Fargo Rock City*, my standing joke was that I'd try to finish before the new Guns N' Roses album came out. It still blows my mind that I did. As I write this coda, it's March of 2002, and it appears that the softcover edition will beat *Chinese Democracy* again. I would also like to note that I've now heard about half of the yet-to-be released GNR album, and at least one song—"The Blues"—is as good as anything Axl has ever recorded. I'm still a fuckin' believer.

going to show why all that "poofy, sexist, shallow glam rock was important." There are some who claim I failed at this attempt, which is fine. Part of me doesn't even care anymore. But part of me still does, so I want to give it one last shot. . . .

Try to look at it like this: I love Radiohead. I've slowly come to the conclusion that Radiohead is the best working band I've experienced since I started listening to music 18 years ago. And even though they get bushels of positive press coverage, I think they're still slightly underrated; people don't seem to realize they've made the best record in the world during three different years (1995, 1997, and 2000). Sometimes, Thom Yorke is perfect. We are watching a band that's at least as good as The Who. But you know what? I could never love Radiohead as much as I loved Mötley Crüe. I could never love Radiohead as much as Mötley Crüe because I'll never be 15 again. I can certainly *appreciate* Radiohead, but they're not an extension of my life. No rock band ever will be again. For 99 percent of the populace (myself included), that kind of mystical connection can only happen during those terrible, magical years when you somehow convince yourself that a guy like Nikki Sixx understands you. And it didn't matter if Nikki didn't write with the poetic prowess of Paul Westerberg; for me, he may as well have been Paul McCartney. It's all about timing, you know?

In 1996, I went to a concert headlined by Vince Neil (this was during his ill-fated "solo" period) that also featured Slaughter and Warrant. All three acts were at the lowest points in their career. But something happened at this show that I will always remember: After his first song, Warrant's Jani Lane promised the crowd he would sing "Cherry Pie" and "Heaven" and all the other songs he knew everyone had paid to hear, but he just asked that we sit through a half dozen of the new (and—to be honest—horrible) songs he had recorded on the unsuccessful *Dog Eat Dog* record. And he didn't ask this in a self-conscious, self-deprecating way; he was almost begging. Basically, he agreed to deliver all the old songs he hated if we would politely listen to the new stuff he cared about.

To me, that was cool. Maybe the 8th grade Chuck would have scoffed at his desperate earnesty, but the 24-year-old Chuck was sort of touched by that sincerity. And when I look back at Jani's request today, I always wonder: Would Thom Yorke ever do that? Well, perhaps he'll never have to. But on that summer night in 1996, I was glad Jani Lane cared enough about his life to give me back 20 minutes of mine.

February 2, 2000

Mr. Charles Klosterman

Dear Mr. Klosterman:

We received a complaint this morning regarding loud music and jumping in your apartment in the early hours of the morning. After reviewing your file, it seems as if this is a recurring problem in your apartment. It distresses us to have to write this letter, but you are keeping your neighbors awake.

We realize that it is sometimes difficult to live with neighbors, but please understand that playing music loudly at any time, if it disturbs your neighbors, is expressly against your lease. Your lack of consideration for your neighbors is also very disrespectful.

Your status as a resident here at Cedarwood Village is very tenuous. You are currently here on a month to month basis. Therefore, if we receive just one more complaint about noise we will give you a 30 day notice to vacate your apartment.

Our hope is that we do not have to take any further action in respect to you disturbing your neighbors. If you have any questions, please give us a call.

Sincerely,

General Manager

.com

MOVE   1055001

n\ 85 fol cutt

rica-
(overs)
Thirlwell

KGM
gerkus
missel.

Snobby.
OT — tell'n bout yr f